Hands-On Deep Learning with Apache Spark

Build and deploy distributed deep learning applications on
Apache Spark

Guglielmo Iozzia

BIRMINGHAM - MUMBAI

Hands-On Deep Learning with Apache Spark

Commissioning Editor: Pravin Dhandre
Acquisition Editor: Nelson Morris
Content Development Editor: Roshan Kumar
Technical Editor: Snehal Dalmet
Copy Editor: Safis Editing
Project Coordinator: Namrata Swetta
Proofreader: Safis Editing
Indexer: Mariammal Chettiyar
Graphics: Jisha Chirayil
Production Coordinator: Jyoti Chauhan

First published: January 2019

Production reference: 1310119

Published by Packt Publishing Ltd.
Livery Place
35 Livery Street
Birmingham
B3 2PB, UK.

ISBN 978-1-78899-461-3

www.packtpub.com

`mapt.io`

Mapt is an online digital library that gives you full access to over 5,000 books and videos, as well as industry leading tools to help you plan your personal development and advance your career. For more information, please visit our website.

Why subscribe?

- Spend less time learning and more time coding with practical eBooks and Videos from over 4,000 industry professionals

- Improve your learning with Skill Plans built especially for you

- Get a free eBook or video every month

- Mapt is fully searchable

- Copy and paste, print, and bookmark content

Packt.com

Did you know that Packt offers eBook versions of every book published, with PDF and ePub files available? You can upgrade to the eBook version at `www.packt.com` and as a print book customer, you are entitled to a discount on the eBook copy. Get in touch with us at `customercare@packtpub.com` for more details.

At `www.packt.com`, you can also read a collection of free technical articles, sign up for a range of free newsletters, and receive exclusive discounts and offers on Packt books and eBooks.

Contributors

About the author

Guglielmo Iozzia is currently a big data delivery manager at Optum in Dublin. He completed his master's degree in biomedical engineering at the University of Bologna. After graduation, he joined a start-up IT company in Bologna that had implemented a new system to manage online payments. There, he worked on complex Java projects for different customers in different areas. He has also worked at the IT department of FAO, an agency of the United Nations. In 2013, he had the chance to join IBM in Dublin. There, he improved his DevOps skills, working mostly on cloud-based applications. He is a golden member, writes articles at DZone, and maintains a personal blog to share his findings and thoughts about various tech topics.

I would like to thank my wife Elena for her patience during the making of this book and my lovely little daughters Katerina and Anna for the joy they bring day by day to our life.

About the reviewer

Nisith Kumar Nanda is a passionate big data consultant who loves to find solutions to complex data problems. He has around 10 years of IT experience from working on multiple technologies with various clients globally. His core expertise involves working with open source big data technologies such as Apache Spark, Kafka, Cassandra, and HBase to build critical next-generation real-time and batch applications. He is very proficient in various programming languages, such as Java, Scala, and Python. He is passionate about AI, machine learning, and NLP.

> *I would like to thank my family and especially to my wife, Samita, for their support. I will also take this opportunity to thank my friends and colleagues who helped me to grow professionally.*

Packt is searching for authors like you

If you're interested in becoming an author for Packt, please visit `authors.packtpub.com` and apply today. We have worked with thousands of developers and tech professionals, just like you, to help them share their insight with the global tech community. You can make a general application, apply for a specific hot topic that we are recruiting an author for, or submit your own idea.

Table of Contents

Preface

Deep learning is a subset of machine learning based on multilayer neural networks that can solve particularly hard and large-scale problems in areas such as natural language processing and image classification. This book addresses the sheer complexity of the technical and analytical parts, and the speed at which deep learning solutions can be implemented on top of Apache Spark.

The book starts with an explanation of the fundamentals of Apache Spark and deep learning (how to set up Spark for deep learning, the principles of distributed modeling, and different types of neural network). Then it moves to the implementation of some deep learning models, such as CNNs, RNNs, and LSTMs, on Spark. The readers will get hands-on experience of what it takes and a general feeling of the complexity of what they are dealing with. During the course of the book, popular deep learning frameworks such as DeepLearning4J (mostly), Keras, and TensorFlow will be used to implement and train distributed models.

The mission of this book is as follows:

- To create a hands-on guide to implementing Scala (and in some cases, Python too) deep learning solutions that scale and perform
- To make readers confident with using Spark via several code examples
- To explain how to choose the model that best addresses a particular deep learning problem or scenario

Who this book is for

If you are a Scala developer, a data scientist, or a data analyst who wants to learn how to use Spark to implement efficient deep learning models, this is the book for you. Knowledge of core machine learning concepts and some experience of using Spark will be helpful.

What this book covers

Chapter 1, *The Apache Spark Ecosystem*, provides a comprehensive overview of the Apache Spark modules and its different deployment modes.

Chapter 2, *Deep Learning Basics*, introduces the basic concepts of deep learning.

Chapter 3, *Extract, Transform, Load*, introduces the DL4J framework and presents training data ETL examples from diverse sources.

Chapter 4, *Streaming*, presents data streaming examples using Spark and DL4J DataVec.

Chapter 5, *Convolutional Neural Networks*, goes deeper into the theory behind CNNs and model implementation through DL4J.

Chapter 6, *Recurrent Neural Networks*, goes deeper into the theory behind RNNs and model implementation through DL4J.

Chapter 7, *Training Neural Networks in Spark*, explains how to train CNNs and RNNs with DL4J and Spark.

Chapter 8, *Monitoring and Debugging Neural Network Training*, goes through the facilities provided by DL4J to monitor and tune a neural network at training time.

Chapter 9, *Interpreting Neural Network Output*, presents some techniques to evaluate the accuracy of a model.

Chapter 10, *Deploying on a Distributed System*, talks about some of the things you need to take into consideration when configuring a Spark cluster, and the possibility of importing and running pre-trained Python models in DL4J.

Chapter 11, *NLP Basics*, introduces the core concepts of **natural language processing (NLP)**.

Chapter 12, *Textual Analysis and Deep Learning*, covers some examples of NLP implementations through DL4J, Keras, and TensorFlow.

Chapter 13, *Convolution*, talks about convolution and object recognition strategies.

Chapter 14, *Image Classification*, drives through the implementation of an end-to-end image classification web application.

Chapter 15, *What's Next for Deep Learning?*, tries to give an overview of what's in store in the future for deep learning.

To get the most out of this book

A basic knowledge of the Scala programming language is required in order to understand the hands-on topics throughout this book. Basic knowledge of machine learning will also be helpful for a better understanding of the deep learning theory. Preliminary knowledge or experience with Apache Spark isn't necessary, as the first chapter covers all of the topics regarding the Spark ecosystem. A good knowledge of Python is required only in order to understand the Keras and TensorFlow models that can be imported in DL4J.

In order to build and execute the code examples in this book, Scala 2.11.x, Java 8, Apache Maven, and your IDE of choice are required.

Download the example code files

You can download the example code files for this book from your account at `www.packt.com`. If you purchased this book elsewhere, you can visit `www.packt.com/support` and register to have the files emailed directly to you.

You can download the code files by following these steps:

1. Log in or register at `www.packt.com`.
2. Select the **SUPPORT** tab.
3. Click on **Code Downloads & Errata**.
4. Enter the name of the book in the **Search** box and follow the onscreen instructions.

Once the file is downloaded, please make sure that you unzip or extract the folder using the latest version of:

- WinRAR/7-Zip for Windows
- Zipeg/iZip/UnRarX for Mac
- 7-Zip/PeaZip for Linux

The code bundle for the book is also hosted on GitHub at `https://github.com/PacktPublishing/Hands-On-Deep-Learning-with-Apache-Spark`. In case there's an update to the code, it will be updated on the existing GitHub repository.

We also have other code bundles from our rich catalog of books and videos available at `https://github.com/PacktPublishing/`. Check them out!

Download the color images

We also provide a PDF file that has color images of the screenshots/diagrams used in this book. You can download it here: https://www.packtpub.com/sites/default/files/downloads/9781788994613_ColorImages.pdf.

Conventions used

There are a number of text conventions used throughout this book.

CodeInText: Indicates code words in text, database table names, folder names, filenames, file extensions, pathnames, dummy URLs, user input, and Twitter handles. Here is an example: "Mount the downloaded WebStorm-10*.dmg disk image file as another disk in your system."

A block of code is set as follows:

```
val spark = SparkSession
    .builder
      .appName("StructuredNetworkWordCount")
      .master(master)
      .getOrCreate()
```

When we wish to draw your attention to a particular part of a code block, the relevant lines or items are set in bold:

```
------------------------------------------
Time: 1527457655000 ms
------------------------------------------
(consumer,1)
(Yet,1)
(another,1)
(message,2)
(for,1)
(the,1)
```

Any command-line input or output is written as follows:

```
$KAFKA_HOME/bin/kafka-server-start.sh $KAFKA_HOME/config/server.properties
```

Bold: Indicates a new term, an important word, or words that you see onscreen. For example, words in menus or dialog boxes appear in the text like this. Here is an example: "Select **System info** from the **Administration** panel."

Warnings or important notes appear like this.

 Tips and tricks appear like this.

Get in touch

Feedback from our readers is always welcome.

General feedback: If you have questions about any aspect of this book, mention the book title in the subject of your message and email us at customercare@packtpub.com.

Errata: Although we have taken every care to ensure the accuracy of our content, mistakes do happen. If you have found a mistake in this book, we would be grateful if you would report this to us. Please visit www.packt.com/submit-errata, selecting your book, clicking on the Errata Submission Form link, and entering the details.

Piracy: If you come across any illegal copies of our works in any form on the Internet, we would be grateful if you would provide us with the location address or website name. Please contact us at copyright@packt.com with a link to the material.

If you are interested in becoming an author: If there is a topic that you have expertise in and you are interested in either writing or contributing to a book, please visit authors.packtpub.com.

Reviews

Please leave a review. Once you have read and used this book, why not leave a review on the site that you purchased it from? Potential readers can then see and use your unbiased opinion to make purchase decisions, we at Packt can understand what you think about our products, and our authors can see your feedback on their book. Thank you!

For more information about Packt, please visit packt.com.

The Apache Spark Ecosystem

1

Apache Spark (`http://spark.apache.org/`) is an open source, fast cluster-computing platform. It was originally created by AMPLab at the University of California, Berkeley. Its source code was later donated to the Apache Software Foundation (`https://www.apache.org/`). Spark comes with a very fast computation speed because data is loaded into distributed memory (RAM) across a cluster of machines. Not only can data be quickly transformed, but also cached on demand for a variety of use cases. Compared to Hadoop MapReduce, it runs programs up to 100 times faster when the data fits in memory, or 10 times faster on disk. Spark provides support for four programming languages: Java, Scala, Python, and R. This book covers the Spark APIs (and deep learning frameworks) for Scala (`https://www.scala-lang.org/`) and Python (`https://www.python.org/`) only.

This chapter will cover the following topics:

- Apache Spark fundamentals
- Getting Spark
- **Resilient Distributed Dataset** (**RDD**) programming
- Spark SQL, Datasets, and DataFrames
- Spark Streaming
- Cluster mode using a different manager

Apache Spark fundamentals

This section covers the Apache Spark fundamentals. It is important to become very familiar with the concepts that are presented here before moving on to the next chapters, where we'll be exploring the available APIs.

As mentioned in the introduction to this chapter, the Spark engine processes data in distributed memory across the nodes of a cluster. The following diagram shows the logical structure of how a typical Spark job processes information:

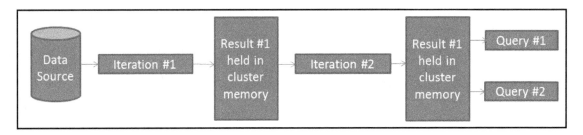

Figure 1.1

Spark executes a job in the following way:

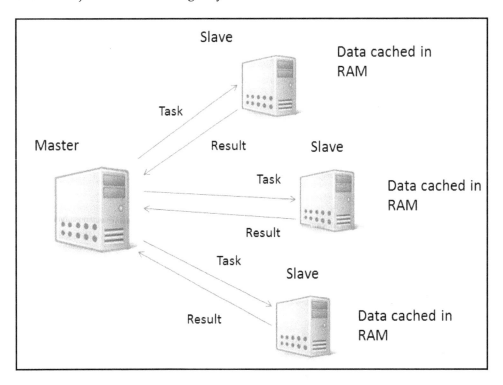

Figure 1.2

The **Master** controls how data is partitioned and takes advantage of data locality while keeping track of all the distributed data computation on the **Slave** machines. If a certain Slave machine becomes unavailable, the data on that machine is reconstructed on another available machine(s). In standalone mode, the Master is a single point of failure. This chapter's *Cluster mode using different managers* section covers the possible running modes and explains fault tolerance in Spark.

Spark comes with five major components:

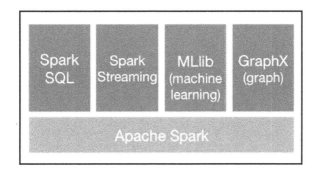

Figure 1.3

These components are as follows:

- The core engine.
- **Spark SQL**: A module for structured data processing.
- **Spark Streaming**: This extends the core Spark API. It allows live data stream processing. Its strengths include scalability, high throughput, and fault tolerance.
- **MLib**: The Spark machine learning library.
- **GraphX**: Graphs and graph-parallel computation algorithms.

Spark can access data that's stored in different systems, such as HDFS, Cassandra, MongoDB, relational databases, and also cloud storage services such as Amazon S3 and Azure Data Lake Storage.

Getting Spark

Now, let's get hands-on with Spark so that we can go deeper into the core APIs and libraries. In all of the chapters of this book, I will be referring to the 2.2.1 release of Spark, however, several examples that are presented here should work with the 2.0 release or later. I will put a note when an example is specifically for 2.2+ releases only.

First of all, you need to download Spark from its official website (`https://spark.apache.org/downloads.html`). The download page should look like this:

Download Apache Spark™

1. Choose a Spark release: **2.2.1 (Dec 01 2017)** ▾

2. Choose a package type: **Pre-built for Apache Hadoop 2.7 and later** ▾

3. Download Spark: spark-2.2.1-bin-hadoop2.7.tgz

4. Verify this release using the 2.2.1 signatures and checksums and project release KEYS.

Figure 1.4

You need to have JDK 1.8+ and Python 2.7+ or 3.4+ (only if you need to develop using this language). Spark 2.2.1 supports Scala 2.11. The JDK needs to be present on your user path system variable, though, alternatively, you could have your user `JAVA_HOME` environment variable pointing to a JDK installation.

Extract the content of the downloaded archive to any local directory. Move to the `$SPARK_HOME/bin` directory. There, among the other executables, you will find the interactive Spark shells for Scala and Python. They are the best way to get familiar with this framework. In this chapter, I am going to present examples that you can run through these shells.

You can run a Scala shell using the following command:

```
$SPARK_HOME/bin/spark-shell.sh
```

If you don't specify an argument, Spark assumes that you're running locally in standalone mode. Here's the expected output to the console:

```
Spark context Web UI available at http://10.72.0.2:4040
Spark context available as 'sc' (master = local[*], app id =
local-1518131682342).
Spark session available as 'spark'.
Welcome to
      ____              __
     / __/__  ___ _____/ /__
    _\ \/ _ \/ _ `/ __/  '_/
   /___/ .__/\_,_/_/ /_/\_\   version 2.2.1
      /_/
```

```
Using Scala version 2.11.8 (Java HotSpot(TM) 64-Bit Server VM, Java
1.8.0_91)
Type in expressions to have them evaluated.
Type :help for more information.

scala>
```

The web UI is available at the following URL: `http://<host>:4040`.

It will give you the following output:

Figure 1.5

From there, you can check the status of your jobs and executors.

From the output of the console startup, you will notice that two built-in variables, `sc` and `spark`, are available. `sc` represents the `SparkContext` (http://spark.apache.org/docs/latest/api/scala/index.html#org.apache.spark.SparkContext), which in Spark < 2.0 was the entry point for each application. Through the Spark context (and its specializations), you can get input data from data sources, create and manipulate RDDs (http://spark.apache.org/docs/latest/api/scala/index.html#org.apache.spark.rdd.RDD), and attain the Spark primary abstraction before 2.0. The *RDD programming* section will cover this topic and other operations in more detail. Starting from release 2.0, a new entry point, `SparkSession` (http://spark.apache.org/docs/latest/api/scala/index.html#org.apache.spark.sql.SparkSession), and a new main data abstraction, the Dataset (http://spark.apache.org/docs/latest/api/scala/index.html#org.apache.spark.sql.Dataset), were introduced. More details on them are presented in the following sections. The `SparkContext` is still part of the Spark API so that compatibility with existing frameworks not supporting Spark sessions is ensured, but the direction the project has taken is to move development to use the `SparkSession`.

Here's an example of how to read and manipulate a text file and put it into a Dataset using the Spark shell (the file used in this example is part of the resources for the examples that are bundled with the Spark distribution):

```
scala>
spark.read.textFile("/usr/spark-2.2.1/examples/src/main/resources/people.txt")
res5: org.apache.spark.sql.Dataset[String] = [value: string]
```

The result is a Dataset instance that contains the file lines. You can then make several operations on this Dataset, such as counting the number of lines:

```
scala> res5.count()
res6: Long = 3
```

You can also get the first line of the Dataset:

```
scala> res5.first()
res7: String = Michael, 29
```

In this example, we used a path on the local filesystem. In these cases, the file should be accessible from the same path by all of the workers, so you will need to copy the file across all workers or use a network-mounted shared filesystem.

To close a shell, you can type the following:

```
:quit
```

To see the list of all of the available shell commands, type the following:

```scala
scala> :help
```

All commands can be abbreviated, for example, `:he` instead of `:help`.

The following is the list of commands:

Commands	Purpose
`:edit <id>|<line>`	Edit history
`:help [command]`	Prints summary or command-specific help
`:history [num]`	Shows history (optional `num` is commands to show)
`:h? <string>`	Search history
`:imports [name name ...]`	Show import history, identifying the sources of names
`:implicits [-v]`	Show the `implicits` in scope
`:javap <path|class>`	Disassemble a file or class name
`:line <id>|<line>`	Place line(s) at the end of history
`:load <path>`	Interpret lines in a file
`:paste [-raw] [path]`	Enter paste mode or paste a file
`:power`	Enable power user mode
`:quit`	Exit the interpreter
`:replay [options]`	Reset the `repl` and `replay` on all previous commands
`:require <path>`	Add a `jar` to the classpath
`:reset [options]`	Reset the `repl` to its initial state, forgetting all session entries
`:save <path>`	Save the replayable session to a file
`:sh <command line>`	Run a shell command (the result is `implicitly =>` `List[String]`)
`:settings <options>`	Update compiler options, if possible; see `reset`
`:silent`	Disable or enable the automatic printing of results
`:type [-v] <expr>`	Display the type of expression without evaluating it
`:kind [-v] <expr>`	Display the kind of expression
`:warnings`	Show the suppressed warnings from the most recent line that had any

Like Scala, an interactive shell is available for Python. You can run it using the following command:

```
$SPARK_HOME/bin/pyspark.sh
```

A built-in variable named `spark` representing the `SparkSession` is available. You can do the same things as for the Scala shell:

```
>>> textFileDf =
spark.read.text("/usr/spark-2.2.1/examples/src/main/resources/people.txt")
>>> textFileDf.count()
3
>>> textFileDf.first()
Row(value='Michael, 29')
```

Unlike Java and Scala, Python is more dynamic and is not strongly typed. Therefore, a `DataSet` in Python is a `DataSet[Row]`, but you can call it a DataFrame so that it's consistent with the DataFrame concept of the Pandas framework (https://pandas.pydata.org/).

To close a Python shell, you can type the following:

```
quit()
```

Interactive shells aren't the only choice for running code in Spark. It is also possible to implement self-contained applications. Here's an example of reading and manipulating a file in Scala:

```scala
import org.apache.spark.sql.SparkSession

object SimpleApp {
  def main(args: Array[String]) {
    val logFile = "/usr/spark-2.2.1/examples/src/main/resources/people.txt"
    val spark = SparkSession.builder.master("local").appName("Simple
Application").getOrCreate()
    val logData = spark.read.textFile(logFile).cache()
    val numAs = logData.filter(line => line.contains("a")).count()
    val numBs = logData.filter(line => line.contains("b")).count()
    println(s"Lines with a: $numAs, Lines with b: $numBs")
    spark.stop()
  }
}
```

Applications should define a `main()` method instead of extending `scala.App`. Note the code to create `SparkSession`:

```scala
val spark = SparkSession.builder.master("local").appName("Simple
Application").getOrCreate()
```

It follows the builder factory design pattern.

Always explicitly close the session before ending the program execution:

```
spark.stop()
```

To build the application, you can use a build tool of your choice (`Maven`, `sbt`, or `Gradle`), adding the dependencies from Spark 2.2.1 and Scala 2.11. Once a JAR file has been generated, you can use the `$SPARK_HOME/bin/spark-submit` command to execute it, specifying the JAR filename, the Spark master URL, and a list of optional parameters, including the job name, the main class, the maximum memory to be used by each executor, and many others.

The same self-contained application could have been implemented in Python as well:

```python
from pyspark.sql import SparkSession

logFile = "YOUR_SPARK_HOME/README.md"  # Should be some file on your system
spark =
SparkSession.builder().appName(appName).master(master).getOrCreate()
logData = spark.read.text(logFile).cache()

numAs = logData.filter(logData.value.contains('a')).count()
numBs = logData.filter(logData.value.contains('b')).count()

print("Lines with a: %i, lines with b: %i" % (numAs, numBs))

spark.stop()
```

This can be saved in a `.py` file and submitted through the same `$SPARK_HOME/bin/spark-submit` command for execution.

RDD programming

In general, every Spark application is a driver program that runs the logic that has been implemented for it and executes parallel operations on a cluster. In accordance with the previous definition, the main abstraction provided by the core Spark framework is the RDD. It is an immutable distributed collection of data that is partitioned across machines in a cluster. Operations on RDDs can happen in parallel.

Two types of operations are available on an RDD:

- Transformations
- Actions

A **transformation** is an operation on an RDD that produces another RDD, while an **action** is an operation that triggers some computation and then returns a value to the master or can be persisted to a storage system. Transformations are lazy—they aren't executed until an action is invoked. Here's the strength point of Spark—Spark masters and their drivers both remember the transformations that have been applied to an RDD, so if a partition is lost (for example, a slave goes down), it can be easily rebuilt on some other node of the cluster.

The following table lists some of the common transformations supported by Spark:

Transformation	Purpose
map(func)	Returns a new RDD by applying the func function on each data element of the source RDD.
filter(func)	Returns a new RDD by selecting those data elements for which the applied func function returns true.
flatMap(func)	This transformation is similar to map: the difference is that each input item can be mapped to zero or multiple output items (the applied func function should return a Seq).
union(otherRdd)	Returns a new RDD that contains the union of the elements in the source RDD and the otherRdd argument.
distinct([numPartitions])	Returns a new RDD that contains only the distinct elements of the source RDD.
groupByKey([numPartiotions])	When called on an RDD of (K, V) pairs, it returns an RDD of (K, Iterable<V>) pairs. By default, the level of parallelism in the output RDD depends on the number of partitions of the source RDD. You can pass an optional numPartitions argument to set a different number of partitions.
reduceByKey(func, [numPartitions])	When called on an RDD of (K, V) pairs, it returns an RDD of (K, V) pairs, where the values for each key are aggregated using the given reduce func function, which must be of type $(V,V) => V$. The same as for the groupByKey transformation, the number of reduce partitions is configurable through an optional numPartitions second argument.

`sortByKey([ascending], [numPartitions])`	When called on an RDD of (K, V) pairs, it returns an RDD of (K, V) pairs sorted by keys in ascending or descending order, as specified in the Boolean `ascending` argument. The number of partitions for the output RDD is configurable through an optional `numPartitions` second argument.
`join(otherRdd, [numPartitions])`	When called on RDDs of type (K, V) and (K, W), it returns an RDD of (K, (V, W)) pairs with all pairs of elements for each key. It supports left outer join, right outer join, and full outer join. The number of partitions for the output RDD is configurable through an optional `numPartitions` second argument.

The following table lists some of the common actions supported by Spark:

Action	Purpose
`reduce(func)`	Aggregates the elements of an RDD using a given function, `func` (this takes two arguments and returns one). To ensure the correct parallelism at compute time, the reduce function, `func`, has to be commutative and associative.
`collect()`	Returns all the elements of an RDD as an array to the driver.
`count()`	Returns the total number of elements in an RDD.
`first()`	Returns the first element of an RDD.
`take(n)`	Returns an array containing the first *n* elements of an RDD.
`foreach(func)`	Executes the `func` function on each element of an RDD.
`saveAsTextFile(path)`	Writes the elements of an RDD as a text file in a given directory (with the absolute location specified through the `path` argument) in the local filesystem, HDFS, or any other Hadoop-supported filesystem. This is available for Scala and Java only.
`countByKey()`	This action is only available on RDDs of type (K, V) – it returns a hashmap of (K, *Int*) pairs, where *K* is a key of the source RDD and its value is the count for that given key, *K*.

Now, let's understand the concepts of transformation and action through an example that could be executed in the Scala shell—this finds the *N* most commonly used words in an input text file. The following diagram depicts a potential implementation for this problem:

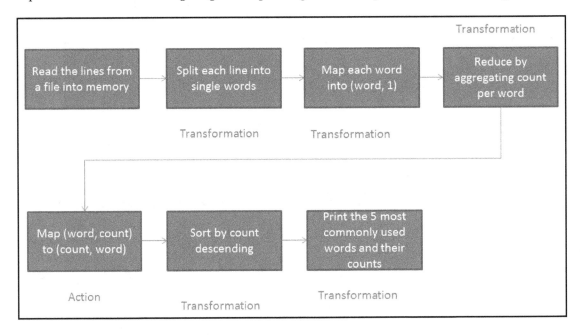

Figure 1.6

Let's translate this into code.

First of all, let's load the content of a text file into an RDD of strings:

```
scala> val spiderman = sc.textFile("/usr/spark-2.2.1/tests/spiderman.txt")
spiderman: org.apache.spark.rdd.RDD[String] =
/usr/spark-2.2.1/tests/spiderman.txt MapPartitionsRDD[1] at textFile at
<console>:24
```

Then, we will apply the necessary transformations and actions:

```
scala> val topWordCount = spiderman.flatMap(str=>str.split("
")).filter(!_.isEmpty).map(word=>(word,1)).reduceByKey(_+_).map{case(word,
count) => (count, word)}.sortByKey(false)
topWordCount: org.apache.spark.rdd.RDD[(Int, String)] = ShuffledRDD[9] at
sortByKey at <console>:26
```

Here, we have the following:

- `flatMap(str=>str.split(" "))`: Splits each line into single words
- `filter(!_.isEmpty)`: Removes empty strings
- `map(word=>(word,1))`: Maps each word into a key-value pair
- `reduceByKey(_+_)`: Aggregates the count
- `map{case(word, count) => (count, word)}`: Reverses the `(word, count)` pairs to `(count, word)`
- `sortByKey(false)`: Sorts by descending order

Finally, print the five most used words in the input content to the console:

```
scala> topWordCount.take(5).foreach(x=>println(x))
(34,the)
(28,and)
(19,of)
(19,in)
(16,Spider-Man)
```

The same could be achieved in Python in the following way:

```
from operator import add
spiderman = spark.read.text("/usr/spark-2.2.1/tests/spiderman.txt")
lines = spiderman.rdd.map(lambda r: r[0])
counts = lines.flatMap(lambda x: x.split(' ')) \
                .map(lambda x: (x, 1)) \
                .reduceByKey(add) \
                .map(lambda x: (x[1],x[0])) \
                .sortByKey(False)
```

The result, of course, is the same as for the Scala example:

```
>> counts.take(5)
[(34, 'the'), (28, 'and'), (19, 'in'), (19, 'of'), (16, 'Spider-Man')]
```

Spark can persist RDDs (and Datasets as well) in memory while executing operations on them. Persisting and caching are synonyms in Spark. When persisting an RDD, each node of the cluster stores the RDD partitions that it needs to compute in memory and reuses them in further actions on the same RDD (or RDDs that have been derived from it through some transformations). This is the reason why future actions execute much faster. It is possible to mark an RDD to be persisted using its `persist()` method. The first time an action is executed on it, it will be kept in memory on the cluster's nodes. The Spark cache is fault-tolerant—this means that, if for any reason all of the partitions of an RDD are lost, it will be automatically recalculated using the transformations that created it. A persisted RDD can be stored using different storage levels. Levels can be set by passing a `StorageLevel` object to the `persist()` method of the RDD. The following table lists all of the available storage levels and their meanings:

Storage Level	Purpose
MEMORY_ONLY	This is the default storage level. It stores RDDs as deserialized Java objects in memory. In those cases where an RDD shouldn't fit in memory, some of its partitions won't be cached and will be recalculated on the fly when needed.
MEMORY_AND_DISK	It stores RDDs as deserialized Java objects in memory first, but, in those cases where an RDD shouldn't fit in memory, it stores some partitions on disk (this is the main difference between MEMORY_ONLY), and reads them from there when needed.
MEMORY_ONLY_SER	It stores RDDs as serialized Java objects. Compared to MEMORY_ONLY, this is more space-efficient, but more CPU-intensive in read operations. This is available for JVM languages only.
MEMORY_AND_DISK_SER	Is similar to MEMORY_ONLY_SER (it stores RDDs as serialized Java objects), with the main difference being that it stores partitions that don't fit in memory to disk. This is available only for JVM languages.
DISK_ONLY	It stores the RDD partitions on disk only.
MEMORY_ONLY_2, MEMORY_AND_DISK_2, and so on	The same as the two preceding levels (MEMORY_ONLY and MEMORY_AND_DISK), but each partition is replicated on two cluster nodes.
OFF_HEAP	Similar to MEMORY_ONLY_SER, but it stores data in off-heap memory (assuming off-heap memory is enabled). Please be careful when using this storage level as it is still experimental.

When a function is passed to a Spark operation, it is executed on a remote cluster node that will work on separate copies of all the variables that are used in the function. Once done, the variables will be copied to each machine. There will be no updates to the variables on the remote machine when propagated back to the driver program. It would be inefficient to support general, read-write shared variables across tasks.

However, there are two limited types of shared variables that are available in Spark for two common usage patterns – broadcast variables and accumulators.

One of the most common operations in Spark programming is to perform joins on RDDs to consolidate data by a given key. In these cases, it is quite possible to have large Datasets sent around to slave nodes that host the partitions to be joined. You can easily understand that this situation presents a huge performance bottleneck, as network I/O is 100 times slower than RAM access. To mitigate this issue, Spark provides broadcast variables, which are broadcast to slave nodes. RDD operations on the nodes can quickly access the broadcast variable value. Spark also attempts to distribute broadcast variables using efficient broadcast algorithms to reduce communication costs. Broadcast variables are created from a variable, *v*, by calling the `SparkContext.broadcast(v)` method. The broadcast variable is a wrapper around *v*, and its value can be obtained by calling the `value` method. Here's an example in Scala that you can run through the Spark shell:

```scala
scala> val broadcastVar = sc.broadcast(Array(1, 2, 3))
broadcastVar: org.apache.spark.broadcast.Broadcast[Array[Int]] =
Broadcast(0)

scala> broadcastVar.value
res0: Array[Int] = Array(1, 2, 3)
```

After its creation, the broadcast variable, `broadcastVar`, can be used in any function that's executed on the cluster, but not the initial value, *v*, as this prevents *v* being shipped to all the nodes more than once. To ensure that all the nodes get the same value of the broadcast variable, *v* must not be modified after `broadcastVar` has been broadcast.

Here's the code for the same example in Python:

```python
>>> broadcastVar = sc.broadcast([1, 2, 3])
 <pyspark.broadcast.Broadcast object at 0x102789f10>

>>> broadcastVar.value
 [1, 2, 3]
```

To aggregate information across executors in a Spark cluster, `accumulator` variables should be used. The fact that they are added through an associative and commutative operation ensures their efficient support in parallel computation. Spark natively provides support for the accumulators of numeric types—they can be created by calling `SparkContext.longAccumulator()` (to accumulate values of type `Long`) or `SparkContext.doubleAccumulator()` (to accumulate values of type `Double`) methods.

However, it is possible to programmatically add support for other types. Any task running on a cluster can add to an accumulator using the add method, but they cannot read its value – this operation is only allowed for the driver program, which uses its value method. Here's a code example in Scala:

```
scala> val accum = sc.longAccumulator("First Long Accumulator")
accum: org.apache.spark.util.LongAccumulator = LongAccumulator(id: 0, name:
Some
(First Long Accumulator), value: 0)

scala> sc.parallelize(Array(1, 2, 3, 4)).foreach(x => accum.add(x))
[Stage 0:>                                                        (0 + 0)
/ 8]


scala> accum.value
res1: Long = 10
```

In this case, an accumulator has been created, and has assigned a name to it. It is possible to create unnamed accumulators, but a named accumulator will display in the web UI for the stage that modifies that accumulator:

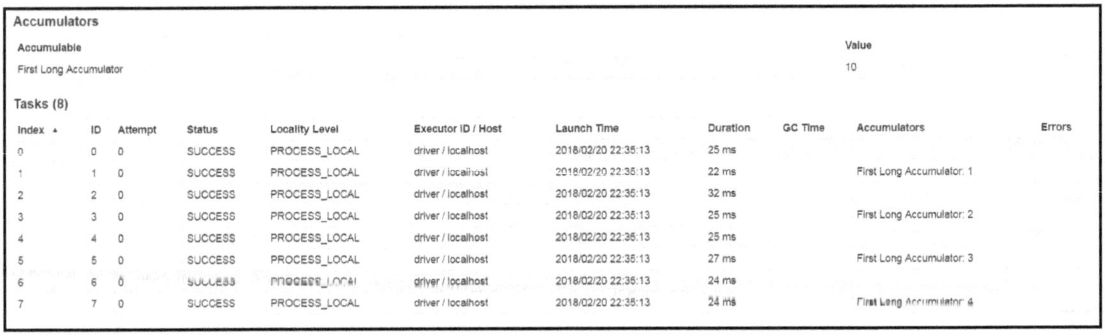

Accumulators									
Accumulable								Value	
First Long Accumulator								10	

Tasks (8)

Index ▲	ID	Attempt	Status	Locality Level	Executor ID / Host	Launch Time	Duration	GC Time	Accumulators	Errors
0	0	0	SUCCESS	PROCESS_LOCAL	driver / localhost	2018/02/20 22:35:13	25 ms			
1	1	0	SUCCESS	PROCESS_LOCAL	driver / localhost	2018/02/20 22:35:13	22 ms		First Long Accumulator: 1	
2	2	0	SUCCESS	PROCESS_LOCAL	driver / localhost	2018/02/20 22:35:13	32 ms			
3	3	0	SUCCESS	PROCESS_LOCAL	driver / localhost	2018/02/20 22:35:13	25 ms		First Long Accumulator: 2	
4	4	0	SUCCESS	PROCESS_LOCAL	driver / localhost	2018/02/20 22:35:13	25 ms			
5	5	0	SUCCESS	PROCESS_LOCAL	driver / localhost	2018/02/20 22:35:13	27 ms		First Long Accumulator: 3	
6	6	0	SUCCESS	PROCESS_LOCAL	driver / localhost	2018/02/20 22:35:13	24 ms			
7	7	0	SUCCESS	PROCESS_LOCAL	driver / localhost	2018/02/20 22:35:13	24 ms		First Long Accumulator: 4	

Figure 1.7

This can be helpful for understanding the progress of running stages.

The same example in Python is as follows:

```
>>> accum = sc.accumulator(0)
>>> accum
Accumulator<id=0, value=0>

>>> sc.parallelize([1, 2, 3, 4]).foreach(lambda x: accum.add(x))
>>> accum.value
10
```

Tracking accumulators in the web UI isn't supported for Python.

Please be aware that Spark guarantees to update accumulators *inside actions only*. When restarting a task, the accumulators will be updated only once. The same isn't true for transformations.

Spark SQL, Datasets, and DataFrames

Spark SQL is the Spark module for structured data processing. The main difference between this API and the RDD API is that the provided Spark SQL interfaces give more information about the structure of both the data and the performed computation. This extra information is used by Spark internally to add extra optimizations through the Catalyst optimization engine, which is the same execution engine that's used regardless of whatever API or programming language is involved.

Spark SQL is commonly used to execute SQL queries (even if this isn't the only way to use it). Whatever programming language supported by Spark encapsulates the SQL code to be executed, the results of a query are returned as a **Dataset**. A Dataset is a distributed collection of data, and was added as an interface in Spark 1.6. It combines the benefits of RDDs (such as strong typing and the ability to apply useful lambda functions) with the benefits of Spark SQL's optimized execution engine (Catalyst, `https://databricks.com/blog/2015/04/13/deep-dive-into-spark-sqls-catalyst-optimizer.html`). You can construct a Dataset by starting with Java/Scala objects and then manipulating it through the usual functional transformations. The Dataset API is available in Scala and Java, while Python doesn't have support for it. However, due to the dynamic nature of this programming language, many of the benefits of the Dataset API are already available for it. Starting from Spark 2.0, the DataFrame and Dataset APIs have been merged into the Dataset API, so a **DataFrame** is just a Dataset that's been organized into named columns and is conceptually equivalent to a table in an RDBMS, but with better optimizations under the hood (being part of the Dataset API, the Catalyst optimization engine works behind the scenes for DataFrames, too). You can construct a DataFrame from diverse sources, such as structured data files, Hive tables, database tables, and RDDs, to name a few. Unlike the Dataset API, the DataFrame API is available in any of the programming languages that are supported by Spark.

Let's start and get hands-on so that we can better understand the concepts behind Spark SQL. The first full example I am going to show is Scala-based. Start a Scala Spark shell to run the following code interactively.

Let's use `people.json` as a data source. One of the files that's available as a resource for this example has been shipped along with the Spark distribution and can be used to create a DataFrame that's a Dataset of Rows (`http://spark.apache.org/docs/latest/api/scala/index.html#org.apache.spark.sql.Row`):

```
val df = spark.read.json("/opt/spark/spark-2.2.1-bin-
hadoop2.7/examples/src/main/resources/people.json")
```

You can print the content of the DataFrame to the console to check that it is what you expected:

```
scala> df.show()
+----+-------+
| age|   name|
+----+-------+
|null|Michael|
|  30|   Andy|
|  19| Justin|
+----+-------+
```

Before you perform DataFrame operations, you need to import the implicit conversions (such as converting RDDs to DataFrames) and use the `$` notation:

```
import spark.implicits._
```

Now, you can print the DataFrame schema in a tree format:

```
scala> df.printSchema()
root
 |-- age: long (nullable = true)
 |-- name: string (nullable = true)
```

Select a single column (let's say `name`):

```
scala> df.select("name").show()
+-------+
|   name|
+-------+
|Michael|
|   Andy|
| Justin|
+-------+
```

Filter the data:

```
scala> df.filter($"age" > 27).show()
+---+----+
|age|name|
+---+----+
| 30|Andy|
+---+----+
```

Then add a `groupBy` clause:

```
scala> df.groupBy("age").count().show()
+----+-----+
| age|count|
+----+-----+
|  19|    1|
|null|    1|
|  30|    1|
+----+-----+
```

Select all rows and increment a numeric field:

```
scala> df.select($"name", $"age" + 1).show()
+-------+---------+
| name|(age + 1)|
+-------+---------+
|Michael| null|
| Andy| 31|
| Justin| 20|
+-------+---------+
```

It is possible to run SQL queries programmatically through the `sql` function of `SparkSession`. This function returns the results of the query in a DataFrame, which, for Scala, is a `Dataset[Row]`. Let's consider the same DataFrame as for the previous example:

```
val df = spark.read.json("/opt/spark/spark-2.2.1-bin-
hadoop2.7/examples/src/main/resources/people.json")
```

You can register it as an SQL temporary view:

```
df.createOrReplaceTempView("people")
```

Then, you can execute an SQL query there:

```scala
scala> val sqlDF = spark.sql("SELECT * FROM people")
sqlDF: org.apache.spark.sql.DataFrame = [age: bigint, name: string]

scala> sqlDF.show()
+----+-------+
| age|   name|
+----+-------+
|null|Michael|
|  30|   Andy|
|  19| Justin|
+----+-------+
```

The same things can be done in Python as well:

```python
>>> df = spark.read.json("/opt/spark/spark-2.2.1-bin-
hadoop2.7/examples/src/main/resources/people.json")
```

Resulting in the following:

```python
>> df.show()
+----+-------+
| age|   name|
+----+-------+
|null|Michael|
|  30|   Andy|
|  19| Justin|
+----+-------+

>>> df.printSchema()
root
 |-- age: long (nullable = true)
 |-- name: string (nullable = true)

>>> df.select("name").show()
+-------+
|   name|
+-------+
|Michael|
|   Andy|
| Justin|
+-------+
```

```
>>> df.filter(df['age'] > 21).show()
+---+----+
|age|name|
+---+----+
| 30|Andy|
+---+----+

>>> df.groupBy("age").count().show()
+----+-----+
| age|count|
+----+-----+
|  19|    1|
|null|    1|
|  30|    1|
+----+-----+

>>> df.select(df['name'], df['age'] + 1).show()
+-------+---------+
|   name|(age + 1)|
+-------+---------+
|Michael|     null|
|   Andy|       31|
| Justin|       20|
+-------+---------+

>>> df.createOrReplaceTempView("people")
>>> sqlDF = spark.sql("SELECT * FROM people")
>>> sqlDF.show()
+----+-------+
| age|   name|
+----+-------+
|null|Michael|
|  30|   Andy|
|  19| Justin|
+----+-------+
```

Other features of Spark SQL and Datasets (data sources, aggregations, self-contained applications, and so on) will be covered in Chapter 3, *Extract, Transform, Load*.

Spark Streaming

Spark Streaming is another Spark module that extends the core Spark API and provides a scalable, fault-tolerant, and efficient way of processing live streaming data. By converting streaming data into *micro* batches, Spark's simple batch programming model can be applied in streaming use cases too. This unified programming model makes it easy to combine batch and interactive data processing with streaming. Diverse sources that ingest data are supported (Kafka, Kinesis, TCP sockets, S3, or HDFS, just to mention a few of the popular ones), as well as data coming from them, and can be processed using any of the high-level functions available in Spark. Finally, the processed data can be persisted to RDBMS, NoSQL databases, HDFS, object storage systems, and so on, or consumed through live dashboards. Nothing prevents other advanced Spark components, such as MLlib or GraphX, being applied to data streams:

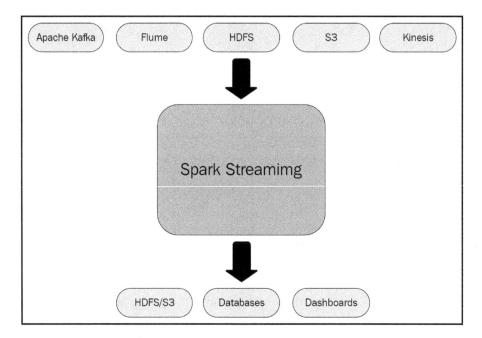

Figure 1.8

The following diagram shows how Spark Streaming works internally—it receives live input data streams and divides them into batches; these are processed by the Spark engine to generate the final batches of results:

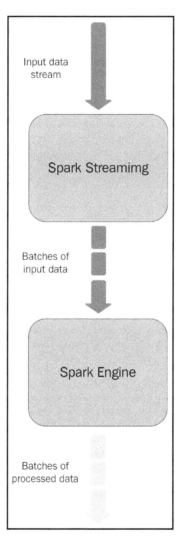

Figure 1.9

The higher-level abstraction of Spark Streaming is the **DStream** (short for **Discretized Stream**), which is a wrapper around a continuous flow of data. Internally, a DStream is represented as a sequence of RDDs. A DStream contains a list of other DStreams that it depends on, a function to convert its input RDDs into output ones, and a time interval at which to invoke the function. DStreams are created by either manipulating existing ones, for example, applying a map or filter function (which internally creates `MappedDStreams` and `FilteredDStreams`, respectively), or by reading from an external source (the base class in these cases is `InputDStream`).

Let's implement a simple Scala example—a streaming word count self-contained application. The code used for this class can be found among the examples that are bundled with the Spark distribution. To compile and package it, you need to add the dependency to Spark Streaming to your `Maven`, `Gradle`, or `sbt` project descriptor, along with the dependencies from Spark Core and Scala.

First, we have to create the `SparkConf` and a `StreamingContext` (which is the main entry point for any streaming functionality) from it:

```
import org.apache.spark.SparkConf
import org.apache.spark.streaming.{Seconds, StreamingContext}
val sparkConf = new
SparkConf().setAppName("NetworkWordCount").setMaster("local[*]")
  val ssc = new StreamingContext(sparkConf, Seconds(1))
```

The batch interval has been set to 1 second. A DStream representing streaming data from a TCP source can be created using the `ssc` streaming context; we need just to specify the source hostname and port, as well as the desired storage level:

```
val lines = ssc.socketTextStream(args(0), args(1).toInt,
StorageLevel.MEMORY_AND_DISK_SER)
```

The returned `lines` DStream is the stream of data that is going to be received from the server. Each record will be a single line of text that we want to split into single words, thus specifying the space character as a separator:

```
val words = lines.flatMap(_.split(" "))
```

Then, we will count those words:

```
val words = lines.flatMap(_.split(" "))
  val wordCounts = words.map(x => (x, 1)).reduceByKey(_ + _)
wordCounts.print()
```

The `words` DStream is mapped (a one-to-one transformation) to a DStream of (*word*, *1*) pairs, which is then reduced to get the frequency of words in each batch of data. The last command will print a few of the counts that are generated every second. Each RDD in a DStream contains data from a certain interval – any operation applied on a DStream translates to operations on the underlying RDDs:

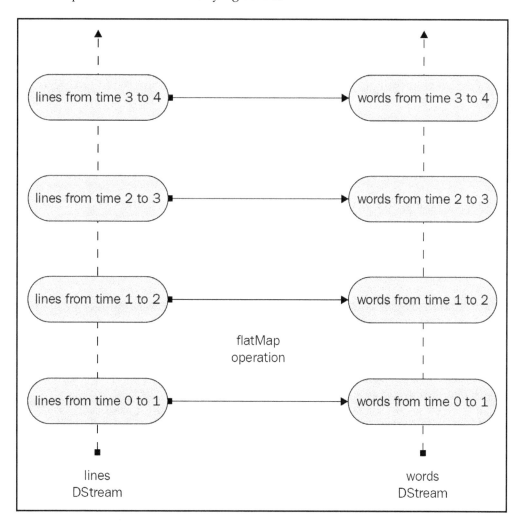

Figure 1.10

To start the processing after all the transformations have been set up, use the following code:

```
ssc.start()
  ssc.awaitTermination()
```

Before running this example, first you will need to run netcat (a small utility found in most Unix-like systems) as a data server:

```
nc -lk 9999
```

Then, in a different Terminal, you can start the example by passing the following as arguments:

```
localhost 9999
```

Any line that's typed into the Terminal and run with the netcat server will be counted and printed on the application screen every second.

Regardless of whether nc shouldn't be available in the system where you run this example, you can implement your own data server in Scala:

```
import java.io.DataOutputStream
import java.net.{ServerSocket, Socket}
import java.util.Scanner

object SocketWriter {
  def main(args: Array[String]) {
    val listener = new ServerSocket(9999)
    val socket = listener.accept()
    val outputStream = new DataOutputStream(socket.getOutputStream())
    System.out.println("Start writing data. Enter close when finish");
    val sc = new Scanner(System.in)
    var str = ""
    /**
     * Read content from scanner and write to socket.
     */
    while (!(str = sc.nextLine()).equals("close")) {
        outputStream.writeUTF(str);
    }
    //close connection now.
    outputStream.close()
    listener.close()
  }
}
```

The same self-contained application in Python could be as follows:

```
from __future__ import print_function

import sys

from pyspark import SparkContext
from pyspark.streaming import StreamingContext

if __name__ == "__main__":
    if len(sys.argv) != 3:
        print("Usage: network_wordcount.py <hostname> <port>",
file=sys.stderr)
        exit(-1)
    sc = SparkContext(appName="PythonStreamingNetworkWordCount")
    ssc = StreamingContext(sc, 1)

    lines = ssc.socketTextStream(sys.argv[1], int(sys.argv[2]))
    counts = lines.flatMap(lambda line: line.split(" "))\
                .map(lambda word: (word, 1))\
                .reduceByKey(lambda a, b: a+b)
    counts.pprint()

    ssc.start()
    ssc.awaitTermination()
```

DStreams support most parts of the transformations that are available for RDDs. This means that data from input DStreams can be modified in the same way as the data in RDDs. The following table lists some of the common transformations supported by Spark DStreams:

Transformation	Purpose
map(func)	Returns a new DStream. The func map function is applied to each element of the source DStream.
flatMap(func)	The same as for map. The only difference is that each input item in the new DStream can be mapped to 0 or more output items.
filter(func)	Returns a new DStream containing only the elements of the source DStream for which the func filter function returned true.
repartition(numPartitions)	This is used to set the level of parallelism by creating a different number of partitions.
union(otherStream)	Returns a new DStream. It contains the union of the elements in the source DStream and the input otherDStream DStream.

count()	Returns a new DStream. It contains single element RDDs that are obtained by counting the number of elements contained in each RDD arriving from the source.
reduce(func)	Returns a new DStream. It contains single element RDDs that are obtained by aggregating those in each RDD of the source by applying the func function (which should be associative and commutative to allow for correct parallel computation).
countByValue()	Returns a new DStream of (K, Long) pairs, where K is the type of the elements of the source. The value of each key represents its frequency in each RDD of the source.
reduceByKey(func, [numTasks])	Returns a new DStream of (K, V) pairs (for a source DStream of (K, V) pairs). The values for each key are aggregated by applying the reduce func function. To do the grouping, this transformation uses Spark's default number of parallel tasks (which is two in local mode, while it is determined by the config property spark.default.parallelism in cluster mode), but this can be changed by passing an optional numTasks argument.
join(otherStream, [numTasks])	Returns a new DStream of (K, (V, W)) pairs when called on two DStreams of (K, V) and (K, W) pairs, respectively.
cogroup(otherStream, [numTasks])	Returns a new DStream of (K, Seq[V], Seq[W]) tuples when called on two DStreams of (K, V) and (K, W) pairs, respectively.
transform(func)	Returns a new DStream. It applies an RDD-to-RDD func function to every RDD of the source.
updateStateByKey(func)	Returns a new state DStream. The state for each key in the new DStream is updated by applying the func input function to the previous state and the new values for the key.

Windowed computations are provided by Spark Streaming. As shown in the following diagram, they allow you to apply transformations over sliding windows of data:

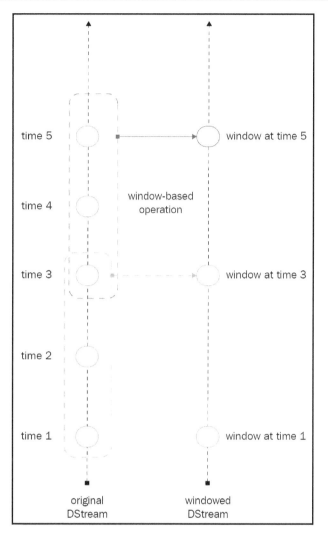

Figure 1.11

When a window slides over a source DStream, all its RDDs that fall within that window are taken into account and transformed to produce the RDDs of the returned windowed DStream. Looking at the specific example that's shown in the preceding diagram, the window-based operation is applied over three time units of data and it slides by two. Two parameters need to be specified by any window operation that's used:

- **Window length**: The duration of the window
- **Sliding interval**: The interval at which the window operation is performed

These two parameters must be multiples of the batch interval of the source DStream.

Let's see how this could be applied to the application that was presented at the beginning of this section. Suppose you want to generate a word count every 10 seconds over the last 60 seconds of data. The `reduceByKey` operation needs to be applied on the (*word, 1*) pairs of the DStream over the last 60 seconds of data. This can be achieved with the `reduceByKeyAndWindow` operation. When translated into Scala code, this is as follows:

```
val windowedWordCounts = pairs.reduceByKeyAndWindow((a:Int,b:Int) => (a +
b), Seconds(60), Seconds(10))
```

For Python, it is as follows:

```
windowedWordCounts = pairs.reduceByKeyAndWindow(lambda x, y: x + y, lambda
x, y: x - y, 60, 10)
```

The following table lists some of the common window operations supported by Spark for DStreams:

Transformation	Purpose
`window(windowLength, slideInterval)`	Returns a new DStream. It is based on windowed batches of the source.
`countByWindow(windowLength, slideInterval)`	Returns a sliding window count (based on the `windowLength` and `slideInterval` parameters) of elements in the source DStream.
`reduceByWindow(func, windowLength, slideInterval)`	Returns a new single element DStream. It is created by aggregating elements in the source DStream over a sliding interval by applying the `func` reduce function (which, to allow for correct parallel computation, is associative and commutative)
`reduceByKeyAndWindow(func, windowLength, slideInterval, [numTasks])`	Returns a new DStream of (*K, V*) pairs (the same *K* and *V* as for the source DStream). The values for each key are aggregated using the `func` input function over batches (defined by the `windowLength` and `slideInterval` arguments) in a sliding window. The number of parallel tasks to do the grouping is two (default) in local mode, while in cluster mode this is given by the Spark configuration property `spark.default.parallelism`. `numTask`, which is an optional argument to specify a custom number of tasks.

reduceByKeyAndWindow(func, invFunc, windowLength, slideInterval, [numTasks])	This is a more efficient version of the reduceByKeyAndWindow transformation. This time, the reduce value of the current window is calculated incrementally using the reduce values of the previous one. This happens by reducing the new data that enters a window while inverse reducing the old data that leaves the same one. Please note that this mechanism only works if the func reduce function has a corresponding inverse reduce function, invFunc.
countByValueAndWindow(windowLength, slideInterval, [numTasks])	Returns a DStream of (*K, Long*) pairs (whatever (*K, V*) pairs the source DStream is made of). The value of each key in the returned DStream is its frequency within a given sliding window (defined by the windowLength and slideInterval arguments). numTask is an optional argument to specify a custom number of tasks.

Cluster mode using different managers

The following diagram shows how Spark applications run on a cluster. They are independent sets of processes that are coordinated by the SparkContext object in the **Driver Program**. SparkContext connects to a **Cluster Manager**, which is responsible for allocating resources across applications. Once the **SparkContext** is connected, Spark gets executors across cluster nodes.

Executors are processes that execute computations and store data for a given Spark application. **SparkContext** sends the application code (which could be a JAR file for Scala or .py files for Python) to the executors. Finally, it sends the tasks to run to the executors:

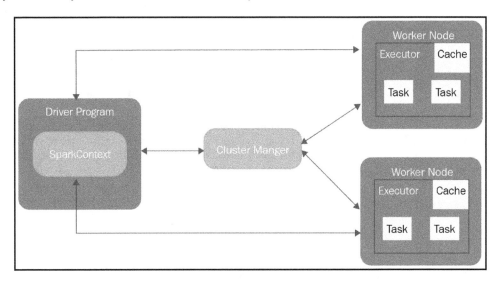

Figure 1.12

To isolate applications from each other, every Spark application receives its own executor processes. They stay alive for the duration of the whole application and run tasks in multithreading mode. The downside to this is that it isn't possible to share data across different Spark applications – to share it, data needs to be persisted to an external storage system.

Spark supports different cluster managers, but it is agnostic to the underlying type.

The driver program, at execution time, must be network addressable from the worker nodes because it has to listen for and accept incoming connections from its executors. Because it schedules tasks on the cluster, it should be executed close to the worker nodes, on the same local area network (if possible).

The following are the cluster managers that are currently supported in Spark:

- **Standalone**: A simple cluster manager that makes it easy to set up a cluster. It is included with Spark.
- **Apache Mesos**: An open source project that's used to manage computer clusters, and was developed at the University of California, Berkeley.
- **Hadoop YARN**: The resource manager available in Hadoop starting from release 2.
- **Kubernetes**: An open source platform for providing a container-centric infrastructure. Kubernetes support in Spark is still experimental, so it's probably not ready for production yet.

Standalone mode

For standalone mode, you only need to place a compiled version of Spark on each node of the cluster. All the cluster nodes need to be able to resolve the hostnames of the other cluster members and are routable to one another. The Spark master URL can be configured in the `$SPARK_HOME/conf/spark-defaults.conf` file on all of the nodes:

```
spark.master                    spark://<master_hostname_or_IP>:7077
```

Then, the hostname or IP address of the Spark master node needs to be specified in the `$SPARK_HOME/conf/spark-env.sh` file on all of the nodes, as follows:

```
SPARK_MASTER_HOST,              <master_hostname_or_IP>
```

It is now possible to start a standalone master server by executing the following script:

```
$SPARK_HOME/sbin/start-master.sh
```

Once the master has completed, a web UI will be available at the `http://<master_hostname_or_IP>:8080` URL. From there, it is possible to obtain the master URL that's to be used when starting the workers. One or more workers can now be started by executing the following script:

```
$SPARK_HOME/sbin/start-slave.sh <master-spark-URL>
```

Each worker, after the start, comes with its own web UI, whose URL is `http://<worker_hostname_or_IP>:8081`.

The list of workers, along with other information about their number of CPUs and memory, can be found in the master's web UI.

The way to do this is to run a standalone cluster manually. It is also possible to use the provided launch scripts. A $SPARK_HOME/conf/slaves file needs to be created as a preliminary step. It must contain the hostnames – one per line – of all of the machines where the Spark workers should start. Passwordless **SSH** (short for **Secure Shell**) for the Spark master to the Spark slaves needs to be enabled to allow remote login for the slave daemon startup and shutdown actions. A cluster can then be launched or stopped using the following shell scripts, which are available in the $SPARK_HOME/sbin directory:

- start-master.sh: Starts a master instance
- start-slaves.sh: Starts a slave instance on each machine specified in the conf/slaves file
- start-slave.sh: Starts a single slave instance
- start-all.sh: Starts both a master and a number of slaves
- stop-master.sh: Stops a master that has been started via the sbin/start-master.sh script
- stop-slaves.sh: Stops all slave instances on the nodes specified in the conf/slaves file
- stop-all.sh: Stops both a master and its slaves

These scripts must be executed on the machine the Spark master will run on.

It is possible to run an interactive Spark shell against a cluster in the following way:

```
$SPARK_HOME/bin/spark-shell --master <master-spark-URL>
```

The $SPARK_HOME/bin/spark-submit script can be used to submit a compiled Spark application to the cluster. Spark currently supports two deploy modes for standalone clusters: client and cluster. In client mode, the driver and the client that submits the application are launched in the same process, while in cluster mode, the driver is launched from one of the worker processes and the client process exits as soon as it completes submitting the application (it doesn't have to wait for the application to finish).
When an application is launched through spark-submit, then its JAR file is automatically distributed to all the worker nodes. Any additional JAR that an application depends on should be specified through the jars flag using a comma as a delimiter (for example, jars, jar1, jar2).

As mentioned in the *Apache Spark fundamentals* section, in standalone mode, the Spark master is a single point of failure. This means that if the Spark master node should go down, the Spark cluster would stop functioning and all currently submitted or running applications would fail, and it wouldn't be possible to submit new applications.

High availability can be configured using Apache ZooKeeper (`https://zookeeper.apache.org/`), an open source and highly reliable distributed coordination service, or can be deployed as a cluster through Mesos or YARN, which we will talk about in the following two sections.

Mesos cluster mode

Spark can run on clusters that are managed by Apache Mesos (`http://mesos.apache.org/`). Mesos is a cross-platform, cloud provider-agnostic, centralized, and fault-tolerant cluster manager, designed for distributed computing environments. Among its main features, it provides resource management and isolation, and the scheduling of CPU and memory across the cluster. It can join multiple physical resources into a single virtual one, and in doing so is different from classic virtualization, where a single physical resource is split into multiple virtual resources. With Mesos, it is possible to build or schedule cluster frameworks such as Apache Spark (though it is not restricted to just this). The following diagram shows the Mesos architecture:

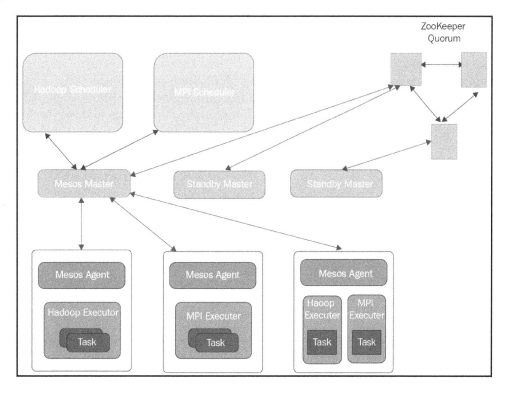

Figure 1.13

Mesos consists of a master daemon and frameworks. The master daemon manages agent daemons running on each cluster node, while the Mesos frameworks run tasks on the agents. The master empowers fine-grained sharing of resources (including CPU and RAM) across frameworks by making them resource offers. It decides how much of the available resources to offer to each framework, depending on given organizational policies. To support diverse sets of policies, the master uses a modular architecture that makes it easy to add new allocation modules through a plugin mechanism. A Mesos framework consists of two components – a scheduler, which registers itself with the master to be offered resources, and an executor, a process that is launched on agent nodes to execute the framework's tasks. While it is the master that determines how many resources are offered to each framework, the frameworks' schedulers are responsible for selecting which of the offered resources to use. The moment a framework accepts offered resources, it passes a description of the tasks it wants to execute on them to Mesos. Mesos, in turn, launches the tasks on the corresponding agents.

The advantages of deploying a Spark cluster using Mesos to replace the Spark Master Manager include the following:

- Dynamic partitioning between Spark and other frameworks
- Scalable partitioning between multiple instances of Spark

Spark 2.2.1 is designed to be used with Mesos 1.0.0+. In this section, I won't describe the steps to deploy a Mesos cluster – I am assuming that a Mesos cluster is already available and running. No particular procedure or patch is required in terms of Mesos installation to run Spark on it. To verify that the Mesos cluster is ready for Spark, navigate to the Mesos master web UI at port 5050:

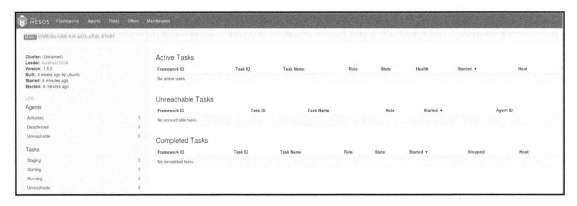

Figure 1.14

Check that all of the expected machines are present in the **Agents** tab.

To use Mesos from Spark, a Spark binary package needs to be available in a place that's accessible by Mesos itself, and a Spark driver program needs to be configured to connect to Mesos. Alternatively, it is possible to install Spark in the same location across all the Mesos slaves and then configure the `spark.mesos.executor.home` property (the default value is `$SPARK_HOME`) to point to that location.

The Mesos master URLs have the form `mesos://host:5050` for a single-master Mesos cluster, or `mesos://zk://host1:2181,host2:2181,host3:2181/mesos` for a multi-master Mesos cluster when using Zookeeper.

The following is an example of how to start a Spark shell on a Mesos cluster:

```
$SPARK_HOME/bin/spark-shell --master mesos://127.0.0.1:5050 -c
spark.mesos.executor.home=`pwd`
```

A Spark application can be submitted to a Mesos managed Spark cluster as follows:

```
$SPARK_HOME/bin/spark-submit --master mesos://127.0.0.1:5050 --total-
executor-cores 2 --executor-memory 3G
$SPARK_HOME/examples/src/main/python/pi.py 100
```

YARN cluster mode

YARN (`http://hadoop.apache.org/docs/stable/hadoop-yarn/hadoop-yarn-site/YARN.html`), which was introduced in Apache Hadoop 2.0, brought significant improvements in terms of scalability, high availability, and support for different paradigms. In the Hadoop version 1 **MapReduce** framework, job execution was controlled by types of processes—a single master process called `JobTracker` coordinates all the jobs running on the cluster and assigns `map` and `reduce` tasks to run on the `TaskTrackers`, which are a number of subordinate processes running assigned tasks and periodically reporting the progress to the `JobTracker`. Having a single `JobTracker` was a scalability bottleneck. The maximum cluster size was a little more than 4,000 nodes, with the number of concurrent tasks limited to 40,000. Furthermore, the `JobTracker` was a single point of failure and the only available programming model was **MapReduce**.

The fundamental idea of YARN is to split up the functionalities of resource management and job scheduling or monitoring into separate daemons. The idea is to have a global **ResourceManager** and per-application **ApplicationMaster** (**App Mstr**). An application is either a single job or a DAG of jobs. The following is a diagram of YARN's architecture:

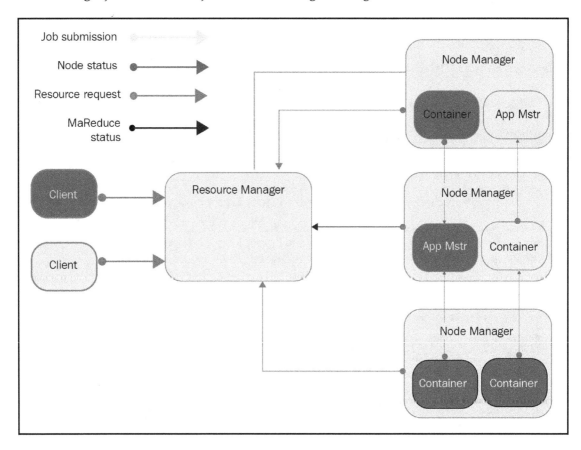

Figure 1.15

The **ResourceManager** and the **NodeManager** form the YARN framework. The **ResourceManager** decides on resource usage across all the running applications, while the **NodeManager** is an agent running on any machine in the cluster and is responsible for the containers by monitoring their resource usage (including CPU and memory) and reporting to the **ResourceManager**. The **ResourceManager** consists of two components – the scheduler and the ApplicationsManager. The scheduler is the component that's responsible for allocating resources to the various applications running, and it doesn't perform any monitoring of applications' statuses, nor offer guarantees about restarting any failed tasks. It performs scheduling based on an application's resource requirements.

The ApplicationsManager accepts job submissions and provides a service to restart the **App Mstr** container on any failure. The per-application **App Mstr** is responsible for negotiating the appropriate resource containers from the scheduler and monitoring their status and progress. YARN, by its nature, is a general scheduler, so support for non-MapReduce jobs (such as Spark jobs) is available for Hadoop clusters.

Submitting Spark applications on YARN

To launch Spark applications on YARN, the `HADOOP_CONF_DIR` or `YARN_CONF_DIR` env variable needs to be set and pointing to the directory that contains the client-side configuration files for the Hadoop cluster. These configurations are needed to connect to the YARN ResourceManager and to write to HDFS. This configuration is distributed to the YARN cluster so that all the containers used by the Spark application have the same configuration. To launch Spark applications on YARN, two deployment modes are available:

- **Cluster mode**: In this case, the Spark driver runs inside an application master process that's managed by YARN on the cluster. The client can finish its execution after initiating the application.
- **Client mode**: In this case, the driver runs and the client runs in the same process. The application master is used for the sole purpose of requesting resources from YARN.

Unlike the other modes, in which the master's address is specified in the `master` parameter, in YARN mode, the ResourceManager's address is retrieved from the Hadoop configuration. Therefore, the `master` parameter value is always `yarn`.

You can use the following command to launch a Spark application in cluster mode:

```
$SPARK_HOME/bin/spark-submit --class path.to.your.Class --master yarn --deploy-mode cluster [options] <app jar> [app options]
```

In cluster mode, since the driver runs on a different machine than the client, the `SparkContext.addJar` method doesn't work with the files that are local to the client. The only choice is to include them using the `jars` option in the `launch` command.

Launching a Spark application in client mode happens the same way—the `deploy-mode` option value needs to change from cluster to client.

Kubernetes cluster mode

Kubernetes (`https://kubernetes.io/`) is an open source system that's used automate the deployment, scaling, and management of containerized applications. It was originally implemented at Google and then open sourced in 2014. The following are the main concepts of Kubernetes:

- **Pod**: This is the smallest deployable unit of computing that can be created and managed. A pod can be seen as a group of one or more containers that share network and storage space, which also contains a specification for how to run those containers.
- **Deployment**: This is a layer of abstraction whose primary purpose is to declare how many replicas of a pod should be running at a time.
- **Ingress**: This is an open channel for communication with a service running in a pod.
- **Node**: This is a representation of a single machine in a cluster.
- **Persistent volume**: This provides a filesystem that can be mounted to a cluster, not to be associated with any particular node. This is the way Kubernetes persists information (data, files, and so on).

The following diagram (source: `https://d33wubrfki0l68.cloudfront.net/518e18713c865fe67a5f23fc64260806d72b38f5/61d75/images/docs/post-ccm-arch.png`) shows the Kubernetes architecture:

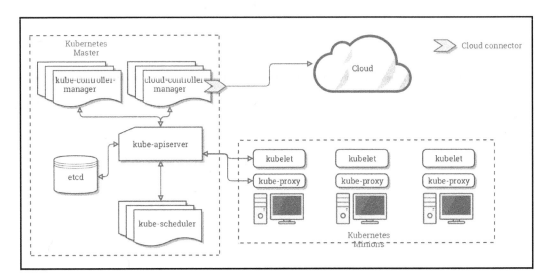

Figure 1.16

The main components of the Kubernetes architecture are as follows:

- **Cloud controller manager**: It runs the Kubernetes controllers
- **Controllers**: There are four of them—node, route, service, and PersistenceVolumeLabels
- **Kubelets**: The primary agents that run on nodes

The submission of Spark jobs to a Kubernetes cluster can be done directly through `spark-submit`. Kubernetes requires that we supply Docker (`https://www.docker.com/`) images that can be deployed into containers within pods. Starting from the 2.3 release, Spark provides a Dockerfile (`$SPARK_HOME/kubernetes/dockerfiles/Dockerfile`, which can also be customized to match specific applications' needs) and a script (`$SPARK_HOME/bin/docker-image-tool.sh`) that can be used to build and publish Docker images that are to be used within a Kubernetes backend. The following is the syntax that's used to build a Docker image through the provided script:

```
$SPARK_HOME/bin/docker-image-tool.sh -r <repo> -t my-tag build
```

This following is the syntax to push an image to a Docker repository while using the same script:

```
$SPARK_HOME/bin/docker-image-tool.sh -r <repo> -t my-tag push
```

A job can be submitted in the following way:

```
$SPARK_HOME/bin/spark-submit \
    --master k8s://https://<k8s_hostname>:<k8s_port> \
    --deploy-mode cluster \
    --name <application-name> \
    --class <package>.<ClassName> \
    --conf spark.executor.instances=<instance_count> \
    --conf spark.kubernetes.container.image=<spark-image> \
    local:///path/to/<sparkjob>.jar
```

Kubernetes requires application names to contain only lowercase alphanumeric characters, hyphens, and dots, and to start and end with an alphanumeric character.

The following diagram shows the way the submission mechanism works:

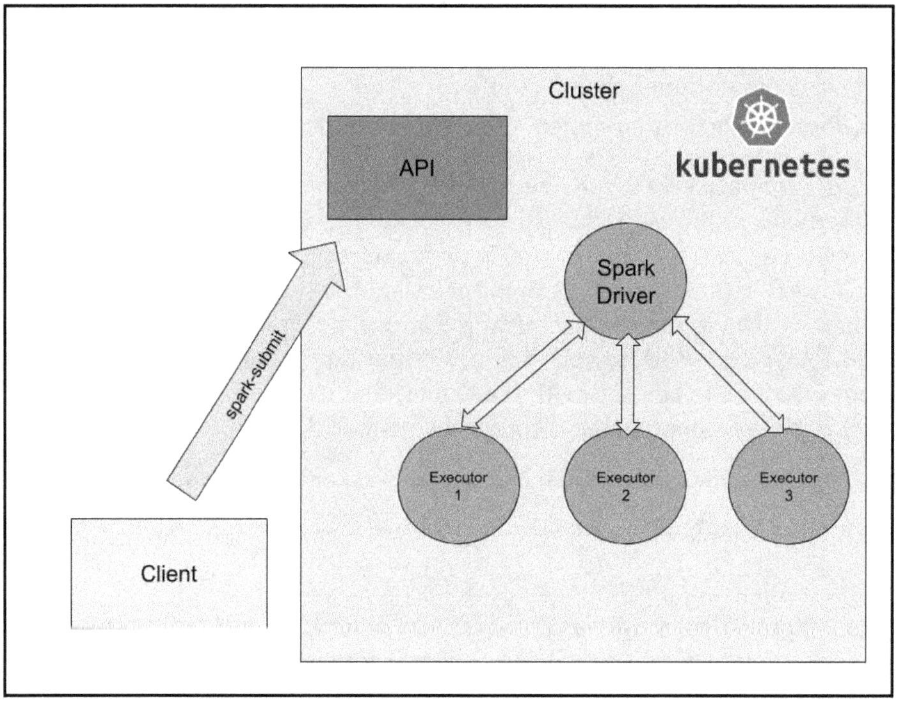

Figure 1.17

Here's what happens:

- Spark creates a driver that's running within a Kubernetes pod
- The driver creates the executors, which also run within Kubernetes pods, and then connects to them and executes application code
- At the end of the execution, the executor pods terminate and are cleaned up, while the driver pod still persists logs and remains in a completed state (which means that it doesn't use cluster computation or memory resources) in the Kubernetes API (until it's eventually garbage collected or manually deleted)

Summary

In this chapter, we became familiar with Apache Spark and most of its main modules. We started to use the available Spark shells and wrote our first self-contained application using the Scala and Python programming languages. Finally, we explored different ways of deploying and running Spark in cluster mode. Everything we have learned about so far is necessary for understanding the topics that are presented from `Chapter 3`, *Extract, Transform, Load*, onward. If you have any doubts about any of the presented topics, I suggest that you go back and read this chapter again before moving on.

In the next chapter, we are going to explore the basics of DL, with an emphasis on some particular implementations of multi-layer neural networks.

2
Deep Learning Basics

In this chapter, I am going to introduce the core concepts of **Deep Learning** (**DL**), the relationship it has with **Machine Learning** (**ML**) and **Artificial Intelligence** (**AI**), the different types of multilayered neural networks, and a list of real-world practical applications. I will try to skip mathematical equations as much as possible and keep the description very high level, with no reference to code examples. The goal of this chapter is to make readers aware of what DL really is and what you can do with it, while the following chapters will go much more into the details of this, with lots of practical code examples in Scala and Python (where this programming language can be used).

This chapter will cover the following topics:

- DL concepts
- **Deep neural networks** (**DNNs**)
- Practical applications of DL

Introducing DL

DL is a subset of ML that can solve particularly hard and large-scale problems in areas such as **Natural Language Processing** (**NLP**) and image classification. The expression DL is sometimes used in an interchangeable way with ML and AI, but both ML and DL are subsets of AI. AI is the broader concept that is implemented through ML. DL is a way of implementing ML, and involves neural network-based algorithms:

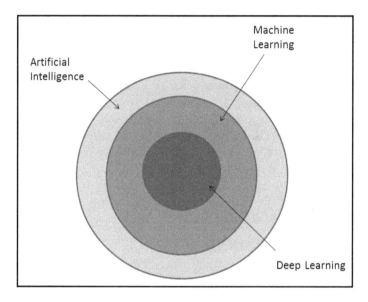

Figure 2.1

AI is considered the ability of a machine (it could be any computer-controlled device or robot) to perform tasks that are typically associated with humans. It was introduced in the 1950s, with the goal of reducing human interaction, thereby making the machine do all the work. This concept is mainly applied to the development of systems that typically require human intellectual processes and/or the ability to learn from past experiences.

ML is an approach that's used to implement AI. It is a field of computer science that gives computer systems the ability to learn from data without being explicitly programmed. Basically, it uses algorithms to find patterns in data and then uses a model that recognizes those patterns to make predictions on new data. The following diagram shows the typical process that's used to train and build a model:

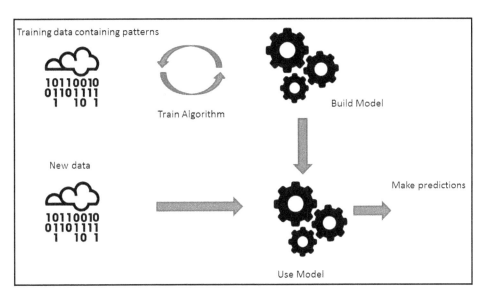

Figure 2.2

ML can be classified into three types:

- Supervised learning algorithms, which use labeled data
- Unsupervised learning algorithms, which find patterns, starting from unlabeled data
- Semi-supervised learning, which uses a mix of the two (labeled and unlabeled data)

At the time of writing, supervised learning is the most common type of ML algorithm. Supervised learning can be divided into two groups – regression and classification problems.

The following graph shows a simple regression problem:

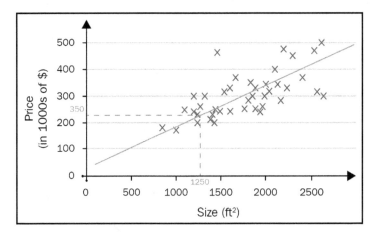

Figure 2.3

As you can see, there are two inputs (or features), **Size** and **Price**, which are used to generate a curve-fitting line and make subsequent predictions of the property price.

The following graph shows an example of supervised classification:

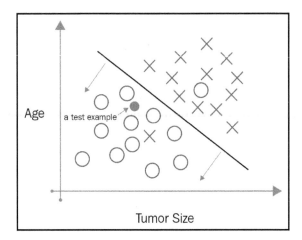

Figure 2.4

The dataset is labeled with benign (circles) and malignant (crosses) tumors for breast cancer patients. A supervised classification algorithm attempts, by fitting a line through the data, to part the tumors into two different classifications. Future data would then be classified as benign or malignant based on that straight-line classification. The case in the preceding graph has only two discrete outputs, but there are cases where there could be more than two classifications as well

While in supervised learning, labeled datasets help the algorithm determine what the correct answer is, in unsupervised learning, an algorithm is provided with an unlabeled dataset and depends on the algorithm itself to uncover structures and patterns in the data. In the following graphs (the graph on the right can be found at `https://leonardoaraujosantos.gitbooks.io/artificial-inteligence/content/Images/supervised_unsupervised.png`), no information is provided about the meaning of each data point. We ask the algorithm to find a structure in the data in a way that is independent of supervision. An unsupervised learning algorithm could find that there are two distinct clusters and then perform straight-line classification between them:

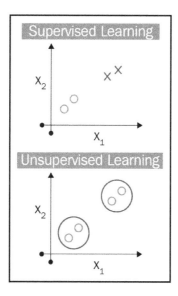

Figure 2.5

DL is the name for multilayered neural networks, which are networks that are composed of several hidden layers of nodes between the input and output. DL is a refinement of **Artificial Neural Networks (ANNs)**, which emulate how the human brain learns (even if not closely) and how it solves problems. ANNs consist of an interconnected group of neurons, similar to the way neurons work in the human brain. The following diagram represents the general model of ANNs:

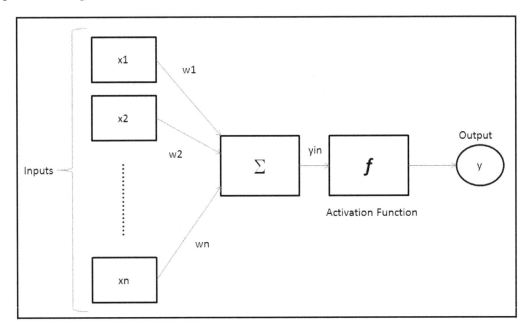

Figure 2.6

A neuron is the atomic unit of an ANN. It receives a given number of input (x_i) before executing computation on it and finally sends the output to other neurons in the same network. The weights (w_j), or *parameters*, represent the strength of the input connection – they can assume positive or negative values. The net input can be calculated as follows:

$$y_{in} = x_1 \times w_1 + x_2 \times w_2 + x_3 \times w_3 + \dots + x_n \times w_n$$

The output can be calculated by applying the activation function over the net input:

$$y = f(y_{in})$$

The activation function allows an ANN to model complex non-linear patterns that simpler models may not represent correctly.

The following diagram represents a neural network:

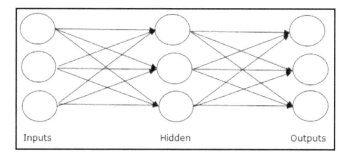

Figure 2.7

The first layer is the input layer – this is where features are put into the network. The last one is the output layer. Any layer in between that is not an input or output layer is a hidden layer. The term DL is used because of the multiple levels of hidden layers in neural networks that are used to resolve complex non-linear problems. At each layer level, any single node receives input data and a weight, and will then output a confidence score to the nodes of the next layer. This process happens until the output layer is reached. The error of the score is calculated on that layer. The errors are then sent back and the weights of the network are adjusted to improve the model (this is called **backpropagation** and happens inside a process called **gradient descent**, which we will discuss in `Chapter 6`, *Recurrent Neural Networks*). There are many variations of neural networks – more about them in the next section.

Before moving on, a final observation. You're probably wondering why most of the concepts behind AI, ML, and DL have been around for decades, but have only been hyped up in the past 4 or 5 years. There are several factors that accelerated their implementation and made it possible to move them from theory to real-world applications:

- **Cheaper computation**: In the last few decades, hardware has been a constraining factor for AI/ML/DL. Recent advances in both hardware (coupled with improved tools and software frameworks) and new computational models (including those around GPUs) have accelerated AI/ML/DL adoption.
- **Greater data availability**: AI/ML/DL needs a huge amount of data to learn. The digital transformation of society is providing tons of raw material to move forward quickly. Big data now comes from diverse sources such as IoT sensors, social and mobile computing, smart cars, healthcare devices, and many others that are or will be used to train models.

- **Cheaper storage**: The increased amount of available data means that more space is needed for storage. Advances in hardware, cost reduction, and improved performance have made the implementation of new storage systems possible, all without the typical limitations of relational databases.
- **More advanced algorithms**: Less expensive computation and storage enable the development and training of more advanced algorithms that also have impressive accuracy when solving specific problems such as image classification and fraud detection.
- **More, and bigger, investments**: Last but not least, investment in AI is no longer confined to universities or research institutes, but comes from many other entities, such as tech giants, governments, start-ups, and large enterprises across almost every business area.

DNNs overview

As stated in the previous section, a DNN is an ANN with multiple hidden layers between the input and output layers. Typically, they are feedforward networks in which data flows from the input layer to the output layer without looping back, but there are different flavors of DNNs – among them, those with the most practical applications are **Convolutional Neural Networks (CNNs)** and **Recurrent Neural Networks (RNNs)**.

CNNs

The most common use case scenarios of CNNs are all to do with image processing, but are not restricted to other types of input, whether it be audio or video. A typical use case is image classification – the network is fed with images so that it can classify the data. For example, it outputs a lion if you give it a lion picture, a tiger when you give it a tiger picture, and so on. The reason why this kind of network is used for image classification is because it uses relatively little preprocessing compared to other algorithms in the same space – the network learns the filters that, in traditional algorithms, were hand-engineered.

Being a multilayered neural network, A CNN consists of an input and an output layer, as well as multiple hidden layers. The hidden layers can be convolutional, pooling, fully connected, and normalization layers. Convolutional layers apply a convolution operation (`https://en.wikipedia.org/wiki/Convolution`) to an input, before passing the result to the next layer. This operation emulates how the response of an individual physical neuron to a visual stimulus is generated. Each convolutional neuron processes only the data for its receptive field (which is the particular region of the sensory space of an individual sensory neuron in which a change in the environment will modify the firing of that neuron). Pooling layers are responsible for combining the outputs of clusters of neurons in a layer into a single neuron in the next layer. There are different implementations of poolings—max pooling, which uses the maximum value from each cluster from the prior layer; average pooling, which uses the average value from any cluster of neurons on the prior layer; and so on. Fully connected layers, instead, as you will clearly realize from their name, connect every neuron in a layer to every other neuron in another layer.

CNNs don't parse all the training data at once, but they usually start with a sort of input scanner. For example, consider an image of 200 x 200 pixels as input. In this case, the model doesn't have a layer with 40,000 nodes, but a scanning input layer of 20 x 20, which is fed using the first 20 x 20 pixels of the original image (usually, starting in the upper-left corner). Once we have passed that input (and possibly used it for training), we feed it using the next 20 x 20 pixels (this will be explained better and in a more detailed manner in `Chapter 5`, *Convolutional Neural Networks*; the process is similar to the movement of a scanner, one pixel to the right). Please note that the image isn't dissected into 20 x 20 blocks, but the scanner moves over it. This input data is then fed through one or more convolutional layers. Each node of those layers only has to work with its close neighboring cells—not all of the nodes are connected to each other. The deeper a network becomes, the more its convolutional layers shrink, typically following a divisible factor of the input (if we started with a layer of 20, then, most probably, the next one would be a layer of 10 and the following a layer of 5). Powers of two are commonly used as divisible factors.

The following diagram (by Aphex34—own work, CC BY-SA 4.0, `https://commons.wikimedia.org/w/index.php?curid=45679374`) shows the typical architecture of a CNN:

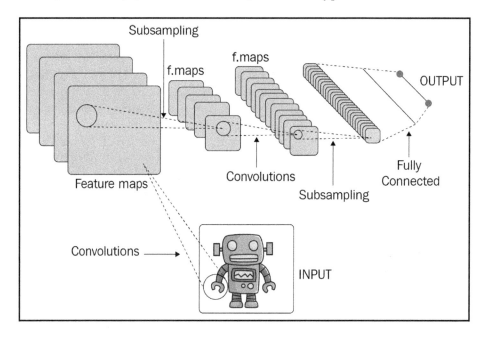

Figure 2.8

RNNs

RNNs are primarily popular for many NLP tasks (even if they are currently being used in different scenarios, which we will talk about in Chapter 6, *Recurrent Neural Networks*). What's different about RNNs? Their peculiarity is that the connections between units form a directed graph along a sequence. This means that an RNN can exhibit a dynamic temporal behavior for a given time sequence. Therefore, they can use their internal state (memory) to process sequences of inputs, while in a traditional neural network, we assume that all inputs and outputs are independent of each other. This makes RNNs suitable for cases such as those, for example, when we want to predict the next word in a sentence – it is definitely better to know which words came before it. Now, you can understand why they are called recurrent – the same task is performed for every element of a sequence, with the output being dependent on the previous computations.

RNNs have loops in them, allowing information to persist, like so:

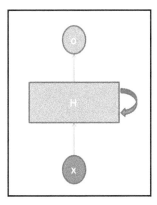

Figure 2.9

In the preceding diagram, a chunk of the neural network, **H**, receives some input, **x** and outputs a value, **o**. A loop allows information to be passed from one step of the network to the next. By unfolding the RNN in this diagram into a full network (as shown in the following diagram), it can be thought of as multiple copies of the same network, each passing information to a successor:

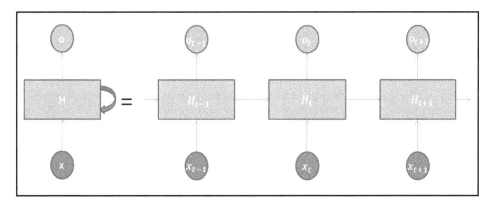

Figure 2.10

Here, x_t is the input at time step t, H_t is the hidden state at time step t (and represents the memory of the network), and o_t is the output at step t. The hidden states capture information about what happened in all the previous time steps. The output at a given step is calculated based only on the memory at time t. An RNN shares the same parameters across every step—that's because the same task is performed at each step; it just has different inputs—drastically reduces the total number of parameters it needs to learn. Outputs aren't necessary at each step, since this depends on the task at hand. Similarly, inputs aren't always needed at each time step.

RNNs were first developed in the 1980s and only lately have they come in many new variants. Here's a list of some of those architectures:

- **Fully recurrent**: Every element has a weighted one-way connection to every other element in the architecture and has a single feedback connection to itself.
- **Recursive**: The same set of weights is applied recursively over a structure, which resembles a graph structure. During this process, the structure is traversed in topological sorting (`https://en.wikipedia.org/wiki/Topological_sorting`).
- **Hopfield**: All of the connections are symmetrical. This is not suitable in scenarios where sequences of patterns need to be processed, as it requires stationary inputs only.
- **Elman network**: This is a three-layer network, arranged horizontally, plus a set of so-called **context units**. The middle hidden layer is connected to all of them, with a fixed weight of 1. What happens at each time step is that the input is fed forward and then a learning rule is applied. Because the back-connections are fixed, a copy of the previous values of the hidden units is saved in the context units. This is the way the network can maintain a state. For this reason, this kind of RNN allows you to perform tasks that are beyond the power of a standard multilayered neural network.
- **Long short-term memory (LSTM)**: This is a DL that prevents back-propagated errors from vanishing or exploding gradients (this will be covered in more detail in `Chapter 6`, *Recurrent Neural Networks*). Errors can flow backward through (in theory) an unlimited number of virtual layers unfolded in space. This means that an LSTM can learn tasks that require memories of events that could have happened several time steps earlier.

- **Bi-directional**: By concatenating the outputs of two RNNs, it can predict each element of a finite sequence. The first RNN processes the sequence from left to right, while the second one does so in the opposite direction.
- **Recurrent multilayer perceptron network**: This consists of cascaded subnetworks, each containing multiple layers of nodes. Each subnetwork, except for the last layer (the only one that can have feedback connections), is feed-forward.

Chapter 5, *Convolutional Neural Networks*, and Chapter 6, *Recurrent Neural Networks*, will go into more detail about CNNs and RNNs.

Practical applications of DL

The DL concepts and models that were illustrated in the previous two sections aren't just pure theory – practical applications have been implemented from them. DL excels at identifying patterns in unstructured data; most use cases are related to media such as images, sound, video, and text. Nowadays, DL is applied in a number of use case scenarios across different business domains, such as the following:

- **Computer vision**: A number of applications in the automotive industry, facial recognition, motion detection, and real-time threat detection
- **NLP**: Sentiment analysis in social media, fraud detection in finance and insurance, augmented search, and log analysis
- **Medical diagnosis**: Anomaly detection, pathology identification
- **Search engines**: Image searching
- **IoT**: Smart homes, predictive analysis using sensor data
- **Manufacturing**: Predictive maintenance
- **Marketing**: Recommendation engines, automated target identification
- **Audio analysis**: Speech recognition, voice searching, and machine translation

There are many others that are yet to come.

Summary

In this chapter, the basics of DL were introduced. This overview was kept very high-level to help readers who are new to this topic and prepare them to tackle the more detailed and hands-on topics that are covered in the following chapters.

3
Extract, Transform, Load

Training and testing DL models requires data. Data is usually hosted on different distributed and remote storage systems. You need them to connect to the data sources and perform data retrieval so that you can start the training phase and you would probably need to do some preparation before feeding your model. This chapter goes through the phases of the **Extract, Transform, Load (ETL)** process applied to DL. It covers several use cases for which the DeepLearning4j framework and Spark would be used. The use cases presented here are related to batch data ingestion. Data streaming will be covered in the next chapter.

The following topics will be covered in this chapter:

- Training data ingestion through Spark
- Data ingestion from a relational database
- Data ingestion from a NoSQL database
- Data ingestion from S3

Training data ingestion through Spark

The first section of this chapter introduces the DeepLearning4j framework and then presents some use cases of training data ingestion from files using this framework along with Apache Spark.

The DeepLearning4j framework

Before jumping into the first example, let's quickly introduce the DeepLearning4j (`https://deeplearning4j.org/`) framework. It is an open source (released under the Apache license 2.0 (`https://www.apache.org/licenses/LICENSE-2.0`)), distributed deep learning framework written for the JVM. Being integrated since its earliest releases with Hadoop and Spark, it takes advantage of such distributed computing frameworks to speed up network training. It is written in Java, so is compatible with any other JVM language (including Scala of course), while the underlying computations are written in lower level languages, such as C, C++, and CUDA. The DL4J API gives flexibility when composing deep neural networks. So it is possible to combine different network implementations as needed in a distributed, production-grade infrastructure on top of distributed CPUs or GPUs. DL4J can import neural net models from most of the major ML or DL Python frameworks (including TensorFlow and Caffe) via Keras (`https://keras.io/`), bridging the gap between the Python and the JVM ecosystems in terms of toolkits for data scientists in particular, but also for data engineers and DevOps. Keras represents the DL4J's Python API.

DL4J is modular. These are the main libraries that comprise this framework:

- **Deeplearning4j**: The neural network platform core
- **ND4J**: The NumPy (`http://www.numpy.org/`) porting for the JVM
- **DataVec**: A tool for ML ETL operations
- **Keras import**: To import pre-trained Python models implemented in Keras
- **Arbiter**: A dedicated library for multilayer neural networks hyperparameter optimization
- **RL4J**: The implementation of deep reinforcement learning for the JVM

We are going to explore almost all of the features of DL4J and its libraries, starting from this chapter and across the other chapters of this book.

The reference release for DL4J in this book is version 0.9.1.

Data ingestion through DataVec and transformation through Spark

Data can come from many sources and in many types, for example:

- Log files
- Text documents
- Tabular data
- Images
- Videos

When working with neural nets, the end goal is to convert each data type into a collection of numerical values in a multidimensional array. Data could also need to be pre-processed before it can be used to train or test a net. Therefore, an ETL process is needed in most cases, which is a sometimes underestimated challenge that data scientists have to face when doing ML or DL. That's when the DL4J DataVec library comes to the rescue. After data is transformed through this library API, it comes into a format (vectors) understandable by neural networks, so DataVec quickly produces open standard compliant vectorized data.

DataVec supports out-of-the-box all the major types of input data (text, CSV, audio, video, image) with their specific input formats. It can be extended for specialized input formats not covered by the current release of its API. You can think about the DataVec input/output format system as the same way Hadoop MapReduce uses `InputFormat` implementations to determine the logical *InputSplits* and the `RecordReaders` implementation to use. It also provides `RecordReaders` to serialize data. This library also includes facilities for feature engineering, data cleanup, and normalization. They work with both static data and time series. All of the available functionalities can be executed on Apache Spark through the DataVec-Spark module.

If you want to know more about the Hadoop MapReduce classes mentioned previously, you can have a look at the following official online Javadocs:

Class name	Link
`InputFormat`	`https://hadoop.apache.org/docs/r2.7.2/api/org/apache/hadoop/mapred/InputFormat.html`
`InputSplits`	`https://hadoop.apache.org/docs/r2.7.2/api/org/apache/hadoop/mapred/InputSplit.html`
`RecordReaders`	`https://hadoop.apache.org/docs/r2.7.2/api/org/apache/hadoop/mapred/RecordReader.html`

Let's see a practical code example in Scala. We want to extract data from a CSV file that contains some e-shop transactions and have the following columns:

- `DateTimeString`
- `CustomerID`
- `MerchantID`
- `NumItemsInTransaction`
- `MerchantCountryCode`
- `TransactionAmountUSD`
- `FraudLabel`

Then, we perform some transformation over them.

We need to import the required dependencies (Scala, Spark, DataVec, and DataVec-Spark) first. Here is a complete list for a Maven POM file (but, of course, you can use SBT or Gradle):

```xml
<properties>
    <scala.version>2.11.8</scala.version>
    <spark.version>2.2.1</spark.version>
    <dl4j.version>0.9.1</dl4j.version>
    <datavec.spark.version>0.9.1_spark_2</datavec.spark.version>
</properties>
<dependencies>
  <dependency>
      <groupId>org.scala-lang</groupId>
      <artifactId>scala-library</artifactId>
      <version>${scala.version}</version>
  </dependency>
  <dependency>
      <groupId>org.apache.spark</groupId>
      <artifactId>spark-core_2.11</artifactId>
      <version>${spark.version}</version>
  </dependency>
  <dependency>
      <groupId>org.datavec</groupId>
      <artifactId>datavec-api</artifactId>
      <version>${dl4j.version}</version>
  </dependency>
  <dependency>
      <groupId>org.datavec</groupId>
      <artifactId>datavec-spark_2.11</artifactId>
      <version>${datavec.spark.version}</version>
  </dependency>
</dependencies>
```

The first thing to do in the Scala application is to define the input data schema, as follows:

```
val inputDataSchema = new Schema.Builder()
        .addColumnString("DateTimeString")
        .addColumnsString("CustomerID", "MerchantID")
        .addColumnInteger("NumItemsInTransaction")
        .addColumnCategorical("MerchantCountryCode", List("USA", "CAN",
"FR", "MX").asJava)
          .addColumnDouble("TransactionAmountUSD", 0.0, null, false, false)
    //$0.0 or more, no maximum limit, no NaN and no Infinite values
        .addColumnCategorical("FraudLabel", List("Fraud", "Legit").asJava)
        .build
```

If input data is numeric and appropriately formatted then a `CSVRecordReader` (`https://deeplearning4j.org/datavecdoc/org/datavec/api/records/reader/impl/csv/CSVRecordReader.html`) may be satisfactory. If, however, the input data has non-numeric fields, then a schema transformation will be required. DataVec uses Apache Spark to perform transform operations. Once we have the input schema, we can define the transformation we want to apply to the input data. Just a couple of transformations are described in this example. We can remove some columns that are unnecessary for our net, for example:

```
val tp = new TransformProcess.Builder(inputDataSchema)
        .removeColumns("CustomerID", "MerchantID")
        .build
```

Filter the `MerchantCountryCode` column in order to get the records related to USA and Canada only, as follows:

```
.filter(new ConditionFilter(
        new CategoricalColumnCondition("MerchantCountryCode",
ConditionOp.NotInSet, new HashSet(Arrays.asList("USA","CAN")))))
```

At this stage, the transformations are only defined, but not applied yet (of course we need to get the data from the input file first). So far, we have used DataVec classes only. In order to read the data and apply the defined transformations, the Spark and DataVec-Spark API need to be used.

Let's create the `SparkContext` first, as follows:

```
val conf = new SparkConf
conf.setMaster(args[0])
conf.setAppName("DataVec Example")
val sc = new JavaSparkContext(conf)
```

Now, we can read the CSV input file and parse the data using a `CSVRecordReader`, as follows:

```
val directory = new ClassPathResource("datavec-example-
data.csv").getFile.getAbsolutePath
val stringData = sc.textFile(directory)
val rr = new CSVRecordReader
val parsedInputData = stringData.map(new StringToWritablesFunction(rr))
```

Then execute the transformation defined earlier, as follows:

```
val processedData = SparkTransformExecutor.execute(parsedInputData, tp)
```

Finally, let's collect the data locally, as follows:

```
val processedAsString = processedData.map(new
WritablesToStringFunction(","))
val processedCollected = processedAsString.collect
val inputDataCollected = stringData.collect
```

The input data is as follows:

```
18/08/01 20:59:11 INFO DAGScheduler: Job 2 finished: collect at BasicDataVecExample.scala:79, took 0.022346 s


---- Original Data ----
2016-01-01 17:00:00.000,830a7u3,u323fy8902,1,USA,100.00,Legit
2016-01-01 18:03:01.256,830a7u3,9732498oeu,3,FR,73.20,Legit
2016-01-03 02:53:32.231,78ueoau32,w234e989,1,USA,1621.00,Fraud
2016-01-03 09:30:16.832,t842uocd,9732498oeu,4,USA,43.19,Legit
2016-01-04 23:01:52.920,t842uocd,cza8873bm,10,MX,159.65,Legit
2016-01-05 02:28:10.648,t842uocd,fgcq9803,6,CAN,26.33,Fraud
2016-01-05 10:15:36.483,rgc707ke3,tn342v7,2,USA,-0.90,Legit
```

The processed data is as follows:

```
---- Processed Data ----
2016-01-01 17:00:00.000,1,USA,100.00,Legit
2016-01-03 02:53:32.231,1,USA,1621.00,Fraud
2016-01-03 09:30:16.832,4,USA,43.19,Legit
2016-01-05 02:28:10.648,6,CAN,26.33,Fraud
2016-01-05 10:15:36.483,2,USA,-0.90,Legit
18/08/01 20:59:11 INFO SparkUI: Stopped Spark web UI at http://192.1
18/08/01 20:59:11 INFO MapOutputTrackerMasterEndpoint: MapOutputTrac
```

The full code of this example is part of the source code included with the book.

Training data ingestion from a database with Spark

Sometimes data has been previously ingested and stored into a database by some other application, so you would need to connect to a database in order to use it for training or testing purposes. This section describes how to get data from a relational database and a NoSQL database. In both cases, Spark would be used.

Data ingestion from a relational database

Suppose the data is stored in a table called `sparkexample` in a MySQL (`https://dev.mysql.com/`) schema with the name `sparkdb`. This is the structure of that table:

```
mysql> DESCRIBE sparkexample;
+----------------------+-------------+------+-----+---------+-------+
| Field                | Type        | Null | Key | Default | Extra |
+----------------------+-------------+------+-----+---------+-------+
| DateTimeString       | varchar(23) | YES  |     | NULL    |       |
| CustomerID           | varchar(10) | YES  |     | NULL    |       |
| MerchantID           | varchar(10) | YES  |     | NULL    |       |
| NumItemsInTransaction| int(11)     | YES  |     | NULL    |       |
| MerchantCountryCode  | varchar(3)  | YES  |     | NULL    |       |
| TransactionAmountUSD | float       | YES  |     | NULL    |       |
| FraudLabel           | varchar(5)  | YES  |     | NULL    |       |
+----------------------+-------------+------+-----+---------+-------+
7 rows in set (0.00 sec)
```

It contains the same data as, for the example, in *Training data ingestion through Spark*, as follows:

```
mysql> select * from sparkexample;
+------------------------+------------+------------+----------------------
-+--------------------+----------------------+------------+
| DateTimeString         | CustomerID | MerchantID | NumItemsInTransaction
| MerchantCountryCode    | TransactionAmountUSD | FraudLabel |
+------------------------+------------+------------+----------------------
-+--------------------+----------------------+------------+
| 2016-01-01 17:00:00.000 | 830a7u3   | u323fy8902 |                     1
| USA                    |                 100 | Legit      |
| 2016-01-01 18:03:01.256 | 830a7u3   | 9732498oeu |                     3
| FR                     |                73.2 | Legit      |
|...                     |            |            |
|                        |            |            |            |
```

The dependencies to add to the Scala Spark project are the following:

- Apache Spark 2.2.1
- Apache Spark SQL 2.2.1
- The specific JDBC driver for the MySQL database release used

Let's now implement the Spark application in Scala. In order to connect to the database, we need to provide all of the needed parameters. Spark SQL also includes a data source that can read data from other databases using JDBC, so the required properties are the same as for a connection to a database through traditional JDBC; for example:

```
var jdbcUsername = "root"
  var jdbcPassword = "secretpw"
  val jdbcHostname = "mysqlhost"
  val jdbcPort = 3306
  val jdbcDatabase ="sparkdb"
  val jdbcUrl = s"jdbc:mysql://${jdbcHostname}:${jdbcPort}/${jdbcDatabase}"
```

We need to check that the JDBC driver for the MySQL database is available, as follows:

```
Class.forName("com.mysql.jdbc.Driver")
```

We can now create a `SparkSession`, as follows:

```
val spark = SparkSession
      .builder()
      .master("local[*]")
      .appName("Spark MySQL basic example")
      .getOrCreate()
```

Import the implicit conversions, as follows:

```
import spark.implicits._
```

You can finally connect to the database and load the data from the `sparkexample` table to a DataFrame, as follows:

```
val jdbcDF = spark.read
      .format("jdbc")
      .option("url", jdbcUrl)
      .option("dbtable", s"${jdbcDatabase}.sparkexample")
      .option("user", jdbcUsername)
      .option("password", jdbcPassword)
      .load()
```

Spark automatically reads the schema from a database table and maps its types back to Spark SQL types. Execute the following method on the DataFrame:

```
jdbcDF.printSchema()
```

It returns the exact same schema as for the table `sparkexample`; for example:

```
root
 |-- DateTimeString: string (nullable = true)
 |-- CustomerID: string (nullable = true)
 |-- MerchantID: string (nullable = true)
 |-- NumItemsInTransaction: integer (nullable = true)
 |-- MerchantCountryCode: string (nullable = true)
 |-- TransactionAmountUSD: double (nullable = true)
 |-- FraudLabel: string (nullable = true)
```

Once the data is loaded into the DataFrame, it is possible to run SQL queries against it using the specific DSL as shown in the following example:

```
jdbcDF.select("MerchantCountryCode",
"TransactionAmountUSD").groupBy("MerchantCountryCode").avg("TransactionAmou
ntUSD")
```

It is possible to increase the parallelism of the reads through the JDBC interface. We need to provide split boundaries based on the DataFrame column values. There are four options available (`columnname`, `lowerBound`, `upperBound`, and `numPartitions`) to specify the parallelism on read. They are optional, but they must all be specified if any of them is provided; for example:

```
val jdbcDF = spark.read
        .format("jdbc")
        .option("url", jdbcUrl)
        .option("dbtable", s"${jdbcDatabase}.employees")
        .option("user", jdbcUsername)
        .option("password", jdbcPassword)
        .option("columnName", "employeeID")
        .option("lowerBound", 1L)
        .option("upperBound", 100000L)
        .option("numPartitions", 100)
        .load()
```

While the examples in this section refer to a MySQL database, they apply the same way to any commercial or open source RDBMS for which a JDBC driver is available.

Data ingestion from a NoSQL database

Data can also come from a NoSQL database. In this section, we are going to explore the code to implement in order to consume the data from a MongoDB (https://www.mongodb.com/) database.

The collection `sparkexample` of the `sparkmdb` database contains the same data as for the examples in *Data ingestion through DataVec and transformation through Spark* and *Data ingestion from a relational database* sections, but in the form of BSON documents; for example:

```
/* 1 */
{
    "_id" : ObjectId("5ae39eed144dfae14837c625"),
    "DateTimeString" : "2016-01-01 17:00:00.000",
    "CustomerID" : "830a7u3",
    "MerchantID" : "u323fy8902",
    "NumItemsInTransaction" : 1,
    "MerchantCountryCode" : "USA",
    "TransactionAmountUSD" : 100.0,
    "FraudLabel" : "Legit"
}

/* 2 */
{
    "_id" : ObjectId("5ae3a15d144dfae14837c671"),
    "DateTimeString" : "2016-01-01 18:03:01.256",
    "CustomerID" : "830a7u3",
    "MerchantID" : "9732498oeu",
    "NumItemsInTransaction" : 3,
    "MerchantCountryCode" : "FR",
    "TransactionAmountUSD" : 73.0,
    "FraudLabel" : "Legit"
}
...
```

The dependencies to add to the Scala Spark project are the following:

- Apache Spark 2.2.1
- Apache Spark SQL 2.2.1
- The MongoDB connector for Spark 2.2.0

We need to create a Spark Session, as follows:

```
val sparkSession = SparkSession.builder()
    .master("local")
    .appName("MongoSparkConnectorIntro")
```

```
        .config("spark.mongodb.input.uri",
"mongodb://mdbhost:27017/sparkmdb.sparkexample")
        .config("spark.mongodb.output.uri",
"mongodb://mdbhost:27017/sparkmdb.sparkexample")
        .getOrCreate()
```

Specify the connection to the database. After the session as been created, it is possible to use it to load data from the `sparkexample` collection through the `com.mongodb.spark.MongoSpark` class, as follows:

```
val df = MongoSpark.load(sparkSession)
```

The returned DataFrame has the same structure as for the `sparkexample` collection. Use the following instruction:

```
df.printSchema()
```

It prints the following output:

```
root
 |-- CustomerID: string (nullable = true)
 |-- DateTimeString: string (nullable = true)
 |-- FraudLabel: string (nullable = true)
 |-- MerchantCountryCode: string (nullable = true)
 |-- MerchantID: string (nullable = true)
 |-- NumItemsInTransaction: integer (nullable = true)
 |-- TransactionAmountUSD: double (nullable = true)
 |-- _id: struct (nullable = true)
 |     |-- oid: string (nullable = true)
```

Of course, the retrieved data is that in the DB collection, as follows:

```
df.collect.foreach { println }
```

It returns the following:

```
[830a7u3,2016-01-01
17:00:00.000,Legit,USA,u323fy8902,1,100.0,[5ae39eed144dfae14837c625]]
[830a7u3,2016-01-01
18:03:01.256,Legit,FR,9732498oeu,3,73.0,[5ae3a15d144dfae14837c671]]
...
```

It is also possible to run SQL queries on the DataFrame. We need first to create a case class to define the schema for the DataFrame, as follows:

```
case class Transaction(CustomerID: String,
                       MerchantID: String,
                       MerchantCountryCode: String,
```

```
                    DateTimeString: String,
                    NumItemsInTransaction: Int,
                    TransactionAmountUSD: Double,
                    FraudLabel: String)
```

Then we load the data, as follows:

```
val transactions = MongoSpark.load[Transaction](sparkSession)
```

We must register a temporary view for the DataFrame, as follows:

```
transactions.createOrReplaceTempView("transactions")
```

Before we can execute an SQL statement, for example:

```
val filteredTransactions = sparkSession.sql("SELECT CustomerID, MerchantID
FROM transactions WHERE TransactionAmountUSD = 100")
```

Use the following instruction:

```
filteredTransactions.show
```

It returns the following:

```
+----------+----------+
|CustomerID|MerchantID|
+----------+----------+
|   830a7u3|u323fy8902|
+----------+----------+
```

Data ingestion from S3

Nowadays, there's a big chance that the training and test data are hosted in some cloud storage system. In this section, we are going to learn how to ingest data through Apache Spark from an object storage such as Amazon S3 (`https://aws.amazon.com/s3/`) or S3-based (such as Minio, `https://www.minio.io/`). The Amazon simple storage service (which is more popularly known as Amazon S3) is an object storage service part of the AWS cloud offering. While S3 is available in the public cloud, Minio is a high performance distributed object storage server compatible with the S3 protocol and standards that has been designed for large-scale private cloud infrastructures.

We need to add to the Scala project the Spark core and Spark SQL dependencies, and also the following:

```
groupId: com.amazonaws
 artifactId: aws-java-sdk-core
 version1.11.234

 groupId: com.amazonaws
 artifactId: aws-java-sdk-s3
 version1.11.234
 groupId: org.apache.hadoop
 artifactId: hadoop-aws
 version: 3.1.1
```

They are the AWS Java JDK core and S3 libraries, plus the Apache Hadoop module for AWS integration.

For this example, we need to have already created one existing bucket on S3 or Minio. For the readers not familiar with the S3 object storage, a bucket is similar to a file system directory, where users can store objects (data and the metadata that describe it). Then we need to upload a file in that bucket that would need to be read by Spark. The file used for this example is one generally available for download at the MonitorWare website (http://www.monitorware.com/en/logsamples/apache.php). It contains HTTP requests log entries in ASCII format. For the purpose of this example, we are assuming that the name of the bucket is d14j-bucket and the uploaded file name is access_log. The first thing to do in our Spark program is to create a SparkSession, as follows

```
val sparkSession = SparkSession
    .builder
    .master(master)
    .appName("Spark Minio Example")
    .getOrCreate
```

In order to reduce noise on the output, let's set the log level for Spark to WARN, as follows

```
sparkSession.sparkContext.setLogLevel("WARN")
```

Now that the SparkSession has been created, we need to set up the S3 or Minio endpoint and the credentials for Spark to access it, plus some other properties, as follows:

```
sparkSession.sparkContext.hadoopConfiguration.set("fs.s3a.endpoint",
"http://<host>:<port>")
sparkSession.sparkContext.hadoopConfiguration.set("fs.s3a.access.key",
"access_key")
sparkSession.sparkContext.hadoopConfiguration.set("fs.s3a.secret.key",
"secret")
```

```
sparkSession.sparkContext.hadoopConfiguration.set("fs.s3a.path.style.access
", "true")
sparkSession.sparkContext.hadoopConfiguration.set("fs.s3a.connection.ssl.en
abled", "false")
sparkSession.sparkContext.hadoopConfiguration.set("fs.s3a.impl",
"org.apache.hadoop.fs.s3a.S3AFileSystem")
```

This is the meaning of the properties that have been set for the minimal configuration:

- `fs.s3a.endpoint`: The S3 or Minio endpoint.
- `fs.s3a.access.key`: The AWS or Minio access key ID.
- `fs.s3a.secret.key`: The AWS or Minio secret key.
- `fs.s3a.path.style.access`: Enables S3 path style access while disabling the default virtual hosting behavior.
- `fs.s3a.connection.ssl.enabled`: Specifies if SSL is enabled at the endpoint. Possible values are `true` and `false`.
- `fs.s3a.impl`: The implementation class of the `S3AFileSystem` that is used.

We are now ready to read the `access_log` file (or any other file) from a S3 or Minio bucket and load its content into a RDD, as follows:

```
val logDataRdd = sparkSession.sparkContext.textFile("s3a://dl4j-
bucket/access_log")
println("RDD size is " + logDataRdd.count)
```

It is also possible to convert the RDD into a DataFrame and show the content on the output, as follows:

```
import sparkSession.implicits._
val logDataDf = logDataRdd.toDF
logDataDf.show(10, false)
```

This will provide the following output:

```
19/01/13 14:83:04 WARN MetricsConfig: Cannot locate configuration: tried hadoop-metrics2-s3a-file-system.properties,hadoop-metrics2.properties
RDD size is 1546
+----------------------------------------------------------------------------------------------------------------------------------------------+
|value                                                                                                                                         |
+----------------------------------------------------------------------------------------------------------------------------------------------+
|64.242.88.10 - - [07/Mar/2004:16:05:49 -0800] "GET /twiki/bin/edit/Main/Double_bounce_sender?topicparent=Main.ConfigurationVariables HTTP/1.1" 401 12846 |
|64.242.88.10 - - [07/Mar/2004:16:06:51 -0800] "GET /twiki/bin/rdiff/TWiki/NewUserTemplate?rev1=1.3&rev2=1.2 HTTP/1.1" 200 4523                  |
|64.242.88.10 - - [07/Mar/2004:16:10:02 -0800] "GET /mailman/listinfo/hsdivision HTTP/1.1" 200 6291                                             |
|64.242.88.10 - - [07/Mar/2004:16:11:58 -0800] "GET /twiki/bin/view/TWiki/WikiSyntax HTTP/1.1" 200 7352                                         |
|64.242.88.10 - - [07/Mar/2004:16:20:55 -0800] "GET /twiki/bin/view/Main/DCCAndPostFix HTTP/1.1" 200 5253                                       |
|64.242.88.10 - - [07/Mar/2004:16:23:12 -0800] "GET /twiki/bin/oops/TWiki/AppendixFileSystem?template=oopsmore&param1=1.12&param2=1.12 HTTP/1.1" 200 11382|
|64.242.88.10 - - [07/Mar/2004:16:24:16 -0800] "GET /twiki/bin/view/Main/PeterThoeny HTTP/1.1" 200 4924                                         |
|64.242.88.10 - - [07/Mar/2004:16:29:16 -0800] "GET /twiki/bin/edit/Main/Header_checks?topicparent=Main.ConfigurationVariables HTTP/1.1" 401 12851|
|64.242.88.10 - - [07/Mar/2004:16:30:29 -0800] "GET /twiki/bin/attach/Main/OfficeLocations HTTP/1.1" 401 12851                                  |
|64.242.88.10 - - [07/Mar/2004:16:31:48 -0800] "GET /twiki/bin/view/TWiki/WebTopicEditTemplate HTTP/1.1" 200 3732                               |
+----------------------------------------------------------------------------------------------------------------------------------------------+
only showing top 10 rows
```

Once data has been loaded from objects stored into S3 or Minio buckets, any operation available in Spark for RDDs and Datasets can be used.

Raw data transformation with Spark

Data coming from a source is often raw data. When we talk about raw data we mean data that is in a format that can't be used as is for the training or testing purposes of our models. So, before using, we need to make it tidy. The cleanup process is done through one or more transformations before giving the data as input for a given model.

For data transformation purposes, the DL4J DataVec library and Spark provide several facilities. Some of the concepts described in this section have been explored in the *Data ingestion through DataVec and transformation through Spark* section, but now we are going to add a more complex use case.

To understand how to use Datavec for transformation purposes, let's build a Spark application for web traffic log analysis. The dataset used is generally available for download at the MonitorWare website (`http://www.monitorware.com/en/logsamples/apache.php`). They are HTTP requests log entries in ASCII format. There is one line per request, with the following columns:

- The host making the request. A hostname or an internet address
- A timestamp in the format *DD/Mon/YYYY:HH:MM:SS*, where *DD* is the day of the month, *Mon* is the name of the month, *YYYY* is the year and *HH:MM:SS* is the time of day using a 24-hour clock. The timezone is *-0800*
- The HTTP request given in quotes
- The HTTP reply code
- The total of bytes in the reply

Here's a sample of the log content used:

```
64.242.88.10 - - [07/Mar/2004:16:05:49 -0800] "GET
/twiki/bin/edit/Main/Double_bounce_sender?topicparent=Main.ConfigurationVar
iables HTTP/1.1" 401 12846
64.242.88.10 - - [07/Mar/2004:16:06:51 -0800] "GET
/twiki/bin/rdiff/TWiki/NewUserTemplate?rev1=1.3&rev2=1.2 HTTP/1.1" 200 4523
64.242.88.10 - - [07/Mar/2004:16:10:02 -0800] "GET
/mailman/listinfo/hsdivision HTTP/1.1" 200 6291
64.242.88.10 - - [07/Mar/2004:16:11:58 -0800] "GET
/twiki/bin/view/TWiki/WikiSyntax HTTP/1.1" 200 7352
```

The first thing to do in our application is to define the schema of the input data, as follows:

```
val schema = new Schema.Builder()
        .addColumnString("host")
        .addColumnString("timestamp")
        .addColumnString("request")
        .addColumnInteger("httpReplyCode")
        .addColumnInteger("replyBytes")
        .build
```

Start a Spark context, as follows:

```
val conf = new SparkConf
  conf.setMaster("local[*]")
  conf.setAppName("DataVec Log Analysis Example")
  val sc = new JavaSparkContext(conf)
```

Load the file, as follows:

```
val directory = new ClassPathResource("access_log").getFile.getAbsolutePath
```

A web log file could contain some invalid lines that don't follow the preceding schema, so we need to include some logic to discard those lines that are useless for our analysis, for example:

```
var logLines = sc.textFile(directory)
logLines = logLines.filter { (s: String) =>
    s.matches("(\\S+) - - \\[(\\S+ -\\d{4})\\] \"(.+)\" (\\d+) (\\d+|-)")
}
```

We are applying a regular expression to filter the log lines that match the expected format. We can now start to parse the raw data using a DataVec RegexLineRecordReader (https://deeplearning4j.org/datavecdoc/org/datavec/api/records/reader/impl/regex/RegexLineRecordReader.html). We need to define a regex for formatting the lines, as follows:

```
val regex = "(\\S+) - - \\[(\\S+ -\\d{4})\\] \"(.+)\" (\\d+) (\\d+|-)"
  val rr = new RegexLineRecordReader(regex, 0)
  val parsed = logLines.map(new StringToWritablesFunction(rr))
```

Through the DataVec-Spark library, it is also possible to check the quality of the data before defining the transformations. We can use the `AnalyzeSpark` (`https://deeplearning4j.org/datavecdoc/org/datavec/spark/transform/AnalyzeSpark.html`) class for this purpose, as follows:

```
val dqa = AnalyzeSpark.analyzeQuality(schema, parsed)
  println("----- Data Quality -----")
  println(dqa)
```

The following is the output produced by the data quality analysis:

```
----- Data Quality -----
  idx    name                   type           quality    details
  0      "host"                 String         ok
StringQuality(countValid=1546, countInvalid=0, countMissing=0,
countTotal=1546, countEmptyString=0, countAlphabetic=0, countNumerical=0,
countWordCharacter=10, countWhitespace=0, countApproxUnique=170)
  1      "timestamp"            String         ok
StringQuality(countValid=1546, countInvalid=0, countMissing=0,
countTotal=1546, countEmptyString=0, countAlphabetic=0, countNumerical=0,
countWordCharacter=0, countWhitespace=0, countApproxUnique=1057)
  2      "request"              String         ok
StringQuality(countValid=1546, countInvalid=0, countMissing=0,
countTotal=1546, countEmptyString=0, countAlphabetic=0, countNumerical=0,
countWordCharacter=0, countWhitespace=0, countApproxUnique=700)
  3      "httpReplyCode"        Integer        ok
IntegerQuality(countValid=1546, countInvalid=0, countMissing=0,
countTotal=1546, countNonInteger=0)
  4      "replyBytes"           Integer        FAIL
IntegerQuality(countValid=1407, countInvalid=139, countMissing=0,
countTotal=1546, countNonInteger=139)
```

From this, we notice that on `139` lines (out of `1546`), the `replyBytes` field isn't an integer as expected. Here are a couple of those lines:

```
10.0.0.153 - - [12/Mar/2004:11:01:26 -0800] "GET / HTTP/1.1" 304 -
10.0.0.153 - - [12/Mar/2004:12:23:11 -0800] "GET / HTTP/1.1" 304 -
```

So, the first transformation to do is to clean up the `replyBytes` field by replacing any non-integer entries with the value `0`. We use the `TransformProcess` class as for the example in the *Data ingestion through DataVec and transformation through Spark* section, as follows:

```
val tp: TransformProcess = new TransformProcess.Builder(schema)
      .conditionalReplaceValueTransform("replyBytes", new IntWritable(0),
new StringRegexColumnCondition("replyBytes", "\\D+"))
```

Then, we can apply any other transformation, for example, grouping by host and pulling out summary metrics (count the number of entries, count the number of unique requests and HTTP reply codes, total the values in the `replyBytes` field); for example:

```
.reduce(new Reducer.Builder(ReduceOp.CountUnique)
        .keyColumns("host")
        .countColumns("timestamp")
        .countUniqueColumns("request", "httpReplyCode")
        .sumColumns("replyBytes")
        .build
    )
```

Rename a number of columns, as follows:

```
.renameColumn("count", "numRequests")
```

Filter out all hosts that requested fewer than 1 million bytes in total, as follows:

```
.filter(new ConditionFilter(new LongColumnCondition("sum(replyBytes)",
ConditionOp.LessThan, 1000000)))
    .build
```

We can now execute the transformations, as follows:

```
val processed = SparkTransformExecutor.execute(parsed, tp)
  processed.cache
```

We can also perform some analysis on the final data, as follows:

```
val finalDataSchema = tp.getFinalSchema
  val finalDataCount = processed.count
  val sample = processed.take(10)
  val analysis = AnalyzeSpark.analyze(finalDataSchema, processed)
```

The final data schema is shown as follows:

```
idx    name                            type           meta data
 0      "host"                          String
StringMetaData(name="host",)
 1      "count(timestamp)"              Long
LongMetaData(name="count(timestamp)",minAllowed=0)
 2      "countunique(request)"          Long
LongMetaData(name="countunique(request)",minAllowed=0)
 3      "countunique(httpReplyCode)"    Long
LongMetaData(name="countunique(httpReplyCode)",minAllowed=0)
 4      "sum(replyBytes)"               Integer
IntegerMetaData(name="sum(replyBytes)",)
```

The following shows that the result count is two:

```
[10.0.0.153, 270, 43, 3, 1200145]
 [64.242.88.10, 452, 451, 2, 5745035]
```

The following code shows the result of the analysis:

```
----- Analysis -----
 idx    name                              type          analysis
 0      "host"                            String
StringAnalysis(minLen=10,maxLen=12,meanLen=11.0,sampleStDevLen=1.4142135623
730951,sampleVarianceLen=2.0,count=2)
 1      "count(timestamp)"                Long
LongAnalysis(min=270,max=452,mean=361.0,sampleStDev=128.69343417595164,samp
leVariance=16562.0,countZero=0,countNegative=0,countPositive=2,countMinValu
e=1,countMaxValue=1,count=2)
 2      "countunique(request)"            Long
LongAnalysis(min=43,max=451,mean=247.0,sampleStDev=288.4995667241114,sample
Variance=83232.0,countZero=0,countNegative=0,countPositive=2,countMinValue=
1,countMaxValue=1,count=2)
 3      "countunique(httpReplyCode)"      Long
LongAnalysis(min=2,max=3,mean=2.5,sampleStDev=0.7071067811865476,sampleVari
ance=0.5,countZero=0,countNegative=0,countPositive=2,countMinValue=1,countM
axValue=1,count=2)
 4      "sum(replyBytes)"                 Integer
IntegerAnalysis(min=1200145,max=5745035,mean=3472590.0,sampleStDev=3213722.
538746928,sampleVariance=1.032801255605E13,countZero=0,countNegative=0,coun
tPositive=2,countMinValue=1,countMaxValue=1,count=2)
```

Summary

This chapter explored different ways of ingesting data from files, relational and NoSQL databases, and S3-based object storage systems using the DeepLearning4j DataVec library and the Apache Spark (core and Spark SQL modules) framework, and showed some examples of how to transform the raw data. All of the examples presented represent data ingestion and transformation in a batch fashion.

The next chapter will focus on ingesting and transforming data to train or test your DL model in streaming mode.

4
Streaming

In the previous chapter, we learned how to ingest and transform data to train or evaluate a model using a batch ETL approach. You would use this approach in the training or evaluation phases in most cases, but when running a model, streaming ingestion is needed. This chapter covers setting up streaming ingestion strategies for DL models using a combination of the Apache Spark, DL4J, DataVec, and Apache Kafka frameworks. Streaming data ingestion frameworks don't simply move data from source to destination such as in the traditional ETL approach. With streaming ingestion, any incoming data in any format can be simultaneously ingested, transformed, and/or enriched with other structured and previously stored data for DL purposes.

In this chapter, we will cover the following topics:

- Streaming data with Apache Spark
- Streaming data with Kafka and Apache Spark
- Streaming data with DL4J and Apache Spark

Streaming data with Apache Spark

In Chapter 1, *The Apache Spark Ecosystem*, the details about Spark Streaming and DStreams were covered. A new and different implementation of streaming, Structured Streaming, was introduced as an alpha release in Apache Spark 2.0.0. It finally became stable starting from Spark 2.2.0.

Structured Streaming (which has been built on top of the Spark SQL engine) is a fault-tolerant, scalable stream-processing engine. Streaming can be done in the same way batch computation is done, that is, on static data, which we presented in Chapter 1, *The Apache Spark Ecosystem*. It is the Spark SQL engine that's responsible for incrementally and continuously running the computation and for finally updating the results as data continues to stream. In this scenario, end-to-end, exactly-once, and fault-tolerance guarantees are ensured through **Write Ahead Logs** (**WAL**) and check-pointing.

The difference between the traditional Spark Streaming and the Structured Streaming programming models is sometimes not easy to grasp, especially so for experienced Spark developers who are approaching this concept for the first time. The best way to describe it is like this: you can think of it as a way of handling a live data stream as a table (where the table is thought of as an RDBMS) that is being continuously appended. The streaming computation is expressed as a standard batch-like query (in the same way it happens on a static table), but Spark runs it incrementally on the unbounded table.

Here's how it works. The input data stream can be considered the input table. Every data item arriving in the stream is like a new row being appended to it:

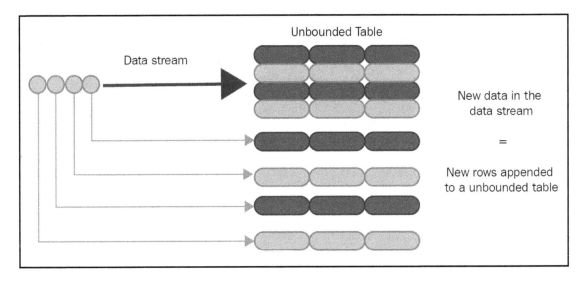

Figure 4.1: A data stream as an unbounded table

A query on the input generates the result table. With every trigger, new interval rows are appended to the input table, which then update the result table (as shown in the following diagram). Any time the result table gets updated, the changed result rows can be written to an external sink. There are different modes for the output that is written to external storage:

- **Complete mode**: In this mode, it is the entire updated result table being written to the external storage. How writing to the storage system of the entire table happens depends on the specific connector configuration or implementation.
- **Append mode**: Only the new rows that are appended in the result table will be written to the external storage system. This means that it is possible to apply this mode in situations where the existing rows in the result table aren't expected to change.

- **Update mode**: Only the rows that have been updated in the result table are written to the external storage system. The difference between this mode and the complete mode is that this one sends out only those rows that have changed since the last trigger:

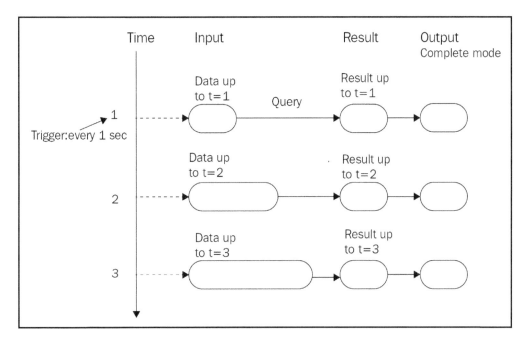

Figure 4.2: Programming model for Structured Streaming

Now, let's implement a simple Scala example – a streaming word count self-contained application, which is the same use case that we used in Chapter 1, *The Apache Spark Ecosystem,* but for Structured Streaming instead. The code that's used for this class can be found among the examples that are bundled with a Spark distribution. The first thing we need to do is initialize a SparkSession:

```
val spark = SparkSession
      .builder
      .appName("StructuredNetworkWordCount")
      .master(master)
      .getOrCreate()
```

We must then create a DataFrame representing the stream of input lines from the connection to `host:port`:

```
val lines = spark.readStream
        .format("socket")
        .option("host", host)
        .option("port", port)
        .load()
```

The `lines` DataFrame represents the unbounded table. It contains the streaming text data. The content of that table is a value, that is, a single column of strings. Each incoming line in the streaming text becomes a row.

Let's split the lines into words:

```
val words = lines.as[String].flatMap(_.split(" "))
```

Then, we need to count the words:

```
val wordCounts = words.groupBy("value").count()
```

Finally, we can start running the query that prints the running counts to the console:

```
val query = wordCounts.writeStream
        .outputMode("complete")
        .format("console")
        .start()
```

We continue running until a termination signal is received:

```
query.awaitTermination()
```

Before running this example, first, you need to run netcat as a data server (or the data server that we implemented in Scala in Chapter 1, *The Apache Spark Ecosystem*):

```
nc -lk 9999
```

Then, in a different Terminal, you can start the example by passing the following as arguments:

```
localhost 9999
```

Any line typed in the Terminal when running the netcat server will be counted and printed to the application screen. An output such as the following will occur:

```
hello spark
 a stream
 hands on spark
```

This will produce the following output:

```
-------------------------------------------
Batch: 0
-------------------------------------------
+------+-----+
| value|count|
+------+-----+
| hello|    1|
| spark|    1|
+------+-----+


-------------------------------------------
Batch: 1
-------------------------------------------
+------+-----+
| value|count|
+------+-----+
| hello|    1|
| spark|    1|
|     a|    1|
|stream|    1|
+------+-----+


-------------------------------------------
Batch: 2
-------------------------------------------
+------+-----+
| value|count|
+------+-----+
| hello|    1|
| spark|    2|
|     a|    1|
|stream|    1|
| hands|    1|
|    on|    1|
+------+-----+
```

The event time is defined as the time that's embedded in the data itself. In many applications, such as those in an IoT context, when the number of events generated by devices every minute needs to be retrieved, the time the data was generated has to be used rather than the time Spark receives it. Event-time is naturally expressed in this programming model—each event from the device is a row in the table, and event-time is a column value in that row. This paradigm makes window-based aggregations simply a special type of aggregation on that event-time column. This grants consistency, because event-time and window-based aggregation queries can be defined in the same way on both static datasets (for example, events logs from devices) and streaming data.

Following the previous consideration, it is evident that this programming model naturally handles data that has arrived later than expected based on its event-time. Since it is Spark itself that updates the result table, it has full control over updating old aggregates when there is late data, as well as limiting the size of intermediate data by cleaning up old aggregates. Starting from Spark 2.1, there is also support for watermarking, which allows you to specify the threshold of late data and allows the underlying engine to clean up old states accordingly.

Streaming data with Kafka and Spark

Spark Streaming with Kafka is a common combination of technologies in data pipelines. This section will present some examples of streaming Kafka with Spark.

Apache Kakfa

Apache Kafka (`http://kafka.apache.org/`) is an open source message broker written in Scala. Originally, it was developed by LinkedIn, but it was then released as open source in 2011 and is currently maintained by the Apache Software Foundation.

Here are some of the reasons why you might prefer Kafka to a traditional JMS message broker:

- **It's fast**: A single Kafka broker running on commodity hardware can handle hundreds of megabytes of reads and writes per second from thousands of clients
- **Great scalability**: It can be easily and transparently expanded without downtime
- **Durability and replication**: Messages are persisted on disk and replicated within the cluster to prevent data loss (by setting a proper configuration using the high number of available configuration parameters, you could achieve zero data loss)
- **Performance**: Each broker can handle terabytes of messages without performance impact
- It allows real-time stream processing
- It can be easily integrated with other popular open source systems for big data architectures such as Hadoop, Spark, and Storm

The following are the core concepts of Kafka that you should become familiar with:

- **Topics**: These are categories or feed names to which upcoming messages are published
- **Producers**: Any entity that publishes messages to a topic
- **Consumers**: Any entity that subscribes to topics and consumes messages from them
- **Brokers**: Services that handle read and write operations

The following diagram shows a typical Kafka cluster architecture:

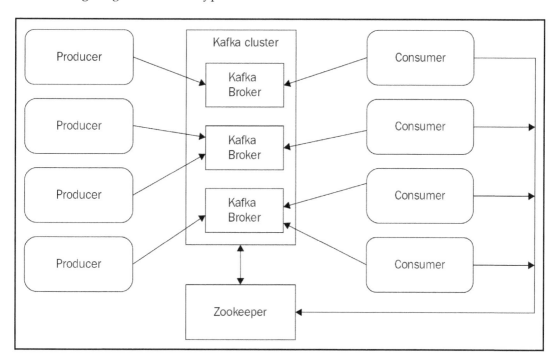

Figure 4.3: Kafka architecture

Kafka uses ZooKeeper (`https://zookeeper.apache.org/`) behind the scenes to keep its nodes in sync. The Kafka binaries provide it, so if hosting machines don't have ZooKeeper on board, you can use the one that comes bundled with Kafka. The communication between clients and servers happens using a highly performant and language-agnostic TCP protocol.

Typical use cases for Kafka are as follows:

- Messaging
- Stream processing
- Log aggregation
- Metrics
- Web activity tracking
- Event sourcing

Spark Streaming and Kafka

To use Spark Streaming with Kafka, you can do two things: either use a receiver or be direct. The first option is similar to streaming from other sources such as text files and sockets – data received from Kafka is stored in Spark executors and processed by jobs that are launched by a Spark Streaming context. This is not the best approach – it can cause data loss in the event of failures. This means that the direct approach (introduced in Spark 1.3) is better. Instead of using receivers to receive data, it periodically queries Kafka for the latest offsets in each topic and partitions, and accordingly defines, the offset ranges to process for each batch. When the jobs to process the data are executed, Kafka's simple consumer API is used to read the defined ranges of offsets (almost in the same way as for reading files from a filesystem). The direct approach brings the following advantages:

- **Simplified parallelism**: There's no need to create multiple input Kafka streams and then struggle trying to unify them. Spark Streaming creates as many RDD partitions as there are Kafka partitions to consume, which read data from Kafka in parallel. This means that there is 1:1 mapping between Kafka and RDD partitions that is easier to understand and tune.
- **Improved efficiency**: Following the receiver approach, to achieve zero-data loss, we need the data to be stored in a WAL. However, this strategy is inefficient, as the data effectively gets replicated twice, by Kafka first and then by the WAL. In the direct approach, there is no receiver, and subsequently no need for WALs—messages can be recovered from Kafka, assuming there is sufficient Kafka retention.

- **Exactly-once semantics**: The receiver approach uses Kafka's high-level API to store consumed offsets in ZooKeeper. While this approach (combined with WALs) can ensure zero data loss, there is a remote possibility that some records will get consumed twice when a failure happens. Inconsistencies between data being reliably received by Spark Streaming and offsets tracked by ZooKeeper lead to this. With the direct approach, the simple Kafka API involved doesn't use ZooKeeper—the offsets are tracked by Spark Streaming itself within its checkpoints. This ensures that each record is received by Spark Streaming effectively exactly once, even when a failure happens.

One disadvantage of the direct approach is that it doesn't update the offsets in ZooKeeper—this means that the ZooKeeper-based Kafka monitoring tools will not show any progress.

Now, let's implement a simple Scala example – a Kafka direct word count. The example that's presented in this section works with Kafka release 0.10.0.0 or later. The first thing to do is to add the required dependencies (Spark Core, Spark Streaming, and Spark Streaming Kafka) to your project:

```
groupId = org.apache.spark
 artifactId = spark-core_2.11
 version = 2.2.1
 groupId = org.apache.spark
 artifactId = spark-streaming_2.11
 version = 2.2.1
 groupId = org.apache.spark
 artifactId = spark-streaming-kafka-0-10_2.11
 version = 2.2.1
```

This application expects two arguments:

- A comma-separated list of one or more Kafka brokers
- A comma-separated list of one or more Kafka topics to consume from:

```
val Array(brokers, topics) = args
```

We need to create the Spark Streaming context. Let's choose a 5-second batch interval:

```
val sparkConf = new
SparkConf().setAppName("DirectKafkaWordCount").setMaster(master)
 val ssc = new StreamingContext(sparkConf, Seconds(5))
```

Now, let's create a direct Kafka stream with the given brokers and topics:

```
val topicsSet = topics.split(",").toSet
val kafkaParams = Map[String, String]("metadata.broker.list" -> brokers)
val messages = KafkaUtils.createDirectStream[String, String,
StringDecoder, StringDecoder](
      ssc, kafkaParams, topicsSet)
```

We can implement the word count now, that is, get the lines from the stream, split them into words, count the words, and then print:

```
val lines = messages.map(_._2)
val words = lines.flatMap(_.split(" "))
val wordCounts = words.map(x => (x, 1L)).reduceByKey(_ + _)
wordCounts.print()
```

Finally, let's start the computation and keep it alive, waiting for a termination signal:

```
ssc.start()
ssc.awaitTermination()
```

To run this example, we first need to start a Kafka cluster and create a topic. The Kafka binaries can be downloaded from the official website (http://kafka.apache.org/downloads). Once it has been downloaded, we can follow the following instructions.

Start a zookeeper node first:

```
$KAFKA_HOME/bin/zookeeper-server-start.sh
$KAFKA_HOME/config/zookeeper.properties
```

It will start listening to the default port, 2181.

Then, start a Kafka broker:

```
$KAFKA_HOME/bin/kafka-server-start.sh $KAFKA_HOME/config/server.properties
```

It will start listening to the default port, 9092.

Create a topic called packttopic:

```
$KAFKA_HOME/bin/kafka-topics.sh --create --zookeeper localhost:2181 --
replication-factor 1 --partitions 1 --topic packttopic
```

Check that the topic has been successfully created:

```
$KAFKA_HOME/bin/kafka-topics.sh --list --zookeeper localhost:2181
```

The topic name, `packttopic`, should be in the list that was printed to the console output.

We can now start to produce messages for the new topic. Let's start a command-line producer:

```
$KAFKA_HOME/bin/kafka-console-producer.sh --broker-list localhost:9092 --topic packttopic
```

Here, we can write some messages to the producer console:

```
First message
 Second message
 Third message
 Yet another message for the message consumer
```

Let's build the Spark application and execute it through the `$SPARK_HOME/bin/spark-submit` command, specifying the JAR filename, the Spark master URL, the job name, the main class name, the maximum memory to be used by each executor, and the job arguments (`localhost:9092` and `packttopic`).

The output printed by the Spark job for each consumed message line will be something like the following:

```
-----------------------------------------
Time: 1527457655000 ms
-----------------------------------------
(consumer,1)
(Yet,1)
(another,1)
(message,2)
(for,1)
(the,1)
```

Streaming data with DL4J and Spark

In this section, we are going to apply data streaming with Kafka and Spark to a use case scenario of a DL4J application. The DL4J module we are going to use is DataVec.

Let's consider the example that we presented in the *Spark Streaming and Kafka* section. What we want to achieve is direct Kafka streaming with Spark, then apply DataVec transformations on the incoming data as soon as it arrives, before using it downstream.

Let's define the input schema first. This is the schema we expect for the messages that are consumed from a Kafka topic. The schema structure is the same as for the classic `Iris` dataset (`https://en.wikipedia.org/wiki/Iris_flower_data_set`):

```
val inputDataSchema = new Schema.Builder()
    .addColumnsDouble("Sepal length", "Sepal width", "Petal length",
"Petal width")
    .addColumnInteger("Species")
    .build
```

Let's define a transformation on it (we are going to remove the petal fields because we are going to do some analysis based on the sepal features only):

```
val tp = new TransformProcess.Builder(inputDataSchema)
    .removeColumns("Petal length", "Petal width")
    .build
```

Now, we can generate the new schema (after applying the transformation to the data):

```
val outputSchema = tp.getFinalSchema
```

The next part of this Scala application is exactly the same as for the example in the *Spark Streaming and Kafka* section. Here, create a streaming context with a 5-second batch interval and a direct Kafka stream:

```
val sparkConf = new
SparkConf().setAppName("DirectKafkaDataVec").setMaster(master)
 val ssc = new StreamingContext(sparkConf, Seconds(5))
 val topicsSet = topics.split(",").toSet
 val kafkaParams = Map[String, String]("metadata.broker.list" -> brokers)
 val messages = KafkaUtils.createDirectStream[String, String,
StringDecoder, StringDecoder](
     ssc, kafkaParams, topicsSet)
```

Let's get the input lines:

```
val lines = messages.map(_._2)
```

`lines` is a `DStream[String]`. We need to iterate for each RDD there, convert it to `javaRdd` (required by the DataVec reader), use a DataVec `CSVRecordReader`, parse the incoming comma-separated messages, apply the schema transformation, and print the result data:

```
lines.foreachRDD { rdd =>
    val javaRdd = rdd.toJavaRDD()
    val rr = new CSVRecordReader
    val parsedInputData = javaRdd.map(new StringToWritablesFunction(rr))
```

```
    if(!parsedInputData.isEmpty()) {
      val processedData = SparkTransformExecutor.execute(parsedInputData,
  tp)
      val processedAsString = processedData.map(new
  WritablesToStringFunction(","))
      val processedCollected = processedAsString.collect
      val inputDataCollected = javaRdd.collect
      println("\n\n---- Original Data ----")
      for (s <- inputDataCollected.asScala) println(s)

      println("\n\n---- Processed Data ----")
      for (s <- processedCollected.asScala) println(s)
    }
  }
```

Finally, we start the streaming context and keep it alive, waiting for a termination signal:

```
ssc.start()
  ssc.awaitTermination()
```

To run this example, we need to start a Kafka cluster and create a new topic called `csvtopic`. The steps are the same as for the example described in the *Spark Streaming and Kafka* section. Once the topic has been created, we can start to produce comma-separated messages on it. Let's start a command-line producer:

$KAFKA_HOME/bin/kafka-console-producer.sh --broker-list localhost:9092 -- topic csvtopic

Now, we can write some messages to the producer console:

```
5.1,3.5,1.4,0.2,0
  4.9,3.0,1.4,0.2,0
  4.7,3.2,1.3,0.2,0
  4.6,3.1,1.5,0.2,0
```

Let's build the Spark application and execute it through the $SPARK_HOME/bin/spark-submit command, specifying the JAR filename, the Spark master URL, the job name, the main class name, the maximum memory to be used by each executor, and the job arguments (localhost:9092 and csvtopic).

The output printed by the Spark job for each consumed message line will be something like the following:

```
4.6,3.1,1.5,0.2,0
  ---- Processed Data ----
  4.6,3.1,0
```

The full code for this example can be found among the source code that's bundled with this book at https://github.com/PacktPublishing/Hands-On-Deep-Learning-with-Apache-Spark.

Summary

To complete our overview of data ingestion possibilities when training, evaluating, and running DL models after exploring them in Chapter 3, *Extract, Transform, Load*, in this chapter, we explored the different options that are available to us when we perform data streaming.

This chapter concludes the exploration of Apache Spark features. Starting from the next chapter, the focus will be on DL4J and some other deep learning framework features. These will be used in different use case scenarios, where they will be implemented on top of Spark.

Convolutional Neural Networks

5

In `Chapter 2`, *Deep Learning Basics*, we learned about a very high level overview of **Convolutional Neural Networks** (**CNNs**). In this chapter, we are going to understand more details about this type of CNN, the possible implementations of their layers, and we will start hands-on implementing CNNs through the DeepLearning4j framework. The chapter ends with examples involving Apache Spark too. Training and evaluation strategies for CNNs will be covered in `Chapter 7`, *Training Neural Networks with Spark*, `Chapter 8`, *Monitoring and Debugging Neural Network Training*, and `Chapter 9`, *Interpreting Neural Network Output*. In the description of the different layers, I have tried to reduce the usage of math concepts and formulas as much as possible in order to make the reading and comprehension easier for developers and data analysts who might have no math or data science background. Therefore, you have to expect more focus on the code implementation in Scala.

The chapter covers the following topics:

- Convolutional layers
- Pooling layers
- Fully connected layers
- Weights
- GoogleNet Inception V3 model
- Hands-on CNN with Spark

Convolutional layers

Since the CNN section was covered in `Chapter 2`, *Deep Learning Basics*, you should know in which context CNNs are commonly used. In that section, we have mentioned that each layer of the same CNN can have a different implementation. The first three sections of this chapter describe possible layer implementations in detail, starting from the convolutional layers. But first, let's recap the process by which CNN perceive images. They perceive images as volumes (3D objects) and not as bi-dimensional canvases (having width and height only). The reason is the following: digital color images have a **Red-Blue-Green** (**RGB**) encoding and it is the mixing of these colors that produces the spectrum that can be perceived by human eyes. This also means that CNNs ingest images as three separate layers of color, one on top of the other. This translates into receiving a color image in the form of a rectangular box where width and height can be measured in pixels and having a three layers (referred as **channels**) depth, one for each RGB color. Cutting a long story short, an input image is seen by a CNN as a multi-dimensional array. Let's give a practical example. If we consider a 480 x 480 image, it is perceived by the network as a 480 x 480 x 3 array, for which each of its elements can have a value of between 0 and 255. These values describe the pixel intensity at a given point. Here's the main difference between the human eyes and a machine: these array values are the only inputs available to it. The output of a computer receiving those numbers as input will be other numbers describing the probability of the image being a certain class. The first layer of a CNN is always **convolutional**. Suppose having an input that is a 32 x 32 x 3 array of pixel values, let's try to imagine a concrete visualization that clearly and simply explains what a convolutional layer is. Let's try to visualize a torch that shines over the top-left part of the image.

This following diagram shows the torch shines, covering a 5 x 5 area:

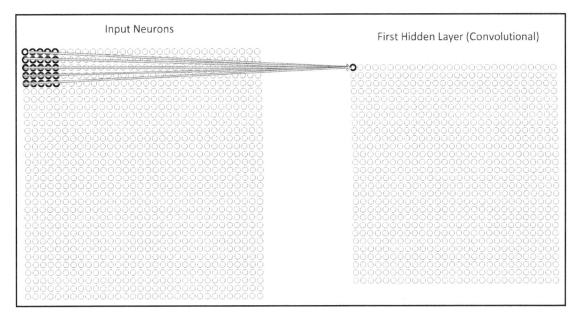

Figure 5.1: 5 x 5 filter

Then the imaginary torch starts sliding over all the other areas of the image. The proper term to call it is **filter** (or **neuron** or **kernel**) and the image region that lights up is called the **receptive field**. In math terms, a filter is an array of numbers (called **weights** or **parameters**). The depth of a filter has to match the depth of the input. Referring to this section example, we have a filter that's dimensions are 5 x 5 x 3. The first position the filter covers (as shown in the diagram in preceding diagram) is the top left corner of the input image. While the filter slides around the image, or convolves (from the Latin verb *convolvere*, which means to wrap up), it multiplies its values with the image original pixel values. The multiplications are then all summed up (in our example, in total we have 75 multiplications). The outcome is a single number, which represents when the filter is only at the top left of the input image. This process is then repeated for every location on the input image. As with the first one, every unique location produces a single number. Once the filter has completed its sliding process over all the locations of the image, the result is a 28 x 28 x 1 (given a 32 x 32 input image, a 5 x 5 filter can fit 784 different locations) numeric array called **activation map** (or **feature map**).

Pooling layers

It is common practice (as you will see next through the code examples of this chapter and from `Chapter 7`, *Training Neural Networks with Spark*, onward) to periodically insert a pooling layer between successive convolution layers in a CNN model. This kind of layers scope is to progressively reduce the number of parameters for the network (which translates into a significant lowering of the computation costs). In fact, spatial pooling (which is also found in literature as downsampling or subsampling) is a technique that reduces the dimensionality of each feature map, while at the same time retaining the most important part of the information. Different types of spatial pooling exist. The most used are max, average, sum, and L2-norm.

Let's take as an example, max pooling. This technique requires defining a spatial neighborhood (typically a 2 × 2 window); the largest element within that window is then taken from the rectified feature map. The average pooling strategy requires taking the average or the sum of all elements in the given window. Several papers and use cases provide evidence that max pooling has been shown to produce better results than other spatial pooling techniques.

The following diagram shows an example of max pooling operation (a 2 × 2 window is used here):

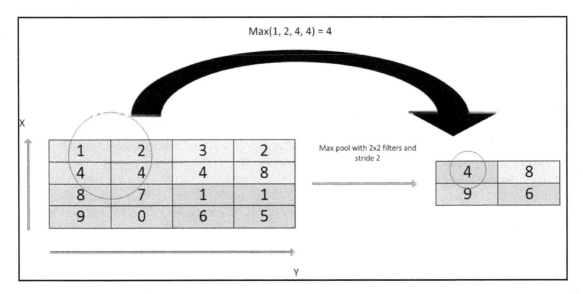

Figure 5.2: Max pooling operation using a 2 × 2 window

Fully connected layers

A fully connected layer is the last layer of a CNN. Fully connected layers, given an input volume, return as output a multi-dimensional vector. The dimension of the output vector matches the number of classes for the particular problem to solve.

This chapter and others in this book present some examples of CNN implementation and training for digit classification purposes. In those cases, the dimension of the output vector would be 10 (the possible digits are 0 to 9). Each number in the 10-dimensional output vector represents the probability of a certain class (digit). The following is an output vector for a digit classification inference:

```
[0 0 0 .1 .75 .1 .05 0 0 0]
```

How do we interpret those values? The network is telling us that it believes that the input image is a four with a 75% probability (which is the highest in this case), with a 10% probability that the image is a three, another 10% probability that the image is a five, and a 5% probability that the image is a six. A fully connected layer looks at the output of the previous layer in the same network and determines which features most correlate to a particular class.

The same happens not only in digit classification. An example of a general use case of image classification is that, if a model that has been trained using images of animals predicts that the input image is, for example, a horse, it will have high values in the activation maps that represent specific high-level features, like four legs or a tail, just to mention a couple. Similarly, if the same model predicts that an image is a different animal, let's say a fish, it will have high values in the activation maps that represent specific high-level features, like fins or a gill. We can then say that a fully connected layer looks at those high-level features that most strongly correlate to a particular class and has particular weights: this ensures that the correct probabilities for each different class are obtained after the products between weights and the previous layer have been calculated.

Weights

CNNs share weights in convolutional layers. This means that the same filter is used for each receptive field in a layer and that these replicated units share the same parameterization (weight vector and bias) and form a feature map.

The following diagram shows three hidden units of a network belonging to the same feature map:

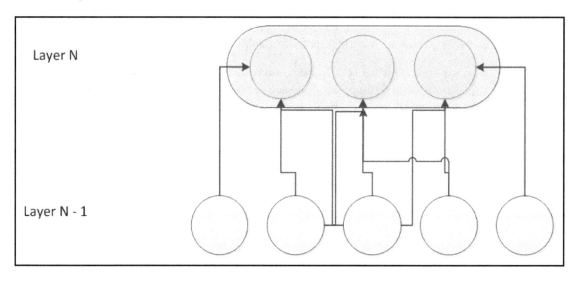

Figure 5.3: Hidden units

The weights in the darker gray color in the preceding diagram are shared and identical. This replication allows features detection regardless of the position they have in the visual field. Another outcome of this weight sharing is the following: the efficiency of the learning process increases by drastically reducing the number of free parameters to be learned.

GoogleNet Inception V3 model

As a concrete implementation of a CNN, in this section, I am going to present the GoogleNet (https://ai.google/research/pubs/pub43022) architecture by Google (https://www.google.com/) and its inception layers. It has been presented at the *ImageNet Large Scale Visual Recognition Challenge 2014* (*ILSVRC2014*, http://www.image-net.org/challenges/LSVRC/2014/). Needless to say, it won that competition. The distinct characteristic of this implementation is the following: increased depth and width and, at the same time, a constant computational budget. Improved computing resources utilization is part of the network design.

This chart summarizes all of the layers for this network implementation presented in the context:

type	patch size/ stride	output size	depth	#1×1	#3×3 reduce	#3×3	#5×5 reduce	#5×5	pool proj	params	ops
convolution	7×7/2	112×112×64	1							2.7K	34M
max pool	3×3/2	56×56×64	0								
convolution	3×3/1	56×56×192	2		64	192				112K	360M
max pool	3×3/2	28×28×192	0								
inception (3a)		28×28×256	2	64	96	128	16	32	32	159K	128M
inception (3b)		28×28×480	2	128	128	192	32	96	64	380K	304M
max pool	3×3/2	14×14×480	0								
inception (4a)		14×14×512	2	192	96	208	16	48	64	364K	73M
inception (4b)		14×14×512	2	160	112	224	24	64	64	437K	88M
inception (4c)		14×14×512	2	128	128	256	24	64	64	463K	100M
inception (4d)		14×14×528	2	112	144	288	32	64	64	580K	119M
inception (4e)		14×14×832	2	256	160	320	32	128	128	840K	170M
max pool	3×3/2	7×7×832	0								
inception (5a)		7×7×832	2	256	160	320	32	128	128	1072K	54M
inception (5b)		7×7×1024	2	384	192	384	48	128	128	1388K	71M
avg pool	7×7/1	1×1×1024	0								
dropout (40%)		1×1×1024	0								
linear		1×1×1000	1							1000K	1M
softmax		1×1×1000	0								

Figure 5.4: GoogleNet layers

There are 22 layers with parameters (excluding the pooling layers; the total is 27 if they are included) and almost 12 times fewer parameters than the winning architecture of the past editions of the same context. This network has been designed keeping in mind computational efficiency and practicality, so that inference can be run also on individual devices having limited resources, in particular those with a low memory footprint. All the convolution layers use **Rectified Linear Unit** (**ReLU**) activation. The of the receptive field is 224 × 224 in the RGB color space (with zero means). Looking at the table in the preceding diagram, the **#3 × 3** and **#5 × 5** reduces are the number of 1 × 1 filters in the reduction layer preceding the 3 × 3 and 5 × 5 convolution layers. The activation function for those reduction layers is ReLU as well.

The diagram at `https://user-images.githubusercontent.com/32988039/33234276-86fa05fc-d1e9-11e7-941e-b3e62771716f.png` shows a schematic view of the network.

In this architecture, each unit from an earlier layer corresponds to a region of the input image—these units are grouped into filter banks. In the layers that are closer to the input, correlated units concentrate in local regions. This results in a lot of clusters concentrated in a single region, so they can be covered by a 1×1 convolution in the following layer. However, there could be a smaller number of more spatially split clusters covered by convolutions over larger chunks, and there would be a decreasing number of chunks over larger regions. To prevent those patch-alignment issues, the inception architecture implementations are restricted to use 1×1, 3×3 and 5×5 filters. The suggested architecture is then a combination of layers which output filter banks are aggregated in a single output vector, which represents the input of the next stage. Additionally, adding an alternative pooling path in parallel to each stage could have a further beneficial effect:

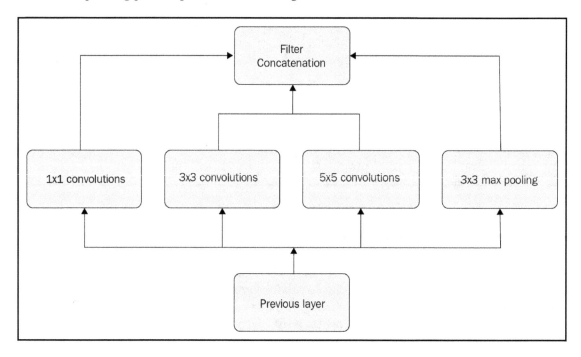

Figure 5.5: Naive version of the inception module

Looking at the preceding diagram, you can understand that, in terms of computational cost, for a layer with a large number of filters, it could be too expensive to have 5 × 5 convolutions (even if there aren't many). And, of course, this becomes a bigger problem when adding more pooling units, because the number of output filters is equal to the number of filters in the previous stage. Definitely merging the output of a pooling layer with outputs of a convolutional layer could inevitably lead to more and more outputs moving from stage to stage. For this reason, a second and more computational idea of the inception architecture has been proposed. The new idea is to reduce dimension where the computational requirements could increase too much. But there's a caveat: low dimensional embeddings could contain lots of information about a large image chunk, but they represent information in a compressed form, making its processing hard. A good compromise is then to keep the representation mostly sparse and at the same time compress the signals only where there is a real need to heavily aggregate them. For this reason, in order to compute reductions, **1 × 1 convolutions** are used before any expensive **3 × 3 and 5 × 5 convolutions**.

The following diagram shows the new module following the preceding consideration:

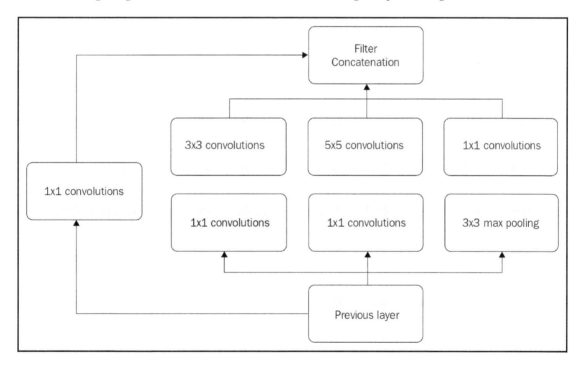

Figure 5.6: Inception module with dimension reductions

Hands-on CNN with Spark

In the previous sections of this chapter, we went through the theory of CNNs and the GoogleNet architecture. If this is the first time you're reading about these concepts, probably you are wondering about the complexity of the Scala code to implement CNN's models, train, and evaluate them. Adopting a high-level framework like DL4J, you are going to discover how many facilities come out-of-the-box with it and that the implementation process is easier than expected.

In this section, we are going to explore a real example of CNN configuration and training using the DL4J and Spark frameworks. The training data used comes from the MNIST database (http://yann.lecun.com/exdb/mnist/). It contains images of handwritten digits, with each image labeled by an integer. It is used to benchmark the performance of ML and DL algorithms. It contains a training set of 60,000 examples and a test set of 10,000 examples. The training set is used to teach the algorithm to predict the correct label, the integer, while the test set is used to check how accurate the trained network can make guesses.

For our example, we download, and extract somewhere locally, the MNIST data. A directory named mnist_png is created. It has two subdirectories: training, containing the training data, and testing, containing the evaluation data.

Let's start using DL4J only first (we would add Spark to the stack later). The first thing we need to do is to vectorize the training data. We use ImageRecordReader (https://deeplearning4j.org/datavecdoc/org/datavec/image/recordreader/ImageRecordReader.html) as reader, because the training data are images, and a RecordReaderDataSetIterator (http://javadox.com/org.deeplearning4j/deeplearning4j-core/0.4-rc3.6/org/deeplearning4j/datasets/canova/RecordReaderDataSetIterator.html) to iterate through the dataset, as follows:

```
val trainData = new ClassPathResource("/mnist_png/training").getFile
val trainSplit = new FileSplit(trainData,
NativeImageLoader.ALLOWED_FORMATS, randNumGen)
val labelMaker = new ParentPathLabelGenerator(); // parent path as the
image label
val trainRR = new ImageRecordReader(height, width, channels, labelMaker)
trainRR.initialize(trainSplit)
val trainIter = new RecordReaderDataSetIterator(trainRR, batchSize, 1,
outputNum)
```

Let's do a min-max scaling of the pixel values from 0-255 to 0-1, as follows:

```
val scaler = new ImagePreProcessingScaler(0, 1)
scaler.fit(trainIter)
trainIter.setPreProcessor(scaler)
```

The same vectorization needs to be done for the testing data as well.

Let's configure the network, as follows:

```
val channels = 1
val outputNum = 10
val conf = new NeuralNetConfiguration.Builder()
      .seed(seed)
      .iterations(iterations)
      .regularization(true)
      .l2(0.0005)
      .learningRate(.01)
      .weightInit(WeightInit.XAVIER)
      .optimizationAlgo(OptimizationAlgorithm.STOCHASTIC_GRADIENT_DESCENT)
      .updater(Updater.NESTEROVS)
      .momentum(0.9)
      .list
      .layer(0, new ConvolutionLayer.Builder(5, 5)
        .nIn(channels)
        .stride(1, 1)
        .nOut(20)
        .activation(Activation.IDENTITY)
        .build)
      .layer(1, new
SubsamplingLayer.Builder(SubsamplingLayer.PoolingType.MAX)
        .kernelSize(2, 2)
        .stride(2, 2)
        .build)
      .layer(2, new ConvolutionLayer.Builder(5, 5)
        .stride(1, 1)
        .nOut(50)
        .activation(Activation.IDENTITY)
        .build)
      .layer(3, new
SubsamplingLayer.Builder(SubsamplingLayer.PoolingType.MAX)
        .kernelSize(2, 2)
        .stride(2, 2)
        .build)
      .layer(4, new DenseLayer.Builder()
        .activation(Activation.RELU)
        .nOut(500)
        .build)
```

```
        .layer(5, new
OutputLayer.Builder(LossFunctions.LossFunction.NEGATIVELOGLIKELIHOOD)
        .nOut(outputNum)
        .activation(Activation.SOFTMAX).build)
    .setInputType(InputType.convolutionalFlat(28, 28, 1))
    .backprop(true).pretrain(false).build
```

The `MultiLayerConfiguration` **object produced** (`https://deeplearning4j.org/doc/ org/deeplearning4j/nn/conf/MultiLayerConfiguration.html`) can then be used to initialize the model (`https://deeplearning4j.org/doc/org/deeplearning4j/nn/ multilayer/MultiLayerNetwork.html`), as follows:

```
val model: MultiLayerNetwork = new MultiLayerNetwork(conf)
model.init()
```

We can now train (and evaluate) the model, as follows:

```
model.setListeners(new ScoreIterationListener(1))
for (i <- 0 until nEpochs) {
    model.fit(trainIter)
    println("*** Completed epoch {} ***", i)
    ...
}
```

Let's now put Apache Spark into the game. Through Spark, it is possible to parallelize the training and evaluation in memory across multiple nodes of a cluster.

As usual, create a Spark context first, as follows:

```
val sparkConf = new SparkConf
sparkConf.setMaster(master)
        .setAppName("DL4J Spark MNIST Example")
val sc = new JavaSparkContext(sparkConf)
```

Then, after vectorizing the training data, parallelize them through the Spark context, as follows:

```
val trainDataList = mutable.ArrayBuffer.empty[DataSet]
while (trainIter.hasNext) {
    trainDataList += trainIter.next
}

val paralleltrainData = sc.parallelize(trainDataList)
```

The same needs to be done for the testing data as well.

After configuring and initializing the model, you can configure Spark for training, as follows:

```
var batchSizePerWorker: Int = 16
val tm = new ParameterAveragingTrainingMaster.Builder(batchSizePerWorker)
    .averagingFrequency(5)
    .workerPrefetchNumBatches(2)
    .batchSizePerWorker(batchSizePerWorker)
    .build
```

Create the Spark network, as follows:

```
val sparkNet = new SparkDl4jMultiLayer(sc, conf, tm)
```

Finally, replace the previous training code with the following:

```
var numEpochs: Int = 15
var i: Int = 0
for (i <- 0 until numEpochs) {
    sparkNet.fit(paralleltrainData)
    println("Completed Epoch {}", i)
}
```

When done, don't forget to delete the temporary training files, as follows:

```
tm.deleteTempFiles(sc)
```

The full example is part of the source code shipped with the book.

Summary

In this chapter, we first went deeper into the CNN main concepts and explored one of the most popular and performing examples of the CNN architecture provided by Google. We started then to implement some code using DL4J and Spark.

In the next chapter, we will follow a similar trail to go deeper into RNNs.

6
Recurrent Neural Networks

In this chapter, we are going to learn more about **Recurrent Neural Networks** (**RNNs**), an overview of their most common use cases, and, finally, a possible implementation by starting to be hands-on using the DeepLearning4j framework. This chapter's code examples involve Apache Spark too. As stated in the previous chapter for CNNs, training and evaluation strategies for RNNs will be covered in Chapter 7, *Training Neural Networks with Spark*, Chapter 8, *Monitoring and Debugging Neural Network Training*, and Chapter 9, *Interpreting Neural Network Output*.

In this chapter, I have tried to reduce the usage of math concepts and formulas as much as possible in order to make the reading and comprehension easier for developers and data analysts who might have no math or data science background.

The chapter covers the following topics:

- **Long short-term memory (LSTM)**
- Use cases
- Hands-on RNN with Spark

LSTM

RNNs are multilayer neural networks that are used to recognize patterns in sequences of data. By sequences of data, we mean text, handwriting, numerical times series (coming for example from sensors), log entries, and so on. The algorithms involved here have a temporal dimension too: they take time (and this is the main difference with CNNs) and sequence both into account. For a better understanding of the need for RNNs, we have to look at the basics of feedforward networks first. Similar to RNNs, these networks channel information through a series of mathematical operations performed at the nodes of the network, but they feed information straight through, never touching a given node twice. The network is fed with input examples that are then transformed into an output: in simple words, they map raw data to categories. Training happens for them on labeled inputs, until the errors made when guessing input categories has been minimized. This is the way a network learns to categorize new data it has never seen before. A feedforward network hasn't any notion of order in time: the only input it considers is the current one it has been exposed to, and it doesn't necessarily alter how it classifies the next one. RNNs take as input the current example they see, plus anything they have perceived previously. A RNN can be then be seen as multiple feedforward neural networks passing information from one to the other.

In the RNNs' use case scenarios, a sequence could be a finite or infinite stream of interdependent data. CNNs can't work well in those cases because they don't have any correlation between previous and next input. From Chapter 5, *Convolutional Neural Networks*, you have learned that a CNN takes an input and then outputs based on the trained model. Running a given number of different inputs, none of them would be biased by taking into account any of the previous outputs. But if you consider a case like that presented in the last sections of this chapter (a sentence generation case), where all the generated words are dependent on the those generated before, there is definitely a need to bias based on previous output. This is where RNNs come to the rescue, because they have memory of what happened earlier in the sequence of data and this helps them to get the context. RNNs in theory can look back indefinitely at all of the previous steps, but really, for performance reasons, they have to restrict looking back at the last few steps only.

Let's go into the details of RNNs. For this explanation, I am going to start from a **Multilayer Perception (MLP)**, a class of feedforward ANN. The minimal implementation of an MLP has at least three layers of nodes. But for the input nodes, each node is a neuron that uses a nonlinear activation function. The input layer, of course, takes the input. It is the first hidden layer that does the activation, passing onto the next hidden layers, and so on. Finally, it reaches the output layer. This is responsible for providing the output. All of the hidden layers behave differently, because each one has different weights, bias, and activation functions. In order to make it possible and easier to merge them, all the layers need to be replaced with the same weights (and also same biases and activation function). This is the only way to combine all the hidden layers into a single recurrent layer. They start looking as shown in the following diagram.

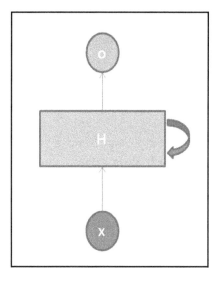

Figure 6.1

With reference to the preceding diagram, the network **H** receives some input **x** and produces an output **o**. Any info passes from one step of the network to the next through a loop mechanism. An input is provided to the hidden layer of the network at each step. Any neuron of an RNN stores the inputs it receives during all of the previous steps and then can merge that information with input passed to it at the current step. This means that a decision taken at a time step *t-1* affects the decision that is taken at a time *t*.

Let's rephrase the preceding explanation with an example: let's say we want to predict what the next letter would be after a sequence of letters. Let's assume the input word is **pizza**, which is of five letters. What happens when the network tries to figure out the fifth letter after the first four letters have been fed to the network? Five iterations happen for the hidden layer. If we unfold the network, it would be a five layers network, one for each letter of the input word (see `Chapter 2`, *Deep Learning Basics*, *Figure 2.11* as reference). We can see it then as a normal neural network repeated multiple times (5). The number of times we unroll it has a direct correlation with how far in the past the network can remember. Going back to the **pizza** example, the total vocabulary of the input data is {*p, i, z, a*}. The hidden layer or the RNN applies a formula to the current input as well as the previous state. In our example, the letter *p* from the word *pizza*, being the first letter, has nothing preceding it, so nothing is done and we can move on to the next letter, which is *i*. The formula is applied by the hidden layer at the time between letter *i* and the previous state, which was letter *p*. If at a given time *t*, the input is *i*, then at time *t-1*, the input is *p*. By applying the formula to both *p* and *i* we get a new state. The formula to calculate the current state can be written as follows:

$$h_t = f(h_{t-1}, x_t)$$

where h_t is the new state, h_{t-1} is the previous state and x_t is the current input. From the previous formula, we can understand that the current state is a function of the previous input (the input neuron has applied transformations on the previous input). Any successive input is used as a time step. In this *pizza* example we have four inputs to the network. The same function and the same weights are applied to the network at each time step. Considering the simplest implementation of an RNN, the activation function is *tanh*, a hyperbolic tangent that ranges from *-1* to *1*, which is one of the most common sigmoid activation function for MLPs. So, the formula looks as follows:

$$h_t = tanh(W_{hh}h_{t-1} + W_{xh}x_t)$$

Here W_{hh} is the weight at the recurrent neuron and W_{xh} is the weight at the input neuron. That formula means that the immediate previous state is taken into account by a recurrent neuron. Of course, the preceding equation can involve multiple states in cases of longer sequence than *pizza*. Once the final state is calculated then the output y_t can be obtained this way:

$$y_t = W_{hy}h_t$$

One final note about the error. It is calculated by comparing the output to the actual output. Once the error has been calculated, then the learning process happens by backpropagating it through the network in order to update the network weights.

Backpropagation Through Time (BPTT)

Multiple variant architectures have been proposed for RNNs (some of them have been listed in `Chapter 2`, *Deep Learning Basics*, in the section *Recurrent Neural Networks*). Before entering into details of the LSTM implementation, a few words must be spent about the problems with the generic RNN architecture described previously. In general for neural networks, forward propagation is the technique used to get the output of a model and check if it is correct or not. Likewise, backward propagation is a technique to go backwards through a neural network to find the partial derivatives of the error over the weights (this makes it possible to subtract the found value from the weights). These derivatives are then used by the Gradient Descent Algorithm, which, in an iterative way, minimizes a function and then does up or down adjustments to the weights (the direction depends on which one decreases the error). At training time, backpropagation is then the way in which it is possible to adjust the weights of a model. BPTT is just a way to define the process of doing backpropagation on an unrolled RNN. With reference to `Chapter 2`, *Deep Learning Basics*, *Figure 2.11*, in doing BPTT, it is mandatory to do the formulation of unrolling, this being the error of a given time step, depending on the previous one. In the BPTT technique, the error is backpropagated from the last time step to the first one, while unrolling all of them. This allows error calculation for each time step, making it possible to update the weights. Please be aware that BPTT can be computationally expensive in those cases where the number of time steps is high.

RNN issues

The two major issues affecting RNNs are the **Exploding Gradients** and **Vanishing Gradients**. We talk about Exploding Gradients when an algorithm assigns, without a reason, a high importance to the model weights. But, the solution to this problem is easy, as this would require just truncating or compressing the gradients. We talk about Vanishing Gradients when the values of a gradient are so small that they cause a model to stop or take too long to learn. This is a major problem if compared with the Exploding Gradients, but it has now been solved through the **LSTM** (Long Short-Term Memory) neural networks. LSTMs are a special kind of RNN, capable of learning long-term dependencies, that were introduced by Sepp Hochreiter (`https://en.wikipedia.org/wiki/Sepp_Hochreiter`) & Juergen Schmidhuber (`https://en.wikipedia.org/wiki/J%C3%BCrgen_Schmidhuber`) in 1997.

They are explicitly designed with the default ability to remember information for long periods of time. This can be achieved because LSTMs retain their information in a memory, which is pretty much like that of a computer: a LSTM can read, write, and delete information from it. The LSTM's memory can be considered as a gated cell: it decides whether or not to store or delete information (open gates or not), depending on the importance it puts on a given information. The process of assigning importance happens through weights: consequently a network learns over time which information has to be considered important and which not. An LSTM has three gates: the input, the forget, and the output gate. The **Input Gate** determines if a new input in should be let in, the **Forget Gate** deletes the non-important information, and the **Output Gate** influences the output of the network at the current time step, as shown in the following diagram:

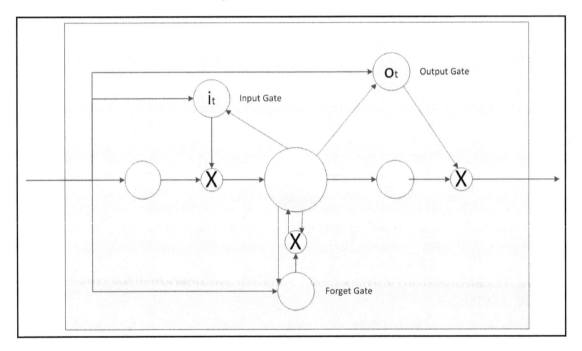

Figure 6.2: The three gates of an LSTM

You can think of each of these three gates as a conventional artificial neuron, as in a feedforward MNN: they compute an activation (using an activation function) of a weighted sum. What enables the LSTM gates to do backpropagation is the fact that they are analog (sigmoids, they range from zero to one). This implementation solves the problems of Vanishing Gradients because it keeps the gradients steep enough, and consequently the training completes in a relatively short time, while maintaining an high accuracy.

Use cases

RNNs have several use cases. Here is a list of the most frequently used:

- **Language modelling and text generation**: This is the attempt to predict the likelihood of the next word, given a sequence of words. This is useful for language translation: the most likely sentence would be the one that is correct.
- **Machine translation**: This is the attempt to translate text from one language to another.
- **Anomaly detection in time series**: It has been demonstrated that LSTM networks in particular are useful for learning sequences containing longer term patterns of unknown length, due to their ability to maintain long-term memory. For this reason they are useful for anomaly or fault detection in time series. Practical use cases are in log analysis and sensor data analysis.
- **Speech recognition**: This is the attempt to predict phonetic segments based on input sound waves and then to formulate a word.
- **Semantic parsing**: Converting a natural language utterance to a logical form—a machine-understandable representation of its meaning. Practical applications include question answering and programming language code generation.
- **Image captioning**: This is a case that usually involves a combination of a CNN and an RNN. The first makes the segmentation, while the other then uses the data segmented by the CNN to recreate the descriptions.
- **Video tagging**: RNNs can be used for video search when doing frame by frame image captioning of a video.
- **Image generation**: This is the process of creating parts of a scene independently from others and to successively refine approximate sketches, generating at the end, images that cannot be distinguished from real data with the naked eye.

Hands-on RNNs with Spark

Let's start now being hands-on with RNNs. This section is divided into two parts—the first one is about using DL4J to implement a network, while the second one will introduce using both DL4J and Spark for the same purpose. As with CNNs, you will discover that, thanks to the DL4J framework, lots of high-level facilities come out-of-the-box with it, so that the implementation process is easier than you might expect.

RNNs with DL4J

The first example presented in this chapter is an LSTM which, after the training, will recite the following characters once the first character of the learning string has been used as input for it.

The dependencies for this example are the following:

- Scala 2.11.8
- DL4J NN 0.9.1
- ND4J Native 0.9.1 and the specific classifier for the OS of the machine where you would run it
- ND4J jblas 0.4-rc3.6

Assuming we have a learn string that is specified through an immutable variable LEARNSTRING, let's start creating a dedicated list of possible characters from it, as follows:

```
val LEARNSTRING_CHARS: util.LinkedHashSet[Character] = new
util.LinkedHashSet[Character]
for (c <- LEARNSTRING) {
        LEARNSTRING_CHARS.add(c)
}
LEARNSTRING_CHARS_LIST.addAll(LEARNSTRING_CHARS)
```

Let's configure the network, as follows:

```
val builder: NeuralNetConfiguration.Builder = new
NeuralNetConfiguration.Builder
builder.iterations(10)
builder.learningRate(0.001)
builder.optimizationAlgo(OptimizationAlgorithm.STOCHASTIC_GRADIENT_DESCENT)
builder.seed(123)
builder.biasInit(0)
builder.miniBatch(false)
builder.updater(Updater.RMSPROP)
builder.weightInit(WeightInit.XAVIER)
```

You will notice that we are using the same `NeuralNetConfiguration.Builder` class as for the CNN example presented in the previous chapter. This same abstraction is used for any network you need to implement through DL4J. The optimization algorithm used is the Stochastic Gradient Descent (`https://en.wikipedia.org/wiki/Stochastic_gradient_descent`). The meaning of the other parameters will be explained in the next chapter that will focus on training.

Let's now define the layers for this network. The model we are implementing is based on the LSTM RNN by Alex Graves (https://en.wikipedia.org/wiki/Alex_Graves_ (computer_scientist)). After deciding their total number assigning a value to an immutable variable HIDDEN_LAYER_CONT, we can define the hidden layers of our network, as follows:

```
val listBuilder = builder.list
for (i <- 0 until HIDDEN_LAYER_CONT) {
  val hiddenLayerBuilder: GravesLSTM.Builder = new GravesLSTM.Builder
  hiddenLayerBuilder.nIn(if (i == 0) LEARNSTRING_CHARS.size else
HIDDEN_LAYER_WIDTH)
  hiddenLayerBuilder.nOut(HIDDEN_LAYER_WIDTH)
  hiddenLayerBuilder.activation(Activation.TANH)
  listBuilder.layer(i, hiddenLayerBuilder.build)
}
```

The activation function is tanh (hyperbolic tangent).

We need then to define the outputLayer (choosing softmax as the activation function), as follows:

```
val outputLayerBuilder: RnnOutputLayer.Builder = new
RnnOutputLayer.Builder(LossFunction.MCXENT)
outputLayerBuilder.activation(Activation.SOFTMAX)
outputLayerBuilder.nIn(HIDDEN_LAYER_WIDTH)
outputLayerBuilder.nOut(LEARNSTRING_CHARS.size)
listBuilder.layer(HIDDEN_LAYER_CONT, outputLayerBuilder.build)
```

Before completing the configuration, we must specify that this model isn't pre-trained and that we use backpropagation, as follows:

```
listBuilder.pretrain(false)
listBuilder.backprop(true)
```

The network (MultiLayerNetwork) can be created starting from the preceding configuration, as follows:

```
val conf = listBuilder.build
val net = new MultiLayerNetwork(conf)
net.init()
net.setListeners(new ScoreIterationListener(1))
```

Some training data can be generated programmatically starting from the learning string character list, as follows:

```
val input = Nd4j.zeros(1, LEARNSTRING_CHARS_LIST.size, LEARNSTRING.length)
val labels = Nd4j.zeros(1, LEARNSTRING_CHARS_LIST.size, LEARNSTRING.length)
var samplePos = 0
for (currentChar <- LEARNSTRING) {
  val nextChar = LEARNSTRING((samplePos + 1) % (LEARNSTRING.length))
  input.putScalar(Array[Int](0,
LEARNSTRING_CHARS_LIST.indexOf(currentChar), samplePos), 1)
  labels.putScalar(Array[Int](0, LEARNSTRING_CHARS_LIST.indexOf(nextChar),
samplePos), 1)
  samplePos += 1
}
val trainingData: DataSet = new DataSet(input, labels)
```

The way the training for this RNN happens will be covered in the next chapter (and the code example will be completed there)—the focus in this section is to show how to configure and build an RNN network using the DL4J API.

RNNs with DL4J and Spark

The example presented in this section is an LSTM that would be trained to generate text, one character at a time. The training is done using Spark.

The dependencies for this example are the following:

- Scala 2.11.8
- DL4J NN 0.9.1
- ND4J Native 0.9.1 and the specific classifier for the OS of the machine where you would run it
- ND4J jblas 0.4-rc3.6
- Apache Spark Core 2.11, release 2.2.1
- DL4J Spark 2.11, release 0.9.1_spark_2

We start configuring the network as usual through the `NeuralNetConfiguration.Builder` class, as follows:

```
val rng = new Random(12345)
val lstmLayerSize: Int = 200
val tbpttLength: Int = 50
val nSamplesToGenerate: Int = 4
val nCharactersToSample: Int = 300
```

```
val generationInitialization: String = null
val conf = new NeuralNetConfiguration.Builder()
    .optimizationAlgo(OptimizationAlgorithm.STOCHASTIC_GRADIENT_DESCENT)
    .iterations(1)
    .learningRate(0.1)
    .rmsDecay(0.95)
    .seed(12345)
    .regularization(true)
    .l2(0.001)
    .weightInit(WeightInit.XAVIER)
    .updater(Updater.RMSPROP)
    .list
    .layer(0, new
GravesLSTM.Builder().nIn(SparkLSTMCharacterExample.CHAR_TO_INT.size).nOut(l
stmLayerSize).activation(Activation.TANH).build())
    .layer(1, new
GravesLSTM.Builder().nIn(lstmLayerSize).nOut(lstmLayerSize).activation(Acti
vation.TANH).build())
    .layer(2, new
RnnOutputLayer.Builder(LossFunction.MCXENT).activation(Activation.SOFTMAX)
        .nIn(lstmLayerSize).nOut(SparkLSTMCharacterExample.nOut).build)
//MCXENT + softmax for classification
.backpropType(BackpropType.TruncatedBPTT).tBPTTForwardLength(tbpttLength).t
BPTTBackwardLength(tbpttLength)
    .pretrain(false).backprop(true)
    .build
```

As for the example presented in the *RNNs with DL4J* section, the LSTM RNN implementation used here is that by Alex Graves. So the configuration, the hidden layers, and the output layer are pretty similar to those for the previous example.

Now this is where Spark comes into play. Let's set up the Spark configuration and context, as follows:

```
val sparkConf = new SparkConf
sparkConf.setMaster(master)
sparkConf.setAppName("LSTM Character Example")
val sc = new JavaSparkContext(sparkConf)
```

Assuming we got some training data and have created a `JavaRDD[DataSet]` named `trainingData` from them, we need to set up for data parallel training. In particular, we need to set up the `TrainingMaster` (`https://deeplearning4j.org/doc/org/deeplearning4j/spark/api/TrainingMaster.html`).

It is an abstraction that controls how learning is actually executed on Spark and allows for multiple different training implementations to be used with `SparkDl4jMultiLayer` (`https://deeplearning4j.org/doc/org/deeplearning4j/spark/impl/multilayer/SparkDl4jMultiLayer.html`). Set up for data parallel training, as follows:

```
val averagingFrequency: Int = 5
val batchSizePerWorker: Int = 8
val examplesPerDataSetObject = 1
val tm = new
ParameterAveragingTrainingMaster.Builder(examplesPerDataSetObject)
    .workerPrefetchNumBatches(2)
    .averagingFrequency(averagingFrequency)
    .batchSizePerWorker(batchSizePerWorker)
    .build
val sparkNetwork: SparkDl4jMultiLayer = new SparkDl4jMultiLayer(sc, conf,
tm)
sparkNetwork.setListeners(Collections.singletonList[IterationListener](new
ScoreIterationListener(1)))
```

Currently, the DL4J framework has only one implementation of the `TrainingMaster`, the `ParameterAveragingTrainingMaster` (`https://deeplearning4j.org/doc/org/deeplearning4j/spark/impl/paramavg/ParameterAveragingTrainingMaster.html`). The parameters that we have set for it in the current example are:

- `workerPrefetchNumBatches`: The number of Spark workers capable of prefetching in an asynchronous way; a number of mini-batches (Dataset objects), in order to avoid waiting for the data to be loaded. Setting this parameter to 0 means disabling this prefetching. Setting it to 2 (such as in our example) is a good compromise (a sensible default with a non-excessive use of memory).
- `batchSizePerWorker`: This is the number of examples used for each parameter update in each Spark worker.
- `averagingFrequency`: To control how frequently the parameters are averaged and redistributed, in terms of a number of mini-batches of size `batchSizePerWorker`. Setting a low averaging period may be inefficient, because of the high network communication and initialization overhead, relative to computation, while setting a large averaging period may result in poor performance. So, a good compromise is to keep its value between 5 and 10.

The `SparkDl4jMultiLayer` requires as parameters the Spark context, the Spark configuration, and the `TrainingMaster`.

The training through Spark can now start. The way it happens will be covered in the next chapter (and this code example will be completed there)—again, the focus in this section is to show how to configure and build an RNN network using the DL4J and Spark API.

Loading multiple CSVs for RNN data pipelines

Before wrapping up this chapter, here are a few notes about how we can load multiple CSV files, each containing one sequence, for RNN training and testing data. We are assuming to have a dataset made of multiple CSV files stored in a cluster (it could be HDFS or an object storage such as Amazon S3 or Minio), where each file represents a sequence, each row of one file contains the values for one time step only, the number of rows could be different across files, and the header row could be present or missing in all files.

With reference to CSV files saved in an S3-based object storage (refer to Chapter 3, *Extract, Transform, Load, Data Ingestion from S3*, for more details), the Spark context has been created as follows:

```
val conf = new SparkConf
conf.setMaster(master)
conf.setAppName("DataVec S3 Example")
val sparkContext = new JavaSparkContext(conf)
```

The Spark job configuration has been set up to access the object storage (as explained in Chapter 3, *Extract, Transform, Load*), and we can get the data as follows:

```
val origData = sparkContext.binaryFiles("s3a://dl4j-bucket")
```

(`dl4j-bucket` is the bucket containing the CSV files). Next we create a DataVec `CSVSequenceRecordReader` specifying if all the CSV files in the bucket have the header row or not (use the value 0 for no, 1 for yes) and the values separator, as follows:

```
val numHeaderLinesEachFile = 0
val delimiter = ","
val seqRR = new CSVSequenceRecordReader(numHeaderLinesEachFile, delimiter)
```

Finally we get the sequence by applying a `map` transformation to the original data in `seqRR`, as follows:

```
val sequencesRdd = origData.map(new SequenceRecordReaderFunction(seqRR))
```

It is very similar in the case of RNN training with non-sequence CSV files, by using the `DataVecDataSetFunction` class of `dl4j-spark` and specifying the index of the label column and the number of labels for classification, as follows:

```
val labelIndex = 1
val numClasses = 4
val dataSetRdd = sequencesRdd.map(new
DataVecSequenceDataSetFunction(labelIndex, numClasses, false))
```

Summary

In this chapter, we first went deeper into the RNNs' main concepts, before understanding how many practical use cases these particular NNs have, and, finally, we started going hands-on, implementing some RNNs using DL4J and Spark.

The next chapter will focus on training techniques for CNN and RNN models. Training techniques have just been mentioned, or skipped from Chapter 3, *Extract, Transform, Load*, to this chapter because the main goal so far has been on understanding how training data can be retrieved and prepared and how models can be implemented through DL4J and Spark.

Training Neural Networks with 7 Spark

In the previous two chapters, we have learned how to programmatically configure and build **convolutional neural networks** (**CNNs**) and **recurrent neural networks** (**RNNs**) using the **DeepLearning4j** (**DL4J**) API in Scala. There, implementing the training of these networks was mentioned, but very little explanation has been provided. This chapter finally goes into details of how to implement the training strategies for both kinds of network. The chapter also explains why Spark is important in the training process and what the fundamental role of DL4J is from a performance perspective.

The second and third sections focus on specific training strategies for CNNs and RNNs respectively. The fourth section of this chapter also provides suggestions, tips, and tricks for a proper Spark environment configuration. The final section describes how to use the DL4J Arbiter component for hyperparameter optimization.

Here is a summary of what we will cover in this chapter:

- CNN distributed training with Spark and DL4J
- RNN distributed training with Spark and DL4J
- Performance considerations
- Hyperparameter optimization

Distributed network training with Spark and DeepLearning4j

The training of **Multilayer Neural Networks** (**MNNs**) is computationally expensive—it involves huge datasets, and there is also the need to complete the training process in the fastest way possible. In Chapter 1, *The Apache Spark Ecosystem*, we have learned about how Apache Spark can achieve high performances when undertaking large-scale data processing. This makes it a perfect candidate to perform training, by taking advantage of its parallelism features. But Spark alone isn't enough—its performances are excellent, in particular for ETL or streaming, but in terms of computation, in an MNN training context, some data transformation or aggregation need to be moved down using a low-level language (such as C++).

Here's where the ND4J (https://nd4j.org/index.html) module of DL4J comes into play. There's no need to learn and program in C++, as ND4J provides the Scala APIs, and those are what we need to use. The underlying C++ library is transparent to Scala or Java developers using ND4J. Here is a simple example of how a Scala application that uses the ND4J API appears (the inline comments explain what the code does):

```scala
object Nd4JScalaSample {
  def main (args: Array[String]) {

    // Create arrays using the numpy syntax
    var arr1 = Nd4j.create(4)
    val arr2 = Nd4j.linspace(1, 10, 10)
    // Fill an array with the value 5 (equivalent to fill method in
numpy)
    println(arr1.assign(5) + "Assigned value of 5 to the array")
    // Basic stats methods
    println(Nd4j.mean(arr1) + "Calculate mean of array")
    println(Nd4j.std(arr2) + "Calculate standard deviation of array")
    println(Nd4j.`var`(arr2), "Calculate variance")
    ...
```

ND4J brings to the JVM an open source, distributed, GPU-enabled, intuitive scientific library, filling the gap between JVM languages and Python programmers in terms of availability of powerful data analysis tools. DL4J relies on Spark for training models in parallel. Large datasets are partitioned, with each partition available to separate neural networks, each one in its own core—DL4J iteratively averages the parameters they produce in a central model.

Just for completeness of information, whether training would be demanded to DL4J only, running multiple models in the same server, `ParallelWrapper` (`https://deeplearning4j.org/api/v1.0.0-beta2/org/deeplearning4j/parallelism/ParallelWrapper.html`) should be used. But please consider that this process is particularly expensive and the server has to be equipped with a large number of CPUs (at least 64) or multiple GPUs.

DL4J provides the following two classes for training neural networks on top of Spark:

- `SparkDl4jMultiLayer` (`https://deeplearning4j.org/api/v1.0.0-beta2/org/deeplearning4j/spark/impl/multilayer/SparkDl4jMultiLayer.html`), a wrapper around `MultiLayerNetwork` (this is the class that has been used in some examples presented in the previous chapters).
- `SparkComputationGraph` (`https://deeplearning4j.org/api/v1.0.0-beta2/org/deeplearning4j/spark/impl/graph/SparkComputationGraph.html`), a wrapper around `ComputationGraph` (`https://deeplearning4j.org/api/v1.0.0-beta2/org/deeplearning4j/nn/graph/ComputationGraph.html`), a neural network with arbitrary connection structure (DAG) that can also have an arbitrary number of inputs and outputs.

These two classes are wrappers around the standard single-machine classes, so the network configuration process is identical in both standard and distributed training.

In order to train a network through DL4J on a Spark cluster you have to follow this standard workflow:

1. Specify the network configuration through the `MultiLayerConfiguration` (`https://static.javadoc.io/org.deeplearning4j/deeplearning4j-nn/0.9.1/org/deeplearning4j/nn/conf/MultiLayerConfiguration.html`) class or the `ComputationGraphConfiguration` (`https://static.javadoc.io/org.deeplearning4j/deeplearning4j-nn/0.9.1/org/deeplearning4j/nn/conf/ComputationGraphConfiguration.html`) class

2. Create an instance of `TrainingMaster` (`https://static.javadoc.io/org.deeplearning4j/dl4j-spark_2.11/0.9.1_spark_2/org/deeplearning4j/spark/api/TrainingMaster.html`) to control how distributed training is executed in practice

3. Create the `SparkDl4jMultiLayer` or `SparkComputationGraph` instance using the network configuration and the `TrainingMaster` object previously created

4. Load the training data
5. Call the appropriate fit method on the `SparkDl4jMultiLayer` (or `SparkComputationGraph`) instance
6. Save the trained network
7. Build the JAR file for the Spark job
8. Submit the JAR for execution

The code examples presented in Chapter 5, *Convolutional Neural Networks*, and Chapter 6, *Recurrent Neural Networks*, have given you an idea of how to configure and build an MNN; those in Chapter 3, *Extract, Transform, Load*, and Chapter 4, *Streaming*, have presented insights about different ways to load the training data and, from Chapter 1, *The Apache Spark Ecosystem*, you have learned how to execute a Spark job. Let's now focus in the next sections on understanding how to implement the missing part: the network training.

At the present time, to train a network, DL4J provides a single approach—parameter averaging (https://arxiv.org/abs/1410.7455). Here's how this process conceptually happens:

- The Spark master starts using the network configuration and parameters
- Depending on the configuration of the `TrainingMaster`, data is partitioned into subsets
- For each subset:
  - Configuration and the parameters are distributed from the master across each worker
  - Each worker executes the fit on its own partition
  - The average of the parameters is calculated and then the results are returned back to the master
- The training completes and a copy of the trained network is available in the master

CNN distributed training with Spark and DL4J

Let's get back to the example that has been presented in Chapter 5, *Convolutional Neural Networks*, *Hands-on CNN with Spark*, about handwritten digits image classification on the MNIST dataset. For convenience, here's a reminder of the network configuration used there:

```
val channels = 1
val outputNum = 10
val conf = new NeuralNetConfiguration.Builder()
    .seed(seed)
```

```
.iterations(iterations)
.regularization(true)
.l2(0.0005)
.learningRate(.01)
.weightInit(WeightInit.XAVIER)
.optimizationAlgo(OptimizationAlgorithm.STOCHASTIC_GRADIENT_DESCENT)
.updater(Updater.NESTEROVS)
.momentum(0.9)
.list
.layer(0, new ConvolutionLayer.Builder(5, 5)
    .nIn(channels)
    .stride(1, 1)
    .nOut(20)
    .activation(Activation.IDENTITY)
    .build)
.layer(1, new
SubsamplingLayer.Builder(SubsamplingLayer.PoolingType.MAX)
    .kernelSize(2, 2)
    .stride(2, 2)
    .build)
.layer(2, new ConvolutionLayer.Builder(5, 5)
    .stride(1, 1)
    .nOut(50)
    .activation(Activation.IDENTITY)
    .build)
.layer(3, new
SubsamplingLayer.Builder(SubsamplingLayer.PoolingType.MAX)
    .kernelSize(2, 2)
    .stride(2, 2)
    .build)
.layer(4, new DenseLayer.Builder()
    .activation(Activation.RELU)
    .nOut(500)
    .build)
.layer(5, new
OutputLayer.Builder(LossFunctions.LossFunction.NEGATIVELOGLIKELIHOOD)
    .nOut(outputNum)
    .activation(Activation.SOFTMAX).build)
    .setInputType(InputType.convolutionalFlat(28, 28, 1))
    .backprop(true).pretrain(false).build
```

We used that `MultiLayerConfiguration` object to initialize the model. Having the model and the training data, the training can be set. As explained in the previous section, the training happens with Spark. Therefore, the next steps would be creating a Spark context, as follows:

```
val sparkConf = new SparkConf
 sparkConf.setMaster(master)
     .setAppName("DL4J Spark MNIST Example")
 val sc = new JavaSparkContext(sparkConf)
```

We then parallelize the training data after loading it in memory, as follows:

```
val trainDataList = mutable.ArrayBuffer.empty[DataSet]
 while (trainIter.hasNext) {
     trainDataList += trainIter.next
 }
 val paralleltrainData = sc.parallelize(trainDataList)
```

Now it is time to create the `TrainingMaster` instance, as follows:

```
var batchSizePerWorker: Int = 16
 val tm = new ParameterAveragingTrainingMaster.Builder(batchSizePerWorker)
     .averagingFrequency(5)
     .workerPrefetchNumBatches(2)
     .batchSizePerWorker(batchSizePerWorker)
     .build
```

We can use the only currently available implementation for the `TrainingMaster` interface, the `ParameterAveragingTrainingMaster` (https://static.javadoc.io/org. deeplearning4j/dl4j-spark_2.11/0.9.1_spark_2/org/deeplearning4j/spark/impl/ paramavg/ParameterAveragingTrainingMaster.html). In the preceding example we have used only three configuration options available for this `TrainingMaster` implementation, but there are more:

- `dataSetObjectSize`: Specifies how many examples are in each `DataSet`.
- `workerPrefetchNumBatches`: The Spark workers are capable of asynchronously prefetching a number of `DataSet` objects, in order to avoid waiting for data to be loaded. It is possible to disable prefetching by setting this property to zero. Setting it to two (such as in our example) is a good compromise (a sensible default with a non-excessive use of memory).

- *rddTrainingApproach*: DL4J provides two approaches when training from an RDD—RDDTrainingApproach.Export and RDDTrainingApproach.Direct (https://static.javadoc.io/org.deeplearning4j/dl4j-spark_2.11/0.9.1_spark_2/org/deeplearning4j/spark/api/RDDTrainingApproach.html). Export is the default approach; it first saves an RDD<DataSet> to disk in batched and serialized form. Then, the executors load asynchronously all the DataSet objects. The choice between the Export and the Direct method depends on the size of the datasets. For large datasets that don't fit into memory and multiple epochs, the Export approach is preferable—in those cases the split and repartition operations overhead typical of the Direct approach doesn't apply and the memory consumption is smaller.
- exportDirectory: The location where the temporary data files are stored (Export method only).
- storageLevel: Applies only when using a Direct approach and training from a RDD<DataSet> or RDD<MultiDataSet>. The default storage level that DL4J persists the *RDDs* at is StorageLevel.MEMORY_ONLY_SER.
- storageLevelStreams: Applies only when using the fitPaths(RDD<String>) method. The default storage level that DL4J persists the RDD<String> at is StorageLevel.MEMORY_ONLY.
- repartitionStrategy: Specifies the strategy by which repartitioning should be done. Possible values are Balanced (default, custom repartitioning strategy defined by DL4J) and SparkDefault (standard repartitioning strategy used by Spark).

Here you can find the full list and their meaning:

```
https://deeplearning4j.org/docs/latest/deeplearning4j-spark-training
```

Once the TrainingMaster configuration and strategy have been defined, an instance of SparkDl4jMultiLayer can be created, as follows:

```
val sparkNet = new SparkDl4jMultiLayer(sc, conf, tm)
```

Then the training can happen, choosing the appropriate fit method, as follows:

```
var numEpochs: Int = 15
 var i: Int = 0
    for (i <- 0 until numEpochs) {
    sparkNet.fit(paralleltrainData)
    println("Completed Epoch {}", i)
 }
```

Chapter 8, *Monitoring and Debugging Neural Network Training*, and Chapter 9, *Interpreting Neural Network Output*, will explain how to monitor, debug, and evaluate the results of network training.

RNN distributed training with Spark and DL4J

Let's reconsider the example that has been presented in Chapter 6, *Recurrent Neural Networks*, section *RNNs with DL4J and Spark*, about an LSTM that would be trained to generate text, one character at a time. For convenience, let's remind ourselves of the network configuration used there (an LSTM RNN implementation of the model proposed by Alex Graves):

```
val rng = new Random(12345)
 val lstmLayerSize: Int = 200
 val tbpttLength: Int = 50
 val nSamplesToGenerate: Int = 4
 val nCharactersToSample: Int = 300
 val generationInitialization: String = null
 val conf = new NeuralNetConfiguration.Builder()
     .optimizationAlgo(OptimizationAlgorithm.STOCHASTIC_GRADIENT_DESCENT)
     .iterations(1)
     .learningRate(0.1)
     .rmsDecay(0.95)
     .seed(12345)
     .regularization(true)
     .l2(0.001)
     .weightInit(WeightInit.XAVIER)
     .updater(Updater.RMSPROP)
     .list
     .layer(0, new
GravesLSTM.Builder().nIn(SparkLSTMCharacterExample.CHAR_TO_INT.size).nOut(l
stmLayerSize).activation(Activation.TANH).build())
     .layer(1, new
GravesLSTM.Builder().nIn(lstmLayerSize).nOut(lstmLayerSize).activation(Acti
vation.TANH).build())
     .layer(2, new
RnnOutputLayer.Builder(LossFunction.MCXENT).activation(Activation.SOFTMAX)
        .nIn(lstmLayerSize).nOut(SparkLSTMCharacterExample.nOut).build)
//MCXENT + softmax for classification
.backpropType(BackpropType.TruncatedBPTT).tBPTTForwardLength(tbpttLength).t
BPTTBackwardLength(tbpttLength)
     .pretrain(false).backprop(true)
     .build
```

All of the considerations made in *CNN distributed training with Spark and DeepLearning4j*, about the creation and configuration of a `TrainingMaster` instance, apply the same way for the creation and configuration of a `SparkDl4jMultiLayer` instance, so they are not repeated. What is different for the `SparkDl4jMultiLayer` is that, in this case, we have to specify the `IteratorListeners` (https://static.javadoc.io/org.deeplearning4j/deeplearning4j-nn/0.9.1/org/deeplearning4j/optimize/api/IterationListener.html) for the model (which would be useful in particular for monitoring and debugging purposes, as will be explained in next chapter). Specify the iterator listeners as follows:

```
val sparkNetwork: SparkDl4jMultiLayer = new SparkDl4jMultiLayer(sc, conf,
tm)
 sparkNetwork.setListeners(Collections.singletonList[IterationListener](new
ScoreIterationListener(1)))
```

And here's one way the training could happen in this case. Define the number of epochs, as follows:

```
val numEpochs: Int = 10
```

Then for each one, apply the appropriate fit method through the `sparkNetwork` and sample some characters, as follows:

```
(0 until numEpochs).foreach { i =>
    //Perform one epoch of training. At the end of each epoch, we are
returned a copy of the trained network
    val net = sparkNetwork.fit(trainingData)

    //Sample some characters from the network (done locally)
    println("Sampling characters from network given initialization \"" +
      (if (generationInitialization == null) "" else
generationInitialization) + "\"")
    val samples = ... // Implement your own sampling method
    samples.indices.foreach { j =>
      println("----- Sample " + j + " -----")
      println(samples(j))
    }
  }
```

Finally, because we decided on an `Export` trained approach, we need to delete the temporary files when done, as follows:

```
tm.deleteTempFiles(sc)
```

Chapter 8, *Monitoring and Debugging Neural Network Training*, and Chapter 9, *Interpreting Neural Network Output*, will explain how to monitor, debug, and evaluate the results of this network training.

Performance considerations

This section presents some recommendations to get the most from DL4J when training on Spark. Let's start with some considerations about memory configuration. It is important to understand how DL4J manages memory first. This framework is built upon the ND4J scientific library (written in C++). ND4J utilizes off-heap memory management—this means that the memory allocated for INDArrays isn't on the JVM heap, as happens for Java objects, but it is allocated outside the JVM. This kind of memory management allows for the efficient use of high-performance native code for numerical operations and it is also necessary for efficient operations with CUDA (https://developer.nvidia.com/cuda-zone) when running on GPUs.

This way, the outcome in terms of extra memory and time overhead is evident—allocating memory on the JVM heap requires that any time there is the need to preliminary copy the data from there, perform then the calculations, and finally copy the result back. ND4J simply passes pointers around for numerical calculations. Heap (JVM) and off-heap (ND4J through JavaCPP (https://github.com/bytedeco/javacpp)) are two separate memory pools. In DL4J, the memory limits of both are controlled via Java command-line arguments through the following system properties:

- Xms: The memory the JVM heap can use at application start
- Xmx: The maximum memory limit the JVM heap could use
- org.bytedeco.javacpp.maxbytes: The off-heap maximum memory limit
- org.bytedeco.javacpp.maxphysicalbytes: To be set typically with the same value as for the maxbytes property

Chapter 10, *Deploying on a Distributed System*, (which focuses on the deployment of a distributed system to train or run a neural network) will present more details about memory management.

Another good practice to improve performance is to configure Spark locality settings. This is an optional configuration, but can bring benefits on this front. Locality refers to where data is, relative to where it can be processed. At execution time, any time data has to be copied across the network to be processed by a free executor; Spark has to decide between waiting for an executor that has local access to the data to become free or executing the network transfer. The default behavior for Spark is to wait a bit before transferring data across the network to a free executor.

Training neural networks with DL4J is computationally intensive, so the amount of computation per input `DataSet` is relatively high. For this reason, the Spark default behavior isn't an ideal fit for maximizing cluster utilization. During Spark training, DL4J ensures there is exactly one task per executor—so it is always better to immediately transfer data to a free executor, rather than waiting for another one to become free. The computation time will become more important than any network transfer time. The way to tell Spark that it hasn't to wait, but start transferring data immediately is simple—when submitting the configuration we have to set the value of the `spark.locality.wait` property to `0`.

Spark has problems handling Java objects with large off-heap components (this could be the case with `DataSet` and `INDArray` objects in DL4J), in particular in caching or persisting them. From `Chapter 1`, *The Apache Spark Ecosystem*, you know that Spark provides different storage levels. Among those, `MEMORY_ONLY` and `MEMORY_AND_DISK` persistence can cause problems with off-heap memory, because Spark can't properly estimate the size of objects in an RDD, leading to out of memory issues. It is then good practice using `MEMORY_ONLY_SER` or `MEMORY_AND_DISK_SER` when persisting an `RDD<DataSet>` or an `RDD<INDArray>`.

Let's go into detail on this. Spark drops part of an RDD based on the estimated size of that block. It estimates the size of a block depending on the selected persistence level. In the case of `MEMORY_ONLY` or `MEMORY_AND_DISK`, the estimate is done by walking the Java object graph. The problem is that this process doesn't take into account the off-heap memory used by DL4J and ND4J, so Spark underestimates the true size of objects, such as `DataSets` or `INDArrays`.

Furthermore, when deciding whether to keep or drop blocks, Spark also only considers the amount of heap memory used. `DataSet` and `INDArray` objects have a very small on-heap size, then Spark will keep too many of them, causing out of memory issues because off-heap memory becomes exhausted. In cases of `MEMORY_ONLY_SER` or `MEMORY_AND_DISK_SER`, Spark stores blocks on the JVM heap in serialized form. Because there is no off-heap memory for the serialized objects, their size can be estimated accurately by Spark—it drops blocks when required, avoiding out of memory issues.

Spark provides two serialization libraries—Java (default serialization) and Kryo (`https://github.com/EsotericSoftware/kryo`). By default, it serializes objects using Java's `ObjectOutputStream` (`https://docs.oracle.com/javase/8/docs/api/java/io/ObjectOutputStream.html`), and can work with any class that implements the serializable interface (`https://docs.oracle.com/javase/8/docs/api/java/io/Serializable.html`). However, it can also use the Kryo library, which is significantly faster and more compact than the Java serialization.

The cons are that Kryo doesn't support all of the serializable types and it doesn't work well with the off-heap data structures by ND4J. So if you want to use Kryo serialization with ND4J on Spark, it is necessary to set some extra configuration, in order to skip potential `NullPointerExceptions` due to incorrect serialization on some of the `INDArray` fields. To use Kryo you need to add the dependency to your project (the following example is for Maven, but you can import the same dependency with Gradle or sbt using the specific syntax for those build tools), as follows:

```
<dependency>
   <groupId>org.nd4j</groupId>
   <artifactId>nd4j-kryo_2.11</artifactId>
   <version>0.9.1</version>
</dependency>
```

Then configure Spark to use the Nd4J Kryo registrator, as follows:

```
val sparkConf = new SparkConf
 sparkConf.set("spark.serializer",
"org.apache.spark.serializer.KryoSerializer")
 sparkConf.set("spark.kryo.registrator", "org.nd4j.Nd4jRegistrator")
```

Hyperparameter optimization

Before any training can begin, ML techniques in general, and so DL techniques, have a set of parameters that have to be chosen. They are referred to as hyperparameters. Keeping focus on DL, we can say that some of these (the number of layers and their size) define the architecture of a neural network, while others define the learning process (learning rate, regularization, and so on). Hyperparameter optimization is an attempt to automate this process (that has a significant impact on the results achieved by training a neural network) using a dedicated software that applies some search strategies. DL4J provides a tool, Arbiter, for hyperparameter optimization of neural nets. This tool doesn't fully automate the process—a manual intervention from data scientists or developers is needed in order to specify the search spaces (the ranges of valid values for hyperparameters). Please be aware that the current Arbiter implementation doesn't prevent failures on finding good models in those cases where the search spaces haven't been manually defined in a good way. The rest of this section covers the details of how Arbiter can be used programmatically.

The Arbiter dependency needs to be added to the DL4J Scala project for which hyperparameter optimization need to be done, as follows:

```
groupId: org.deeplearning4j
 artifactId: arbiter-deeplearning4j
 version: 0.9.1
```

The sequence of steps to follow to set up and execute a hyperparameter optimization through Arbiter is always the same, as follows:

- Define a hyperparameter search space
- Define a candidate generator for that hyperparameter search space
- Define a data source
- Define a model saver
- Choose a score function
- Choose a termination condition
- Use the previously defined data source, model saver, score function, and termination condition to construct an optimization configuration
- Execute the process using the optimization runner

Let's now see the details on how to programmatically implement these steps. The setup of the hyperparameter configuration space is very similar to the configuration of an MNN in DL4J. It happens through the `MultiLayerSpace` class (https://deeplearning4j.org/api/latest/org/deeplearning4j/arbiter/MultiLayerSpace.html). `ParameterSpace<P>` (https://deeplearning4j.org/api/latest/org/deeplearning4j/arbiter/optimize/api/ParameterSpace.html) is the arbiter class through which it is possible to define acceptable ranges of values for a given hyperparameter. Here are some examples:

```
val learningRateHyperparam = new ContinuousParameterSpace(0.0001, 0.1)
val layerSizeHyperparam = new IntegerParameterSpace(16, 256)
```

The lower and upper bound values specified in the `ParameterSpace` constructors are included in the interval. Interval values are generated uniformly at random between the given boundary. The hyperparameters space can then be built, such as in the following example:

```
val hyperparameterSpace = new MultiLayerSpace.Builder
    .weightInit(WeightInit.XAVIER)
    .l2(0.0001)
    .updater(new SgdSpace(learningRateHyperparam))
    .addLayer(new DenseLayerSpace.Builder
        .nIn(784)
        .activation(Activation.LEAKYRELU)
        .nOut(layerSizeHyperparam)
        .build())
    .addLayer(new OutputLayerSpace.Builder
        .nOut(10)
        .activation(Activation.SOFTMAX)
        .lossFunction(LossFunctions.LossFunction.MCXENT)
        .build)
```

```
.numEpochs(2)
.build
```

In DL4J, two classes, `MultiLayerSpace` and `ComputationGraphSpace` (`https://deeplearning4j.org/api/latest/org/deeplearning4j/arbiter/ComputationGraphSpace.html`), are available for the hyperparameters search space setup (they represent what `MultiLayerConfiguration` and `ComputationGraphConfiguration` are for MNNs configuration.)

The next step is the definition of candidate generator. It could be a random search, such as in the following line of code:

```
val candidateGenerator:CandidateGenerator = new
RandomSearchGenerator(hyperparameterSpace, null)
```

Alternatively, it could be a grid search.

In order to define the data source (the origin of the data to be used to train and test the different candidates), the `DataSource` interface (`https://deeplearning4j.org/api/latest/org/deeplearning4j/arbiter/optimize/api/data/DataSource.html`) is available in Arbiter and needs to be implemented (it requires a no-argument constructor) for a given origin.

At this point we need to define where to save the model that would be generated and tested. Arbiter supports saving models to disk or storing results in-memory. Here is an example of usage of the `FileModelSaver` class (`https://deeplearning4j.org/api/latest/org/deeplearning4j/arbiter/saver/local/FileModelSaver.html`) to save to disk:

```
val baseSaveDirectory = "arbiterOutput/"
val file = new File(baseSaveDirectory)
if (file.exists) file.delete
file.mkdir
val modelSaver: ResultSaver = new FileModelSaver(baseSaveDirectory)
```

We have to choose a score function. Arbiter provides three different choices—`EvaluationScoreFunction` (`https://deeplearning4j.org/api/latest/org/deeplearning4j/arbiter/scoring/impl/EvaluationScoreFunction.html`), `ROCScoreFunction` (`https://deeplearning4j.org/api/latest/org/deeplearning4j/arbiter/scoring/impl/ROCScoreFunction.html`), and `RegressionScoreFunction` (`https://deeplearning4j.org/api/latest/org/deeplearning4j/arbiter/scoring/impl/RegressionScoreFunction.html`).

More details on evaluation, ROC, and regression will be discussed in Chapter 9, *Interpreting Neural Network Output*. Here's an example with EvaluationScoreFunction:

```
val scoreFunction:ScoreFunction = new
EvaluationScoreFunction(Evaluation.Metric.ACCURACY)
```

Finally we specify a list of termination conditions. The current implementation of Arbiter provides only two termination conditions, MaxTimeCondition (https://deeplearning4j.org/api/latest/org/deeplearning4j/arbiter/optimize/api/termination/MaxTimeCondition.html) and MaxCandidatesCondition (https://deeplearning4j.org/api/latest/org/deeplearning4j/arbiter/optimize/api/termination/MaxCandidatesCondition.html). Searching stops when one of the specified termination conditions is satisfied for a hyperparameters space. In the following example, the search stops after 15 minutes or after 20 candidates (depending on the one that happens first):

```
val terminationConditions = Array(new MaxTimeCondition(15,
TimeUnit.MINUTES), new MaxCandidatesCondition(20))
```

Now that all of the options have been set, it is possible to build the OptimizationConfiguration (https://deeplearning4j.org/api/latest/org/deeplearning4j/arbiter/optimize/config/OptimizationConfiguration.html), as follows:

```
val configuration: OptimizationConfiguration = new
OptimizationConfiguration.Builder
    .candidateGenerator(candidateGenerator)
    .dataSource(dataSourceClass,dataSourceProperties)
    .modelSaver(modelSaver)
    .scoreFunction(scoreFunction)
    .terminationConditions(terminationConditions)
    .build
```

Then run it through an IOptimizationRunner (https://deeplearning4j.org/api/latest/org/deeplearning4j/arbiter/optimize/runner/IOptimizationRunner.html), such as in the following example:

```
val runner = new LocalOptimizationRunner(configuration, new
MultiLayerNetworkTaskCreator())
runner.execute
```

At the end of the execution, the application stores the generated candidate in separate directories inside the base save directory preliminary specified for the model saver. Each subdirectory is named with a progressive number.

With reference to this section's examples, it would be `./arbiterOutput/0/` for the first candidate, `./arbiterOutput/1/` for the second, and so on. A JSON representation of the model is also generated (as shown in following screenshot) and it could be stored as well for further re-use:

```
Best score: 0.9499
Index of model with best score: 7
Number of configurations evaluated: 10


Configuration of best model:

{
  "backprop" : true,
  "backpropType" : "Standard",
  "cacheMode" : "NONE",
  "confs" : [ {
    "cacheMode" : "NONE",
    "epochCount" : 2,
    "iterationCount" : 0,
    "layer" : {
      "@class" : "org.deeplearning4j.nn.conf.layers.DenseLayer",
      "activationFn" : {
        "@class" : "org.nd4j.linalg.activations.impl.ActivationLReLU",
        "alpha" : 0.01
      },
      "biasInit" : 0.0,
      "biasUpdater" : null,
      "constraints" : null,
      "dist" : null,
      "gradientNormalization" : "None",
      "gradientNormalizationThreshold" : 1.0,
      "hasBias" : true,
      "idropout" : null,
      "iupdater" : {
        "@class" : "org.nd4j.linalg.learning.config.Sgd",
        "learningRate" : 0.09824433809279995
      },
      "l1" : 0.0,
      "l1Bias" : 0.0,
      "l2" : 1.0E-4,
      "l2Bias" : 0.0,
      "layerName" : "layer0",
      "nin" : 784,
      "nout" : 139,
      "pretrain" : false,
      "weightInit" : "XAVIER",
      "weightNoise" : null
    },
    "maxNumLineSearchIterations" : 5,
    "miniBatch" : true,
    "minimize" : true,
    "optimizationAlgo" : "STOCHASTIC_GRADIENT_DESCENT",
    "pretrain" : false,
    "seed" : 1546984851275,
    "stepFunction" : null,
    "variables" : [ "W", "b" ]
```

Figure 7.1: Candidate JSON serialization in Arbiter

The Arbiter UI

To get the results of a hyperparameter optimization, you have to wait for the process execution to end and finally retrieve them using the Arbiter API, such as in the following example:

```
val indexOfBestResult: Int = runner.bestScoreCandidateIndex
val allResults = runner.getResults

val bestResult = allResults.get(indexOfBestResult).getResult
val bestModel = bestResult.getResult

println("Configuration of the best model:\n")
println(bestModel.getLayerWiseConfigurations.toJson)
```

But, depending on the specific case, this process could be long and take hours before it ends and the results become available. Luckily, Arbiter provides a web UI to monitor it at runtime and get insights of potential issues and hints about tuning the optimization configuration, with no need to wait in vain until it completes. In order to begin using this web UI, a further dependency should be added to the project, as follows:

```
groupId: org.deeplearning4j
  artifactId: arbiter-ui_2.11
  version: 1.0.0-beta3
```

The server that manages the web UI needs to be configured before the `IOptimizationRunner` starts, as follows:

```
val ss: StatsStorage = new FileStatsStorage(new
File("arbiterUiStats.dl4j"))
runner.addListeners(new ArbiterStatusListener(ss))
UIServer.getInstance.attach(ss)
```

In the preceding example we are persisting the Arbiter stats to file. Once the optimization process has started, the web UI can be accessed at the following URL, as follows:

```
http://:9000/arbiter
```

It has a single view, which, at the top, shows a summary of the ongoing optimization process, as seen in the following screenshot:

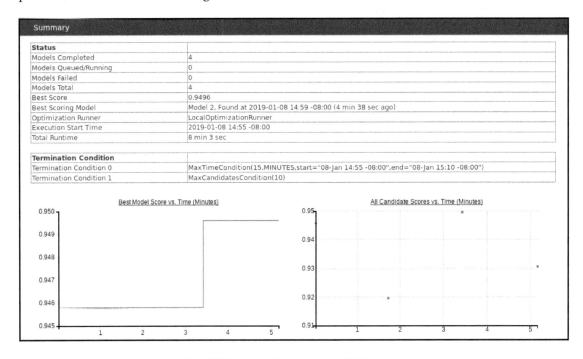

Figure 7.2: Live summary of a hyperparameters optimization process

In its central area, it shows a summary of the optimization settings, as seen in the following screenshot:

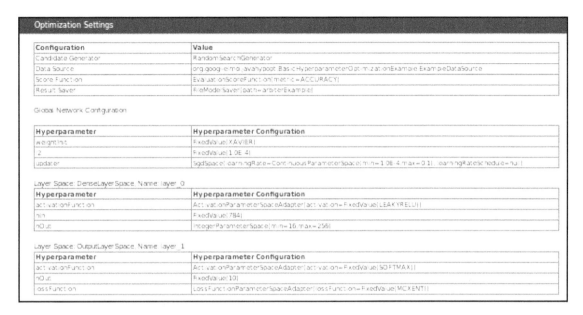

Figure 7.3: Summary of a hyperparameter optimization settings

And, at the bottom, it shows a list of the results, as seen in the following screenshot:

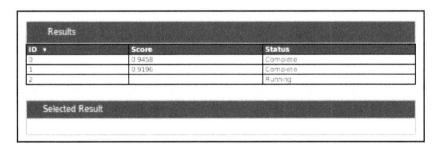

Figure 7.4: Live summary of the results of a hyperparameter optimization process

By clicking on a result id, extra details about that particular candidate, extra charts, and the model configuration are shown in the following screenshot:

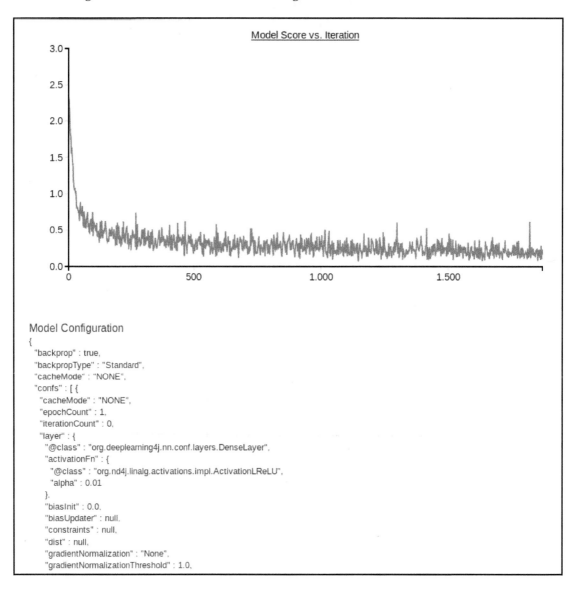

Figure 7.5: Candidate details in the Arbiter web UI

The Arbiter UI uses the same implementation and persistence strategy of the DL4J UI to monitor the training process. These details will be covered in the next chapter.

Summary

In this chapter, you have learned how training happens for CNNs and RNNs with DL4J, ND4J, and Apache Spark. You now also have insights into memory management, a number of tips to improve performance for the training process, and details of how to use Arbiter for hyperparameter optimization.

The next chapter will focus on how to monitor and debug CNNs and RNNs during their training phases.

8
Monitoring and Debugging Neural Network Training

The previous chapter focused on training **Multilayer Neural Networks** (**MNNs**), and presenting code examples for CNNs and RNNs in particular. This chapter describes how monitoring a network can be done while training is in progress and how to use this monitoring information to tune a model. DL4J provides UI facilities for monitoring and tuning purposes, and will be the centerpiece of this chapter. These facilities also work in a training context with DL4J and Apache Spark. Examples for both situations (training using DL4J only and DL4J with Spark) will be presented. A list of potential baseline steps or tips for network training will also be discussed.

Monitoring and debugging neural networks during their training phases

Between `Chapter 5`, *Convolutional Neural Networks*, and `Chapter 7`, *Training Neural Networks with Spark*, a full example was presented regarding a CNN model's configuration and training. This was an example of image classification. The training data that was used came from the `MNIST` database. The training set contained 60,000 examples of handwritten digits, with each image labeled by an integer. Let's use the same example to show the visual facilities that are provided by DL4J for monitoring and debugging a network at training time.

At the end of training, you can programmatically save the generated model as a ZIP archive and throw the `writeModel` method of the `ModelSerializer` class (`https://static. javadoc.io/org.deeplearning4j/deeplearning4j-nn/0.9.1/org/deeplearning4j/util/ ModelSerializer.html`):

```
ModelSerializer.writeModel(net, new File(System.getProperty("user.home") +
"/minist-model.zip"), true)
```

The generated archive contains three files:

- `configuration.json`: The model configuration in JSON format
- `coefficients.bin`: The estimated coefficients
- `updaterState.bin`: The historical states for updaters

It is possible to implement a standalone UI using, for example, the JavaFX (`https://en.wikipedia.org/wiki/JavaFX`) features of the JDK to test the model that is built after training a network. Check out the following screenshot:

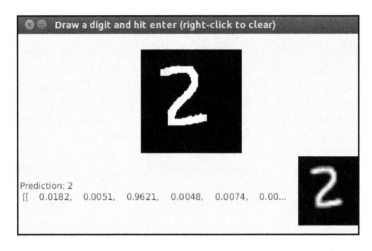

Figure 8.1: The test UI for the handwritten digit classification CNN example

However, this is almost useless for monitoring purposes, where you would like to check in the current network status and the progress of its training in real time. The DL4J training UI, which we will go into the details of in the next two sections of this chapter, fulfills all of your monitoring needs. The implementation details of the test UI, as shown in the preceding screenshot, will be described in the next chapter, which discusses network evaluation – this implementation will make more sense after you've read this.

8.1.1 The DL4J training UI

The DL4J framework provides a web user interface to visualize the current network status and progress of training in real time. It is used to understand how to tune a neural network. In this section, we are going to examine a use case with CNN training where only DL4J is involved. The next section will show the differences between when the training is done through both DL4J and Spark.

The first thing we need to do is add the following dependency to the project:

```
groupId = org.deeplearning4j
 artifactId = deeplearning4j-ui_2.11
 version = 0.9.1
```

Then, we can start adding the necessary code.

Let's initialize the backend for the UI:

```
val uiServer = UIServer.getInstance()
```

Configure the information that is generated for the network during its training:

```
val statsStorage:StatsStorage = new InMemoryStatsStorage()
```

In the preceding example, we have chosen to store the information in memory. It is also possible to store it on disk so that it can be loaded for later use:

```
val statsStorage:StatsStorage = new FileStatsStorage(file)
```

Add a listener (https://deeplearning4j.org/api/latest/org/deeplearning4j/ui/stats/StatsListener.html) so that you can collect information from the network while it is training:

```
val listenerFrequency = 1
net.setListeners(new StatsListener(statsStorage, listenerFrequency))
```

Finally, to allow for visualization, attach the StatsStorage (https://deeplearning4j.org/api/latest/org/deeplearning4j/ui/storage/InMemoryStatsStorage.html) instance to the backend:

```
uiServer.attach(statsStorage)
```

By running the application as soon as the training starts (the fit method is executed), it is possible to access the UI through a web browser at the following URL:

```
http://localhost:<ui_port>/
```

The default listening port is 9000. It is possible to choose a different port through the org.deeplearning4j.ui.port system property, for example:

```
-Dorg.deeplearning4j.ui.port=9999
```

The landing page of the UI is the **Overview** page:

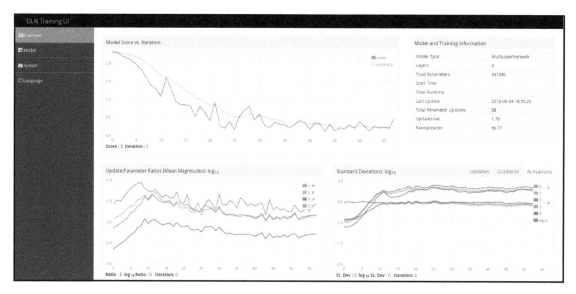

Figure 8.2: The Overview page of the DL4J UI

As we can see in the preceding screenshot, you can see four different sections. On the top left of the page there's the **Score vs. Iteration** chart. It presents the loss function for the current minibatch. On the top right, there's information about the model and its training. On the bottom left, there is a chart presenting the ratio of parameters to update (by layer) for all networks in **Weights vs. Iteration**. The values are displayed as logarithm base 10. On the bottom right, there is a chart presenting the standard deviations of updates, gradients, and activations. For this last chart, the values are displayed as logarithm base 10 too.

Another page of the UI is the **Model** page:

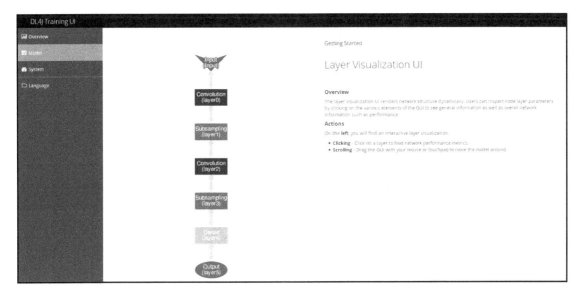

Figure 8.3: The Model page of the DL4J UI

It shows a graphical representation of the neural network. By clicking on a layer in the graph, detailed information about it is given:

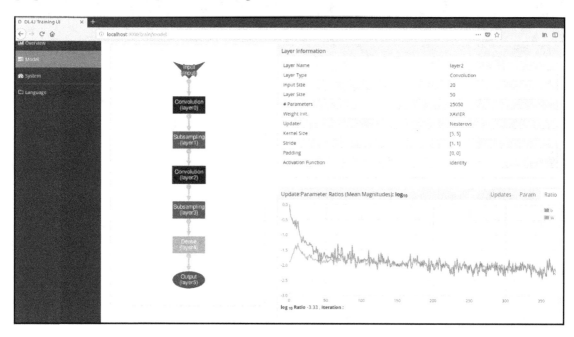

Figure 8.4: Single layer details in the Model page of the DL4J UI

On the right-hand side section of the page, we can find a table containing the details for the selected layer and a chart presenting the update to parameter ratio for this layer (as per the **Overview** page). Scrolling down, we can also find in the same section, other charts presenting the layer activations over time, histograms of parameters, and updates for each parameter type and the learning **Rate vs. Time**.

The third page of the UI is the **System** page:

Figure 8.5: The System page of the DL4J UI

It presents system information (JVM and off-heap memory utilization percentages, hardware, and software details) for each of the machines where the training is happening.

The left menu of the UI presents a fourth item, **Language**, which lists all of the supported language translations for this UI:

Figure 8.6: The list of supported languages for the DL4J UI

8.1.2 The DL4J training UI and Spark

The DL4J UI can also be used when training and including Spark into the tech stack. The main difference with a case where only DL4J is involved is as follows: some conflicting dependencies require that UI and Spark are running on different JVMs. There are two possible alternatives:

1. Collect and save the relevant training stats at runtime, and then visualize them offline later.
2. Execute the DL4J UI and use the remote UI functionality in separate JVMs (servers). The data is then uploaded from the Spark master to the UI server.

Let's take a look at how to implement an alternative to *Step 1*.

Let's reference the CNN example we presented in `Chapter 5`, *Convolutional Neural Networks*, in the *Hands-on CNN with Spark* section, once the Spark network has been created:

```
val sparkNet = new SparkDl4jMultiLayer(sc, conf, tm)
```

We need to create a `FileStatsStorage` object so that we can save the results to a file and set a listener for the Spark network:

```
val ss:StatsStorage = new FileStatsStorage(new
File("NetworkTrainingStats.dl4j"))
  sparkNet.setListeners(ss, Collections.singletonList(new
StatsListener(null)))
```

Later, we can load and display the saved data offline by implementing the following:

```
val statsStorage:StatsStorage = new
FileStatsStorage("NetworkTrainingStats.dl4j")
  val uiServer = UIServer.getInstance()
  uiServer.attach(statsStorage)
```

Now, let's explore an alternative to *Step 2*.

As we mentioned previously, the UI server needs to run on a separate JVM. From there, we need to start the UI server:

```
val uiServer = UIServer.getInstance()
```

Then, we need to enable the remote listener:

```
uiServer.enableRemoteListener()
```

The dependency that we need to set is the same one (DL4J UI) that we used for the example we presented in the *The DL4J training UI* section:

```
groupId = org.deeplearning4j
  artifactId = deeplearning4j-ui_2.11
  version = 0.9.1
```

In the Spark application (we are still referring to the CNN example we presented in Chapter 5, *Convolutional Neural Networks*), after the Spark network has been created, we need to create an instance of `RemoteUIStatsStorageRouter` (`https://static.javadoc.io/org.deeplearning4j/deeplearning4j-core/0.9.1/org/deeplearning4j/api/storage/impl/RemoteUIStatsStorageRouter.html`), which asynchronously posts all updates to the remote UI and finally sets it as a listener for the Spark network:

```
val sparkNet = new SparkDl4jMultiLayer(sc, conf, tm)
 val remoteUIRouter:StatsStorageRouter = new
RemoteUIStatsStorageRouter("http://UI_HOST_IP:UI_HOST_PORT")
 sparkNet.setListeners(remoteUIRouter, Collections.singletonList(new
StatsListener(null)))
```

`UI_HOST_IP` is the IP address of the machine where the UI server is running and `UI_HOST_PORT` is the listening port of the UI server.

To avoid dependency conflicts with Spark, we need to add to the dependency list for this application, and not the full DL4J UI model:

```
groupId = org.deeplearning4j
 artifactId = deeplearning4j-ui-model
 version = 0.9.1
```

Choosing the alternative to *Step 2*, the monitoring of the network happens in real-time during training and not offline after the training execution has completed.

The DL4J UI pages and content are the same as those shown for the scenario of network training without Spark (*The DL4J training UI* section of this chapter).

8.1.3 Using visualization to tune a network

Now, let's look at how we can interpret the visual results presented in the DL4J UI and use them to tune a neural network. Let's start from the **Overview** page. The **Model Score vs. Iteration** chart, which presents the loss function for the current minibatch, should go down over time (as shown in the example in *Figure 8.2*). Regardless of whether the observed score should increase consistently, the learning rate is likely set too high. In this case, it should be reduced until the scores become more stable. Observing increasing scores could also be indicative of other issues, such as incorrect data normalization. On the other hand, if the score is flat or decreases very slowly, this means that the learning rate may be too low or that optimization is difficult. In this second case, training should be tried again using a different updater.

In the example presented in the *The DL4J training UI* section, the Nesterov's momentum updater was used (see *Figure 8.4*) and came up with good results (see *Figure 8.2*). You can change the updater through the `updater` method of the `NeuralNetConfiguration.Builder` class:

```
val conf = new NeuralNetConfiguration.Builder()
  ...
      .updater(Updater.NESTEROVS)
```

Some noise in this line chart should be expected, but if the scores vary quite significantly between runs, this is a problem. The root cause could be one of the issues that we mentioned previously (learning rate, normalization) or data shuffling. Also, setting the minibatch size to a very small number of examples can also contribute in terms of noise for this chart – this might also lead to optimization difficulties.

Other important information that's useful for understanding how to tune a neural network during training comes from combining some details from the **Overview** and **Model** pages. The mean magnitude for parameters (or updates) is the average of their absolute values at a given time step. At training runtime, the ratio of mean magnitudes is provided by the **Overview** page (for the overall network) and the **Model** page (for a given layer). We can use these ratio values when selecting a learning rate. The general rule, which applies to most part of the networks (not all of them, but it is always a good starting point) is that the ratio should be around 0.001 (1:1000), which in the log_{10} chart (like those in the **Overview** and **Model** pages) corresponds to -3. When the ratio diverges significantly from this value, it means that the network parameters may be too unstable or that they may change too slowly to learn useful features. By adjusting the learning rate for the overall network or one or more layers, it is possible to change the ratio of mean magnitudes.

Now, let's explore other useful information from the **Model** page that could help a lot during the tuning process.

The **Layer Activations** chart of the **Model** page (see the following diagram) can be used to detect vanishing or exploding activations. This chart should ideally stabilize over time. A good standard deviation for activations is between 0.5 and 2.0.

Values significantly outside of this range indicate that some problem in terms of lack of data normalization, high learning rate, or poor weight initialization is happening:

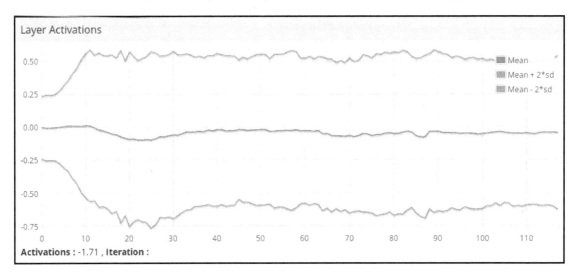

Figure 8.7: The Layer Activations chart of the Model page

The **Layer Parameters Histogram** chart for the weight and biases of the **Model** page (see the following diagram), which is displayed for the most recent iteration only, provides other usual insights:

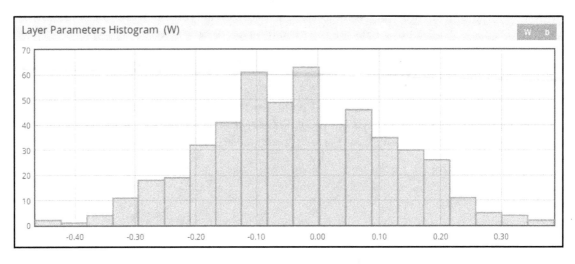

Figure 8.8: The Layer Parameters Histogram chart (weights)

After some time, during the training process, these histograms for weights should assume an approximately Gaussian normal distribution, while for biases, they generally start at **0** and then usually end up being approximately Gaussian. Parameters that are diverging toward +/- infinity may be a good sign of too high a learning rate or insufficient regularization on the network. Biases becoming very large means that the distribution of classes is very imbalanced.

The **Layer Updates Histogram** chart for weight and biases of the **Model** page (see the following diagram), which is displayed for the most recent iteration only for the **Layer Parameters Histogram**, provides other usual information too:

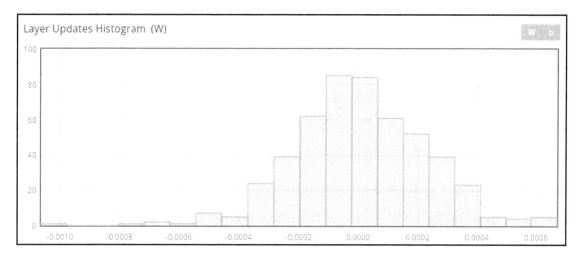

Figure 8.9: The Layer Updates Histogram chart (weights)

This is the same as the parameter graphs – after some time, they should assume an approximately Gaussian normal distribution. Very large values indicate exploding gradients in the network. In those cases, the root cause could be in weight initialization, input or labels data normalization, or the learning rate.

Summary

In this chapter, we have learned about the details of the UI that DL4J provides for the monitoring and tuning purposes of a neural network at training time. We have also learned how to use the UI when training with DL4J and when Apache Spark is part of the game too. Finally, we understood what useful insights we could obtain from the charts that are presented in the DL4J UI pages to spot potential issues and some ways to remedy them.

The next chapter focuses on how to evaluate a neural network so that we can understand the accuracy of a model. Different evaluation techniques will be presented before we dive into practical examples of implementation through the DL4J API and the Spark API.

Interpreting Neural Network Output

9

In the previous chapter, the ability to use the DL4J UI to monitor and debug a **Multilayer Neural Network** (**MNN**) was fully described. The last part of the previous chapter also explained how to interpret and use the real-time visual results in the UI charts to tune training. In this chapter, we will explain how to evaluate the accuracy of a model after its training and before it is moved to production. Several evaluation strategies exist for neural networks. This chapter covers the principal ones and all their implementations, which are provided by the DL4J API.

While describing the different evaluation techniques, I have tried to reduce the usage of math and formulas as much as possible and keep the focus on the Scala implementation with DL4J and Spark.

In this chapter, we will cover the following topics:

- Interpreting the output of a neural network
- Evaluation techniques with DL4J, including the following:
    - Evaluation for classification
    - Evaluation for classification in a Spark context
    - Other types of evaluation that are supported by DL4J

Evaluation techniques with DL4J

At training time and before deploying a MNN, it is important to know the accuracy of the model and understand its performance. In the previous chapter, we learned that at the end of a training phase, the model can be saved in a ZIP archive. From there, it is possible to run it and test it implementing a custom UI, like that shown in *Figure 8.1* (it has been implemented using the JavaFX features; the example code is part of the source code that's bundled with this book). But more significant strategies can be utilized to perform an evaluation. DL4J provides an API that can be used to evaluate the performance of both binary and multi-class classifiers.

This first section and its subsections cover all the details of doing evaluation for classification (DL4J and Spark), while the next section provides an overview of other evaluation strategies that can be done, all of which rely on the DL4J API.

Evaluation for classification

The core DL4J class when implementing evaluations is called **evaluation** (`https://static. javadoc.io/org.deeplearning4j/deeplearning4j-nn/0.9.1/org/deeplearning4j/eval/ Evaluation.html`, part of the DL4J NN module).

The dataset that will be used for the example presented in this subsection is the Iris dataset (it is available for download at `https://archive.ics.uci.edu/ml/datasets/iris`). It is a multivariate dataset that was introduced in 1936 by the British statistician and biologist Ronald Fisher (`https://en.wikipedia.org/wiki/Ronald_Fisher`). It contains 150 records – 50 samples – from three species of Iris flower (Iris setosa, Iris virginica, and Iris versicolor). Four attributes (features) have been measured from each sample – the length and width of the sepals and petals (in centimeters). The structure of this dataset was used for the example that was presented in `Chapter 4`, *Streaming*, in the *Streaming data with DL4J and Spark* section. Here's a sample of the data that's contained in this set:

```
sepal_length,sepal_width,petal_length,petal_width,species
5.1,3.5,1.4,0.2,0
4.9,3.0,1.4,0.2,0
4.7,3.2,1.3,0.2,0
4.6,3.1,1.5,0.2,0
5.0,3.6,1.4,0.2,0
5.4,3.9,1.7,0.4,0
...
```

Typically, for cases of supervised learning like this, a dataset is split into two parts: 70% and 30%. The first part is for the training, while the second is used to calculate the error and modify the network if necessary. This is also the case for this section example – we are going to use 70% of the dataset for the network training and the remaining 30% for evaluation purposes.

The first thing we need to do is get the dataset using a `CSVRecordReader` (the input file is a list of comma-separated records):

```
val numLinesToSkip = 1
 val delimiter = ","
 val recordReader = new CSVRecordReader(numLinesToSkip, delimiter)
 recordReader.initialize(new FileSplit(new
ClassPathResource("iris.csv").getFile))
```

Now, we need to convert the data that's going to be used in the neural network:

```
val labelIndex = 4
 val numClasses = 3
 val batchSize = 150

 val iterator: DataSetIterator = new
RecordReaderDataSetIterator(recordReader, batchSize, labelIndex,
numClasses)
 val allData: DataSet = iterator.next
 allData.shuffle()
```

Each row of the input file contains five values – the four input features, followed by an integer label (class) index. This means that the labels are the fifth value (`labelIndex` is 4). The dataset has three classes representing the types of Iris flowers. They have integer values of either zero (setosa), one (versicolor), or two (virginica).

As we mentioned previously, we split the dataset into two parts – 70% of the data is for training, while the rest is for evaluation:

```
val iterator: DataSetIterator = new
RecordReaderDataSetIterator(recordReader, batchSize, labelIndex,
numClasses)
 val allData: DataSet = iterator.next
 allData.shuffle()
 val testAndTrain: SplitTestAndTrain = allData.splitTestAndTrain(0.70)

 val trainingData: DataSet = testAndTrain.getTrain
 val testData: DataSet = testAndTrain.getTest
```

The split happens through the `SplitTestAndTrain` class (`https://deeplearning4j.org/api/latest/org/nd4j/linalg/dataset/SplitTestAndTrain.html`) of ND4J.

We also need to normalize the input data (for both the training and evaluation sets) using the ND4J `NormalizeStandardize` class (`https://deeplearning4j.org/api/latest/org/nd4j/linalg/dataset/api/preprocessor/NormalizerStandardize.html`) so that we have a zero mean and a standard deviation of one:

```
val normalizer: DataNormalization = new NormalizerStandardize
 normalizer.fit(trainingData)
 normalizer.transform(trainingData)
 normalizer.transform(testData)
```

We can now configure and build the model (a simple feedforward neural network):

```
val conf = new NeuralNetConfiguration.Builder()
   .seed(seed)
   .activation(Activation.TANH)
   .weightInit(WeightInit.XAVIER)
   .l2(1e-4)
   .list
   .layer(0, new DenseLayer.Builder().nIn(numInputs).nOut(3)
     .build)
   .layer(1, new DenseLayer.Builder().nIn(3).nOut(3)
     .build)
   .layer(2, new
OutputLayer.Builder(LossFunctions.LossFunction.NEGATIVELOGLIKELIHOOD)
     .activation(Activation.SOFTMAX)
     .nIn(3).nOut(outputNum).build)
   .backprop(true).pretrain(false)
   .build
```

The following screenshot shows a graphical representation of the network for this example:

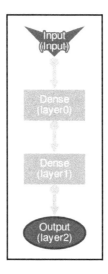

The MNN can be created by starting from the preceding configuration:

```
val model = new MultiLayerNetwork(conf)
 model.init()
 model.setListeners(new ScoreIterationListener(100))
```

The training can be started if we use the portion (70%) of the input dataset that has been reserved for it:

```
for(idx <- 0 to 2000) {
   model.fit(trainingData)
 }
```

At the end of training, the evaluation can be done using the reserved portion (30%) of the input dataset:

```
val eval = new Evaluation(3)
 val output = model.output(testData.getFeatureMatrix)
 eval.eval(testData.getLabels, output)
 println(eval.stats)
```

The value that's passed to the evaluation class constructor is the number of classes to account for in the evaluation – this is 3 here because we have 3 classes of flowers in the dataset. The eval method compares the labels array from the test dataset with the labels that were generated by the model. The result of the evaluation is finally printed to the output:

```
Predictions labeled as 0 classified by model as 0: 18 times
Predictions labeled as 0 classified by model as 1: 1 times
Predictions labeled as 1 classified by model as 1: 4 times
Predictions labeled as 1 classified by model as 2: 13 times
Predictions labeled as 2 classified by model as 0: 1 times
Predictions labeled as 2 classified by model as 2: 16 times


========================Scores========================================
# of classes:    3
Accuracy:        0.7170
Precision:       0.7664
Recall:          0.7079
F1 Score:        0.6689
Precision, recall & F1: macro-averaged (equally weighted avg. of 3 classes)
=====================================================================
```

By default, the stats method of the Evaluation class displays the confusion matrix entries (one entry per line), **Accuracy**, **Precision**, **Recall**, and **F1 Score**, but other information can be displayed. Let's talk about what these stats are.

The **confusion matrix** is a table that is used to describe the performance of a classifier on a test dataset for which the true values are known. Let's consider the following example (for a binary classifier):

Prediction count = 200	Predicted as no	Predicted as yes
Actual: no	55	5
Actual: yes	10	130

These are the insights we can get from the preceding matrix:

- There are two possible predicted classes, yes and no
- The classifier made 200 predictions in total
- Out of those 200 cases, the classifier predicted yes 135 times and no 65 times
- In reality, 140 cases in the sample are yes and 60 are no

When this is translated into proper terms, the insights are as follows:

- **True positives** (**TP**): These are cases in which yes has been predicted and it is really a yes
- **True negatives** (**TN**): No has been predicted and it is really a no
- **False positives** (**FP**): Yes has been predicted, but really it is a no
- **False negatives** (**FN**): No has been predicted, but really it is a yes

Let's consider the following example:

	Predicted as no	Predicted as yes
Actual: no	TN	FP
Actual: yes	FN	TP

This is done in terms of numbers. A list of rates can be calculated from a confusion matrix. With reference to the code example in this section, they are as follows:

- **Accuracy**: Represents how often a classifier is correct: *(TP+TN)/total*.
- **Precision**: Represents how often a classifier is correct when it predicts a positive observation.
- **Recall**: The average recall for all classes (labels) in the evaluation dataset: *TP/TP+FN*.
- **F1 Score**: This is the weighted average of precision and recall. It takes into account both false positives and false negatives: *2 * TP / (2TP + FP + FN)*.

The `Evaluation` class can also display other information such as the G-measure or the Matthews Correlation Coefficient, and much more. The confusion matrix can be also displayed in its full form:

```
println(eval.confusionToString)
```

The preceding command returns the following output:

```
    Predicted:      0    1    2
    Actual:
0   0            |  21   1    0
1   1            |   0   3   13
2   2            |   0   1   14
```

The confusion matrix can be also accessed directly and converted into CSV format:

```
eval.getConfusionMatrix.toCSV
```

The preceding command returns the following output:

```
,,Predicted Class,
,,0,1,2,Total
Actual Class,0,13,0,0,13
,1,1,2,14,17
,2,1,1,21,23
,Total,15,3,35,
```

It can also be converted into HTML:

```
eval.getConfusionMatrix.toHTML
```

The preceding command returns the following output:

```
<table>
<tr><th class="empty-space" colspan="2" rowspan="2"><th class="predicted-class-header" colspan="4">Predicted Class</th></tr>
<tr><th class="predicted-class-header">0</th><th class="predicted-class-header">1</th><th class="predicted-class-header">2</t
<tr><th class="actual-class-header" rowspan="4">Actual Class</th><th class="actual-class-header" >0</th><td class="count-eler
<tr><th class="actual-class-header" >1</th><td class="count-element">1</td><td class="count-element">0</td><td class="count-e
<tr><th class="actual-class-header" >2</th><td class="count-element">0</td><td class="count-element">0</td><td class="count-e
<tr><th class="actual-class-header">Total</th><td class="count-element">19</td><td class="count-element">0</td><td class="cou
</tr>
</table>
```

Evaluation for classification – Spark example

Let's examine another example of evaluation for classification, but in a context where Spark is involved too (distributed evaluation). We are going to complete the example that was presented in Chapter 5, *Convolutional Neural Networks*, in the *Hands-on CNN with Spark* section, Chapter 7, *Training Neural Networks with Spark*, in the *CNN distributed training with Spark and DL4J* section, and Chapter 8, *Monitoring and Debugging Neural Network Training*, in the *The DL4J Training UI and Spark* section. Remember that this is an example of handwritten digits image classification that's trained on the MNIST dataset.

In these chapters, we used only a portion of the MNIST dataset for training purposes, but the downloaded archive also includes a separate directory named testing, which contains the portion of the dataset that's reserved for evaluation purposes. The evaluation dataset also needs to be vectorized, just like the training dataset:

```
val testData = new ClassPathResource("/mnist_png/testing").getFile
 val testSplit = new FileSplit(testData, NativeImageLoader.ALLOWED_FORMATS,
randNumGen)
 val testRR = new ImageRecordReader(height, width, channels, labelMaker)
 testRR.initialize(testSplit)
 val testIter = new RecordReaderDataSetIterator(testRR, batchSize, 1,
```

```
outputNum)
  testIter.setPreProcessor(scaler)
```

We need to do this before we load it into memory at evaluation time and parallelize it:

```
val testDataList = mutable.ArrayBuffer.empty[DataSet]
  while (testIter.hasNext) {
      testDataList += testIter.next
  }

  val paralleltesnData = sc.parallelize(testDataList)
```

Then, the evaluation can be done through the `Evaluation` class, which is what we did for the example in the previous section:

```
val sparkNet = new SparkDl4jMultiLayer(sc, conf, tm)
  var numEpochs: Int = 15
  var i: Int = 0
  for (i <- 0 until numEpochs) {
      sparkNet.fit(paralleltrainData)
      val eval = sparkNet.evaluate(parallelTestData)
      println(eval.stats)
      println("Completed Epoch {}", i)
      trainIter.reset
      testIter.reset
  }
```

The produced output of the `stas` method of the `Evaluation` class is the same as for any other network implementation that's trained and evaluated through DL4J. For example:

```
Predictions labeled as 0 classified by model as 0: 980 times
Predictions labeled as 1 classified by model as 0: 1135 times
Predictions labeled as 2 classified by model as 0: 1032 times
Predictions labeled as 3 classified by model as 0: 1010 times
Predictions labeled as 4 classified by model as 0: 982 times
Predictions labeled as 5 classified by model as 0: 892 times
Predictions labeled as 6 classified by model as 0: 958 times
Predictions labeled as 7 classified by model as 0: 1028 times
Predictions labeled as 8 classified by model as 0: 974 times
Predictions labeled as 9 classified by model as 0: 1009 times

Warning: 9 classes were never predicted by the model and were excluded from average precision
Classes excluded from average precision: [1, 2, 3, 4, 5, 6, 7, 8, 9]

=========================Scores=====================================
 # of classes:    10
 Accuracy:        0.0980
 Precision:       0.0980        (9 classes excluded from average)
 Recall:          0.1000
 F1 Score:        0.1785        (9 classes excluded from average)
Precision, recall & F1: macro-averaged (equally weighted avg. of 10 classes)
====================================================================
```

It is also possible to perform multiple evaluations in the same pass using the `doEvaluation` method of the `SparkDl4jMultiLayer` class. This method expects three input parameters: the data to evaluate on (in the form of a `JavaRDD<org.nd4j.linalg.dataset.DataSet>`), an empty `Evaluation` instance, and a integer that represents the evaluation batch size. It returns the populated `Evaluation` object.

Other types of evaluation

Other evaluations are available through the DL4J API. This section lists them.

It is possible to evaluate a network performing regression through the `RegressionEvaluation` class (`https://static.javadoc.io/org.deeplearning4j/deeplearning4j-nn/1.0.0-alpha/org/deeplearning4j/eval/RegressionEvaluation.html`, DL4J NN). With reference to the example that we used in the *Evaluation for classification* section, evaluation for regression can be done the following way:

```
val eval = new RegressionEvaluation(3)
 val output = model.output(testData.getFeatureMatrix)
 eval.eval(testData.getLabels, output)
 println(eval.stats)
```

The produced output of the `stats` method includes the **MSE**, the **MAE**, the **RMSE**, the **RSE**, and the **R^2**:

```
Column   MSE          MAE          RMSE         RSE          PC           R^2
col_0    8.06825e-02  2.59285e-01  2.84047e-01  3.59742e-01  9.76614e-01  6.40258e-01
col_1    2.08553e-01  4.21093e-01  4.56676e-01  9.57232e-01  4.64832e-01  4.27680e-02
col_2    1.63564e-01  3.60942e-01  4.04430e-01  7.29286e-01  5.43598e-01  2.70714e-01
```

ROC (short for **Receiver Operating Characteristic**, `https://en.wikipedia.org/wiki/Receiver_operating_characteristic`) is another commonly used metric for the evaluation of classifiers. DL4J provides three different implementations for ROC:

- ROC: `https://deeplearning4j.org/api/1.0.0-beta2/org/deeplearning4j/eval/ROC.html`, the implementation for binary classifiers
- ROCBinary: `https://deeplearning4j.org/api/1.0.0-beta2/org/deeplearning4j/eval/ROCBinary.html`, for multi-task binary classifiers
- ROCMultiClass: `https://deeplearning4j.org/api/1.0.0-beta2/org/deeplearning4j/eval/ROCMultiClass.html`, for multi-class classifiers

All of the three preceding classes have the ability to calculate the area under **ROC curve** (**AUROC**), through the `calculateAUC` method, and the area under **Precision-Recall curve** (**AUPRC**), through the `calculateAUPRC` method. These three ROC implementations support two modes of calculation:

- **Thresholded**: It uses less memory and approximates the calculation of the AUROC and AUPRC. This is suitable for very large datasets.
- **Exact**: This is the default. It is accurate, but requires more memory. This is not suitable for very large datasets.

It is possible to export the AUROC and AUPRC in HTML format so that they can be viewed using a web browser. The `exportRocChartsToHtmlFile` method of the `EvaluationTools` class (`https://deeplearning4j.org/api/1.0.0-beta2/org/deeplearning4j/evaluation/EvaluationTools.html`) has to be used to do this export. It expects the ROC implementation to export and a File object (the destination HTML file) as parameters. It saves both curves in a single HTML file.

To evaluate networks with binary classification outputs, the `EvaluationBinary` class (`https://deeplearning4j.org/api/1.0.0-beta2/org/deeplearning4j/eval/EvaluationBinary.html`) is used. The typical classification metrics (**Accuracy**, **Precision**, **Recall**, **F1 Score**, and so on) are calculated for each output. The following is the syntax for this class:

```
val size:Int = 1
  val eval: EvaluationBinary = new EvaluationBinary(size)
```

What about time series evaluation (in the case of RNNs)? It is quite similar to the evaluation approaches for classification that we have described so far in this chapter. For time series in DL4J, the evaluation is performed on all the non-masked time steps in a separate way. But what is masking for RNNs? RNNs require that inputs have a fixed length. Masking is a technique that's used to handle this because it marks missing time steps. The only difference between the other evaluation cases that were presented previously is the optional presence of mask arrays. This means that, in many time series cases, you can just use the `evaluate` or `evaluateRegression` methods of the `MultiLayerNetwork` class – regardless of whether mask arrays should be present, they can be properly handled by those two methods.

DL4J also provides a way to analyze the calibration of a classifier – the `EvaluationCalibration` class (`https://deeplearning4j.org/api/1.0.0-beta2/org/deeplearning4j/eval/EvaluationCalibration.html`). It provides a number of tools for this, such as the following:

- The counts of the number of labels and predictions for each class
- The reliability diagram (`http://www.bom.gov.au/wmo/lrfvs/reliability.shtml`)
- The residual plot (`http://www.statisticshowto.com/residual-plot/`)
- Histograms of probabilities for each class

The evaluation of a classifier using this class is performed in a similar manner to the other evaluation classes. It is possible to export its plots and histograms in HTML format through the `exportevaluationCalibrationToHtmlFile` method of the `EvaluationTools` class. This method expects an `EvaluationCalibration` instance and a file object (the destination HTML file) as arguments.

Summary

In this chapter, we have learned how to programmatically evaluate a model's efficiency using the different facilities that are provided by the DL4J API. We have now closed the full circle in terms of the implementation, training, and evaluation of MNN using DL4J and Apache Spark.

The next chapter will give us some insight into the deployment of a distribution environment and importing and executing pre-trained Python models, as well as a comparison of DL4J with some alternative DL frameworks for the Scala programming language.

10
Deploying on a Distributed System

The upcoming chapters of this book will show what we have learned so far in order to implement some practical and real-world use cases of CNNs and RNNs. But before doing that, let's consider DL4J in a production environment. This chapter is divided into four main sections:

- Some considerations about the setup for a DL4J environment in production, with focus in particular on memory management, CPU, and GPU setup, and job submission for training
- Distributed training architecture details (data parallelism and strategies implemented in DL4J)
- The practical way to import, train, and execute Python (Keras and TensorFlow) models in a DL4J (JVM)-based production environment
- A comparison between DL4J and a couple of alternative DL frameworks for the Scala programming language (with particular focus on their readiness for production)

Setup of a distributed environment with DeepLearning4j

This section explains some tricks to do when setting up a production environment for DL4J neural network model training and execution.

Memory management

In Chapter 7, *Training Neural Networks with Spark*, in the *Performance considerations* section, we learned how DL4J handles memory when training or running a model. Because it relies on ND4J, it also utilizes off-heap memory and not only heap memory. Being off-heap, it means that it is outside the scope managed by the JVM's **Garbage Collection** (**GC**) mechanism (the memory is allocated outside the JVM). At the JVM level, there are only pointers to off-heap memory locations; they can be passed to the C++ code via the Java Native Interface (JNI, https://docs.oracle.com/javase/8/docs/technotes/guides/jni/spec/jniTOC.html) for use in ND4J operations.

In DL4J, it is possible to manage memory allocations using two different approaches:

- JVM GC and weak reference tracking
- Memory workspaces

In this section, both approaches are going to be covered. The idea behind both is the same: once an INDArray is no longer required, the off-heap memory associated with it should be released so that it can be reused. The difference between the two approaches is as follows:

- **JVM GC**: When an INDArray is collected by the garbage collector, its off-heap memory is deallocated, with the assumption that it is not used elsewhere
- **Memory workspaces**: When an INDArray leaves the workspace scope, its off-heap memory may be reused, without deallocation and reallocation

Please refer to Chapter 7, *Training Neural Networks with Spark*, in the *Performance considerations* section, for details on how to configure the limits for the heap and off-heap memory.

The memory workspaces approach needs more explanation. Compared to the JVM GC approach, it gives the best results in terms of performance in cyclic workloads. Within a workspace, any operation is possible with INDArrays. Then at the end of the workspace loop, all INDArrays content in memory is invalidated. Whether an INDArray should be needed outside a workspace (which could be the case when moving results out of it), it is possible to use the detach method of the INDArray itself to create an independent copy of it.

Workspaces are enabled by default in DL4J releases from 1.0.0-alpha or later. In order to use them, they need to be activated for DL4J release 0.9.1 or older. In DL4J 0.9.1, at network configuration time, workspaces can be activated this way (for training):

```
val conf = new NeuralNetConfiguration.Builder()
    .trainingWorkspaceMode(WorkspaceMode.SEPARATE)
```

Or for inference, they can be activated as follows:

```
val conf = new NeuralNetConfiguration.Builder()
    .inferenceWorkspaceMode(WorkspaceMode.SINGLE)
```

A SEPARATE workspace is slower, but it uses less memory, while a SINGLE workspace is faster, but requires more memory. The choice between SEPARATE and SINGLE depends on the compromise you choose between memory footprint and performance. When workspaces are enabled, all the memory used during training is made reusable and tracked without interference by the JVM GC. Only the output method, which uses workspaces internally for the feed-forward loop, is an exception, but then it detaches the resulting INDArray from the workspaces, so it can then be handled by the JVM GC. Starting from release 1.0.0-beta, the SEPARATE and SINGLE modes have been deprecated. The available modes are ENABLED (default) and NONE.

Please remember that, when a training process uses workspaces, in order to get the most from this approach, periodic GC calls need to be disabled, as follows:

```
Nd4j.getMemoryManager.togglePeriodicGc(false)
```

Or their frequency needs to be reduced, as follows:

```
val gcInterval = 10000 // In milliseconds
Nd4j.getMemoryManager.setAutoGcWindow(gcInterval)
```

This setting should be done before invoking the fit method for the model in training. The workspace modes are available also for ParallelWrapper (in the case of training demanded to DL4J only, running multiple models on the same server).

In some cases, to save memory, it would be necessary to release all the workspaces created during training or evaluation. This can be done by invoking the following method of WorkspaceManager:

```
Nd4j.getWorkspaceManager.destroyAllWorkspacesForCurrentThread
```

It destroys all workspaces that have been created within the calling thread. Workspaces created in some external threads that are no longer needed can be destroyed using the same method in that thread.

In DL4J release 1.0.0-alpha and later, when using the `nd4j-native` backend, it is also possible to use a memory-mapped file instead of RAM. While it is slower, it allows memory allocation in a manner that is impossible to achieve using RAM. This option is mostly workable in those cases where `INDArrays` can't fit into RAM. Here's how this could be done programmatically:

```
val mmap = WorkspaceConfiguration.builder
    .initialSize(1000000000)
    .policyLocation(LocationPolicy.MMAP)
    .build
try (val ws = Nd4j.getWorkspaceManager.getAndActivateWorkspace(mmap, "M2"))
{
    val ndArray = Nd4j.create(20000) //INDArray
}
```

In this example, a temporary file of 2 GB is created, a workspace is mapped there, and the `ndArray INDArray` is created in that workspace.

CPU and GPU setup

As mentioned before in this book, any application implemented through DL4J can be executed on CPUs or GPUs. To switch from CPUs to GPUs, a change in the application dependencies for ND4J is needed. Here's an example for CUDA release 9.2 (or later) and NVIDIA-compatible hardware (the example is for Maven, but the same dependency could be set for Gradle or sbt), as follows:

```
<dependency>
  <groupId>org.nd4j</groupId>
  <artifactId>nd4j-cuda-9.2</artifactId>
  <version>0.9.1</version>
</dependency>
```

This dependency replaces that for `nd4j-native`.

When you have multiple GPUs in your system, whether it should restrict their usage and force to execute on a single one, it is possible to change this programmatically through the `CudaEnvironment` helper class (https://deeplearning4j.org/api/latest/org/nd4j/jita/conf/CudaEnvironment.html) of the `nd4j-cuda` library. The following line of code needs to be executed as the first instruction in a DL4J application entry point:

```
CudaEnvironment.getInstance.getConfiguration.allowMultiGPU(true)
```

In section 10.1.1, we have learned how to configure heap and off-heap memory in DL4J. Some considerations need to be made when executing on GPUs. It should be clear that the settings for the command-line arguments `org.bytedeco.javacpp.maxbytes` and `org.bytedeco.javacpp.maxphysicalbytes` define the memory limits for the GPU(s), because for `INDArrays`, the off-heap memory is mapped to the GPU (`nd4j-cuda` is used).

Also, when running on GPUs, most probably less RAM would be used in the JVM heap, while more would be used in the off-heap, as this is where all of the `INDArrays` are stored. Allocating too much to the JVM heap would leave a real risk of having not enough memory left off-heap. Anyway, while doing proper settings, in some situations, execution could lead to the following exception:

```
RuntimeException: Can't allocate [HOST] memory: [memory]; threadId:
[thread_id];
```

This means that we have run out of off-heap memory. In situations like this (in particular for training), we need to consider `WorkspaceConfiguration` to handle the `INDArrays` memory allocation (as learned in the *Memory management* section). If not, the `INDArrays` and their off-heap resources would be reclaimed through the JVM GC approach, which might severely increase latency and generate other potential out of memory issues.

The command-line arguments to set the memory limits are optional. Not specifying anything means that by default 25% of the total system RAM is set as the limit for the heap memory, while by default twice the RAM reserved for the heap memory would be set for the off-heap memory. It is up to us to find the perfect balance, particularly in cases of execution on GPUs, considering the expected amount of off-heap memory for the `INDArrays`.

Typically, CPU RAM is greater than GPU RAM. For this reason, how much RAM is being used off-heap needs to be monitored. DL4J allocates memory on the GPU equivalent to the amount of off-heap memory specified through the previously mentioned command-line arguments. In order to make the communication between CPU and GPU more efficient, DL4J allocates off-heap memory on the CPU RAM too. This way, a CPU can access data from an `INDArray` with no need to fetch data from a GPU any time there is a call for it.

However there is one caveat: if a GPU has less than 2 GB of RAM, it's probably not suitable for DL production workloads. In that case, a CPU should be used. Typically, DL workloads require a minimum of 4 GB of RAM (8 GB of RAM is recommended on a GPU).

Here is a final consideration: with a CUDA backend and using workspaces, it is also possible to use HOST_ONLY memory. Programmatically, this could be set up as in the following example:

```
val basicConfig = WorkspaceConfiguration.builder
    .policyAllocation(AllocationPolicy.STRICT)
    .policyLearning(LearningPolicy.FIRST_LOOP)
    .policyMirroring(MirroringPolicy.HOST_ONLY)
    .policySpill(SpillPolicy.EXTERNAL)
    .build
```

This reduces performance, but it can be useful as in-memory cache pairs when using the unsafeDuplication method of INDArray, which performs efficient (but unsafe) INDArray duplication.

Building a job to be submitted to Spark for training

At this stage, I am assuming you have already started browsing and trying the code examples in the GitHub repository (https://github.com/PacktPublishing/Hands-On-Deep-Learning-with-Apache-Spark) associated with this book. If so, you should have noticed that all of the Scala examples use Apache Maven (https://maven.apache.org/) for packaging and dependency management. In this section, I am going to refer to this tool in order to build a DL4J job that will then be submitted to Spark to train a model.

Once you are confident that the job that you have developed is ready for training in the destination Spark cluster, the first thing to do is to build the uber-JAR file (also called the fat JAR file), which contains the Scala DL4J Spark program classes and dependencies. Check that all of the required DL4J dependencies for the given project are present in the <dependencies> block of the project POM file. Check that the correct version of the dl4j-Spark library has been selected; all of the examples in this book are meant to be used with Scala 2.11.x and Apache Spark 2.2.x. The code should look as follows:

```
<dependency>
    <groupId>org.deeplearning4j</groupId>
    <artifactId>dl4j-spark_2.11</artifactId>
    <version>0.9.1_spark_2</version>
</dependency>
```

If your project POM file, as well as the other dependencies, contains references to Scala and/or any of the Spark libraries, please declare their scope as `provided`, as they are already available across the cluster nodes. This way, the uber-JAR would be lighter.

Once you have checked for the proper dependencies, you need to instruct the POM file on how to build the uber-JAR. There are three techniques to build an uber-JAR: unshaded, shaded, and JAR of JARs. The best approach for this case would be a shaded uber-JAR. Along with the unshaded approach, it works with the Java default class loader (so there is no need to bundle an extra special class loader), but brings the advantage of skipping some dependency version conflicts and the possibility, when there are files present in multiple JARs with the same path, to apply an appending transformation to them. Shading can be achieved in Maven through the Shade plugin (`http://maven.apache.org/plugins/maven-shade-plugin/`). The plugin needs to be registered in the `<plugins>` section of the POM file as follows:

```
<plugin>
    <groupId>org.apache.maven.plugins</groupId>
    <artifactId>maven-shade-plugin</artifactId>
    <version>3.2.1</version>
    <configuration>
      <!-- put your configurations here -->
    </configuration>
    <executions>
      <execution>
        <phase>package</phase>
        <goals>
          <goal>shade</goal>
        </goals>
      </execution>
    </executions>
</plugin>
```

This plugin executes when the following command is issued:

```
mvn package -DskipTests
```

At the end of the packaging process, the latest versions of this plugin replace the slim JAR with the uber-JAR, renaming it with the original filename. For a project with the following coordinates, the name of the uber-JAR would be `rnnspark-1.0.jar`:

```
<groupId>org.googlielmo</groupId>
<artifactId>rnnspark</artifactId>
<version>1.0</version>
```

The slim JAR is preserved anyway, but it is renamed as `original-rnnspark-1.0.jar`. They both can be found inside the `target` sub-directory of the project root directory.

The JAR can then be submitted to the Spark cluster for training using the `spark-submit` script, the same way as for any other Spark job, as follows:

```
$SPARK_HOME/bin/spark-submit --class <package>.<class_name> --master
<spark_master_url> <uber_jar>.jar
```

Spark distributed training architecture details

The *Distributed network training with Spark and DeepLearning4J* section in Chapter 7, *Training Neural Networks with Spark*, explains why it is important to train MNNs in a distributed way across a cluster, and states that DL4J uses a parameter averaging approach to parallel training. This section goes through the architecture details of the distributed training approaches (parameter averaging and gradient sharing, which replaced the parameter averaging approach in DL4J starting from release 1.0.0-beta of the framework). The way DL4J approaches distributed training is transparent to developers, but it is good to have knowledge of it anyway.

Model parallelism and data parallelism

Parallelizing/distributing training computation can happen as **model parallelism** or **data parallelism**.

In model parallelism (see following diagram), different nodes of the cluster are responsible for the computation in different parts of a single MNN (an approach could be that each layer in the network is assigned to a different node):

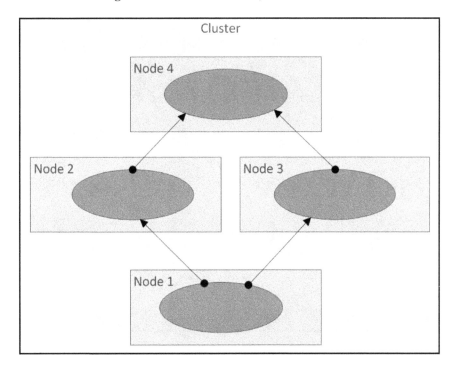

Figure 10.1: Model parallelism

In data parallelism (see the following diagram), different cluster nodes have a complete copy of the network model, but they get a different subset of the training data. The results from each node are then combined, as demonstrated in the following diagram:

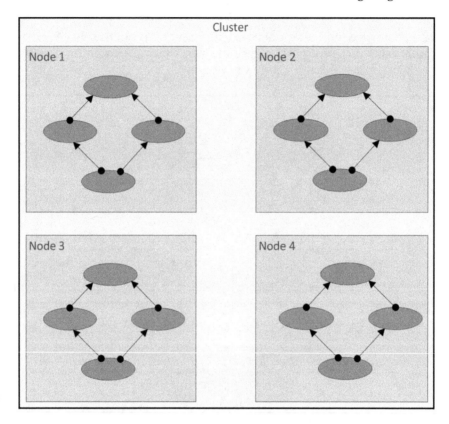

Figure 10.2: Data parallelism

These two approaches can also be combined; they aren't mutually exclusive. Model parallelism works well in practice, but data parallelism has to be preferred for distributed training; matters like implementation, fault tolerance, and optimized cluster resource utilization (just to mention a few) are definitely easier for data parallelism than for model parallelism.

The data parallelism approach requires some way of combining the results and synchronizing the model parameters across workers. In the next two subsections, we are going to explore just the two (parameter averaging and gradient sharing) that have been implemented in DL4J.

Parameter averaging

Parameter averaging happens as follows:

1. The master first initializes the neural network parameters based on the model configuration
2. Then, it distributes a copy of the current parameters to each worker
3. The training starts on each worker using its own subset of data
4. The master sets the global parameters to the average parameters for each worker
5. In those cases where there is more data to process, the flow repeats from *Step 2*

The following diagram shows a representation from *Step 2* to *Step 4*:

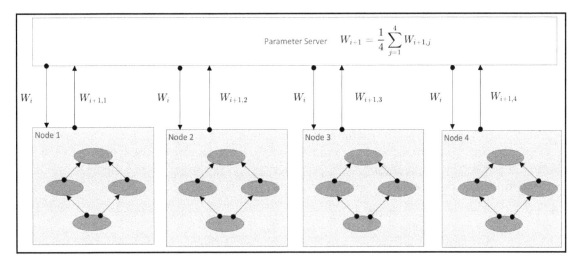

Figure 10.3: Parameter averaging

In this diagram, **W** represents the parameters (weights and biases) in the network. In DL4J, this implementation uses Spark's TreeAggregate (`https://umbertogriffo.gitbooks.io/apache-spark-best-practices-and-tuning/content/treereduce_and_treeaggregate_demystified.html`).

Parameter averaging is a simple approach, but it comes with some challenges. The most intuitive idea for doing averaging is to simply average the parameters after each iteration. While this approach can work, the added overhead could be extremely high and the network communication and synchronization costs may nullify any benefit from scaling the cluster by adding extra nodes. For this reason, parameter averaging is typically implemented with an averaging period (number of minibatches per worker) greater than one. If the averaging period is too infrequent, the local parameters in each worker may significantly diverge, resulting in a poor model. Good averaging periods are of the order of once in every 10 to 20 minibatches per worker. Another challenge is related to the optimization methods (the updaters of DL4J). It has been demonstrated that these methods (`http://ruder.io/optimizing-gradient-descent/`) improve the convergence properties during neural network training. But they have an internal state that could probably be averaged as well. This results in a faster convergence in each worker, but at the cost of doubling the size of the network transfers.

Asynchronous stochastic gradient sharing

Asynchronous stochastic gradient sharing is the approach that has been chosen in the latest release of DL4J (and future ones as well). The main difference between asynchronous stochastic gradient sharing and parameter averaging is that in asynchronous stochastic gradient sharing, updates instead of parameters are transferred from the workers to the parameter server. From an architectural perspective, this is similar to parameter averaging (see the following diagram):

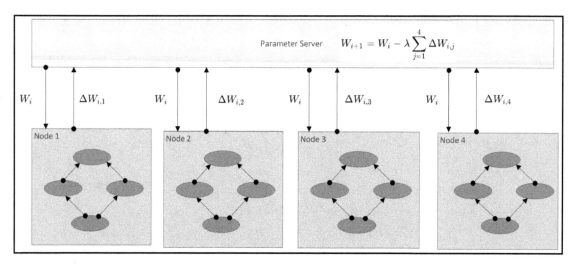

Figure 10.4: Asynchronous stochastic gradient sharing architecture

What is different is the formula through which the parameters are calculated:

$$W_{i+1} = W_i - \lambda \sum_{j=1}^{N} \Delta W_{i,j}$$

Here, λ is the scaling factor. The asynchronous stochastic gradient sharing algorithm is obtained by allowing the updates $\Delta W_{i,j}$ to be applied to the parameter vectors as soon as they are computed.

One of the main benefits of asynchronous stochastic gradient sharing is that it is possible to obtain higher throughput in a distributed system, rather than waiting for the parameter averaging step to be completed, so the workers can spend more time performing useful computations. Another benefit is the following: the workers can potentially incorporate parameter updates from other workers sooner, when compared to the case of using synchronous updating.

One downside of asynchronous stochastic gradient sharing is the so-called stale gradient problem. The calculation of gradients (updates) requires time, and by the time a worker has finished his calculations and applied the results to the global parameter vector, the parameters may have been updated more than once (a problem you can't see in the parameter averaging, as this has a synchronous nature). Several approaches have been proposed in order to mitigate the stale gradient problem. Among these, one is by scaling the value λ separately for each update, based on the staleness of the gradients. Another way is called soft synchronization: rather than updating the global parameter vector immediately, the parameter server waits to collect a given number of updates from any of the learners. Then, the formula through which the parameters are updated becomes this:

$$W_{i+1} = W_i - \frac{1}{s} \sum_{j=1}^{s} \lambda(\Delta W_j) \Delta W_j$$

Here, s is the number of updates that the parameter server waits to collect and $\lambda(\Delta W_j)$ is a Scalar staleness-dependent scaling factor.

In DL4J, while the parameter averaging implementation has always been fault tolerant, the gradient sharing implementation has been made fully fault tolerant starting from release 1.0.0-beta3.

Importing Python models into the JVM with DL4J

In the previous chapter, we have learned how powerful and, at the same time, how easy the DL4J APIs are when it comes to configuring, building, and training multilayer neural network models. The possibilities to implement new models are almost innumerable relying on this framework only in Scala or Java.

But, let's have a look at the following search results from Google; they concern TensorFlow neural network models that are available on the web:

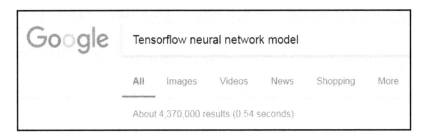

Figure 10.5: The result of a Google search about TensorFlow neural network models

You can see that it is quite an impressive number in terms of results. And this is just a raw search. Refining the search to more specific model implementations means that the numbers are pretty high. But what's TensorFlow? TensorFlow (https://www.tensorflow.org/) is a powerful and comprehensive open source framework for ML and DL, developed by the Google Brain team. At present, it is the most popularly used framework by data scientists. So it has a big community, and lots of shared models and examples are available for it. This explains the big numbers. Among those models, the chances of finding a pre-trained model that fits your specific use case needs are high. So, where's the problem? TensorFlow is mostly Python.

It provides support for other programming languages, such as Java for the JVM, but its Java API is currently experimental and isn't covered by the TensorFlow API stability guarantees. Furthermore, the TensorFlow Python API presents a steep learning curve for non-Python developers and software engineers with no or a basic data science background. How then can they benefit from this framework? How can we reuse an existing valid model in a JVM-based environment? Keras (`https://keras.io/`) comes to the rescue. It is an open source, high-level neural network library written in Python that can be used to replace the TensorFlow high-level API (the following diagram shows the TensorFlow framework architecture):

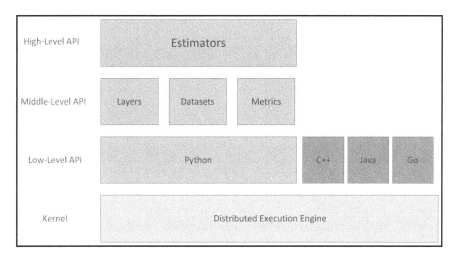

Figure 10.6: The TensorFlow architecture

Compared to TensorFlow, Keras is lightweight and allows easier prototyping. It can run not only on top of TensorFlow, but also on other backend Python engines. And last but not least, it can be used to import Python models into DL4J. The Keras Model Import DL4J library provides facilities for importing neural network models configured and trained through the Keras framework.

The following diagram shows that once a model has been imported into DL4J, the full production stack is at disposal for using it:

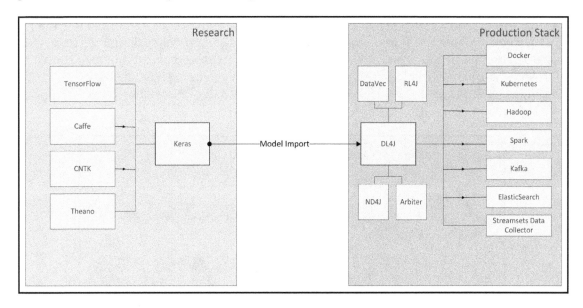

Figure 10.7: Importing a Keras model into DL4J

Let's now go into detail to understand how this happens. For the examples in this section, I am assuming you have already Python 2.7.x and the pip (https://pypi.org/project/pip/) package installer for Python on your machine. In order to implement a model in Keras, we have to install Keras itself and choose a backend (TensorFlow for the examples presented here). TensorFlow has to be installed first, as follows:

```
sudo pip install tensorflow
```

That's for the CPU only. If you need to run it on GPUs, you need to install the following:

```
sudo pip install tensorflow-gpu
```

We can now install Keras, as follows:

```
sudo pip install keras
```

Keras uses TensorFlow as its default tensor manipulation library, so no extra action has to be taken if TensorFlow is our backend of choice.

Let's start simple, implementing an MLP model using the Keras API. After the necessary imports, enter the following lines of code:

```
from keras.models import Sequential
  from keras.layers import Dense
```

We create a `Sequential` model, as follows:

```
model = Sequential()
```

Then, we add layers through the `add` method of `Sequential`, as follows:

```
model.add(Dense(units=64, activation='relu', input_dim=100))
  model.add(Dense(units=10, activation='softmax'))
```

The configuration of the learning process for this model can be done through the `compile` method, as follows:

```
model.compile(loss='categorical_crossentropy',
              optimizer='sgd',
              metrics=['accuracy'])
```

Finally, we serialize the model in HDF5 format, as follows:

```
model.save('basic_mlp.h5')
```

Hierarchical Data Format (**HDF**) is a set of file formats (with the extensions .hdf5 and .h5) to store and manage large amounts of data, in particular multidimensional numeric arrays. Keras uses it to save and load models.

After saving this simple program, `basic_mlp.py`, and running it, as follows the model will be serialized and saved in the `basic_mlp.h5` file:

```
sudo python basic_mlp.py
```

Now, we are ready to import this model into DL4J. We need to add to the Scala project the usual DataVec API, DL4J core, and ND4J dependencies, plus the DL4J model import library, as follows:

```
groupId: org.deeplearning4j
  artifactId: deeplearning4j-modelimport
  version: 0.9.1
```

Copy the `basic_mlp.h5` file in the resource folder of the project, then programmatically get its path, as follows:

```
val basicMlp = new ClassPathResource("basic_mlp.h5").getFile.getPath
```

Then, load the model as DL4J `MultiLayerNetwork`, using the `importKerasSequentialModelAndWeights` method of the `KerasModelImport` class (`https://static.javadoc.io/org.deeplearning4j/deeplearning4j-modelimport/1.0.0-alpha/org/deeplearning4j/nn/modelimport/keras/KerasModelImport.html`), as follows:

```
val model = KerasModelImport.importKerasSequentialModelAndWeights(basicMlp)
```

Generate some mock data, as follows:

```
val input = Nd4j.create(256, 100)
  var output = model.output(input)
```

Now, we can train the model the usual way in DL4J, as follows:

```
model.fit(input, output)
```

All the considerations made in Chapter 7, *Training Neural Networks with Spark,* Chapter 8, *Monitoring and Debugging Neural Network Training,* and Chapter 9, *Interpreting Neural Network Output,* about training, monitoring, and evaluation with DL4J, apply here too.

It is possible, of course, to train the model in Keras (as in the following example):

```
model.fit(x_train, y_train, epochs=5, batch_size=32)
```

Here, `x_train` and `y_train` are NumPy (`http://www.numpy.org/`) arrays) and evaluate it before saving it in serialized form, as follows:

```
loss_and_metrics = model.evaluate(x_test, y_test, batch_size=128)
```

You can finally import the pre-trained model in the same way as explained previously, and just run it.

The same as for `Sequential` model imports, DL4J allows also the importing of Keras `Functional` models.

The latest versions of DL4J, also allow the importing of TensorFlow models. Imagine you want to import this (`https://github.com/tensorflow/models/blob/master/official/mnist/mnist.py`) pre-trained model (a CNN estimator for the `MNIST` database). At the end of the training, which happens in TensorFlow, you can save the model in a serialized form. TensorFlow's file format is based on Protocol Buffers (`https://developers.google.com/protocol-buffers/?hl=en`), which is a language and platform neutral extensible serialization mechanism for structured data.

Copy the serialized `mnist.pb` file into the resource folder of the DL4J Scala project and then programmatically get it and import the model, as follows:

```
val mnistTf = new ClassPathResource("mnist.pb").getFile
 val sd = TFGraphMapper.getInstance.importGraph(mnistTf)
```

Finally, feed the model with images and start to do predictions, as follows:

```
for(i <- 1 to 10){
    val file = "images/img_%d.jpg"
    file = String.format(file, i)
    val prediction = predict(file) //INDArray
    val batchedArr = Nd4j.expandDims(arr, 0) //INDArray
    sd.associateArrayWithVariable(batchedArr, sd.variables().get(0))
    val out = sd.execAndEndResult //INDArray
    Nd4j.squeeze(out, 0)
    ...
}
```

Alternatives to DL4J for the Scala programming language

DL4J isn't the only framework for deep learning available for the Scala programming language. Two open source alternatives exist. In this section, we are going to learn more about them and do a comparison with DL4J.

BigDL

BigDL (`https://bigdl-project.github.io/0.6.0/`) is an open source, distributed, deep learning framework for Apache Spark implemented by Intel (`https://www.intel.com`). It is licensed with the Apache 2.0 license, the same as for DL4J. It has been implemented in Scala and exposes APIs for Scala and Python. It doesn't provide support for CUDA. While DL4J allows cross-platform execution in standalone mode (including Android mobile devices) and distributed mode (with and without Spark), BigDL has been designed to execute in a Spark cluster only. The available benchmarks state that training/running this framework is faster than the most popular Python frameworks, such as TensorFlow or Caffe, because BigDL uses the Intel Math Kernel Library (MKL, `https://software.intel.com/en-us/mkl`), assuming it is running on Intel processor-based machines.

It provides high-level APIs for neural networks and the possibility to import Python models from Keras, Caffe, or Torch.

While it has been implemented in Scala, at the time this chapter was written, it supports only Scala 2.10.x.

Looking at the latest evolution of this framework, it seems that Intel is going to provide more support for importing Python models implemented with other frameworks (and is starting also to provide support for some TensorFlow operations) and enhancements of the Python API, rather than the Scala API.

What about community and contributions? BigDL is supported and driven by Intel, which keeps an eye in particular on how this framework is used on hardware based on their microprocessors. So, this could be a potential risk in adopting this framework in other production hardware contexts. While DL4J is supported by Skymind (`https://skymind.ai/`), the company owned by Adam Gibson, who is one of the authors of this framework, the vision, in terms of future evolution, isn't restricted to the company business. The goal is to make the framework more comprehensive in terms of capabilities and try to further reduce the gap between the JVM languages and Python in relation to available numeric computation and DL tools/features. Also, the number of contributors, commits, and releases are increasing for DL4J.

Compared to the Scala BigDL API, the DL4J API for Scala (and Java) is more high level (some sort of DSL), which is in particular of great help for Scala developers approaching the DL world for the first time, as it speeds up the the process of getting familiar with the framework, and allows programmers to focus more on the model being trained and implemented.

If your plan is to stay in the JVM world, I definitely believe DL4J is a better choice than BigDL.

DeepLearning.scala

DeepLearning.scala (`https://deeplearning.thoughtworks.school/`) is a DL framework from ThoughtWorks (`https://www.thoughtworks.com/`). Implemented in Scala, the goal since the start has been, to get the most from the functional programming and object-oriented paradigms for this language. It supports GPU-accelerated N-dimensional arrays. Neural networks in this framework can be built from mathematical formulas, so it can calculate derivatives of the weights in the formulas used.

This framework supports plugins, so it could be extended by writing custom plugins, which can then coexist along with the plugin set available out of the box (a significant set of plugins is currently available in terms of models, algorithms, hyperparameters, calculation features, and so on).

DeepLearning.scala applications can run as standalone on the JVM, as Jupyter (http://jupyter.org/) notebooks, or as scripts in Ammonite (http://ammonite.io/).

Numerical computing happens through ND4J, the same as for DL4J.

It doesn't have support for Python, nor facilities to import models implemented through Python DL frameworks.

One big difference between this framework and others, such as DL4J and BigDL, is the following: the structure of the neural networks is dynamically determined at runtime. All the Scala language features (functions, expressions, control flows, and so on) are available for implementation. Neural networks are Scala Monads, so they can be created by composing higher order functions, but that's not the only option in DeepLearning.scala; the framework also provides a type class called `Applicative` (through the Scalaz library, http://eed3si9n.com/learning-scalaz/Applicative.html), which allows multiple calculations in parallel.

No native support for Spark or Hadoop was available for this framework at the time this chapter was written.

DeepLearning.scala can be a good alternative to DL4J in those contexts where there's no need for Apache Spark distributed training, and where you want to implement things in pure Scala. In terms of APIs for this programming language, it is more observant of the principles of pure Scala programming than DL4J, which has targeted all of the languages that run on the JVM (starting from Java, then extending to Scala, Clojure, and others, including Android).

The initial visions for these two frameworks are also different: DL4J started to target software engineers, while DeepLearning.scala has an approach more oriented toward data scientists. Still to be verified is its level of stability and performance in production, as it is younger than DL4J and has a smaller number of adopters in real use cases. The lack of support to import existing models from Python frameworks could also be a limitation, because you would need to build and train your model from scratch and can't rely on existing Python models that may be an excellent fit for your specific use case. In terms of community and releases, at present it can't of course compare with DL4J and BigDL (even if there is the chance that it could grow in the very near future). Last but not least, the official documentation and examples are limited and not yet as mature and comprehensive as they are for DL4J.

Summary

In this chapter, some concepts to think about when moving DL4J to production have been discussed. In particular, we understood how heap and off-heap memory management should be set up, looked at extra considerations on GPUs setup, saw how to prepare job JARs to be submitted to Spark for training, and also saw how it is possible to import and integrate Python models into an existing DL4J JVM infrastructure. Finally, a comparison between DL4J and two other DL frameworks for Scala (BigDL and DeepLearning.scala) was presented, and the reasons why DL4J could be a better choice from a production perspective were detailed.

In the next chapter, the core concepts of Natural Language Processing (NLP) will be explained, and a complete Scala implementation of NLP using Apache Spark and its MLLib (Machine Learning Library) will be detailed. We will go through the potential limitations of this approach, before in Chapter 12, *Textual Analysis and Deep Learning*, presenting the same solution using DL4J and/or Keras/TensorFlow.

11
NLP Basics

In the previous chapter, several topics were covered concerning the undertaking of DL distributed training in a Spark cluster. The concepts presented there are common to any network model. Starting from this chapter, specific use cases for RNNs or LSTMs will be looked at first, and then CNNs will be covered. This chapter starts by introducing the following core concepts of **Natural Language Processing** (**NLP**):

- Tokenizers
- Sentence segmentation
- Part-of-speech tagging
- Named entity extraction
- Chunking
- Parsing

The theory behind the concepts in the preceding list will be detailed before finally presenting two complete Scala examples of NLP, one using Apache Spark and the Stanford core NLP library, and the other using the Spark core and the `Spark-nlp` library (which is built on top of Apache Spark MLLib). The goal of the chapter is to make readers familiar with NLP, before moving to implementations based on DL (RNNs) through DL4J and/or Keras/Tensorflow in combination with Spark, which will be the core topic of the next chapter.

NLP

NLP is the field of using computer science and AI to process and analyze natural language data and then make machines able to interpret it as humans do. During the 1980s, when this concept started to get hyped, language processing systems were designed by hand coding a set of rules. Later, following increases in calculation power, a different approach, mostly based on statistical models, replaced the original one. A later ML approach (supervised learning first, also semi-supervised or unsupervised at present time) brought advances in this field, such as voice recognition software and human language translation, and will probably lead to more complex scenarios, such as natural language understanding and generation.

Here is how NLP works. The first task, called the speech-to-text process, is to understand the natural language received. A built-in model performs speech recognition, which does the conversion from natural to programming language. This happens by breaking down speech into very small units and then comparing them to previous units coming speech that has been input previously. The output determines the words and sentences that most probably have been said. The next task, called **part-of-speech** (**POS**) tagging (or word-category disambiguation in some literature), identifies words as their grammatical forms (nouns, adjectives, verbs, and so on) using a set of lexicon rules. At the end of these two phases, a machine should understand the meaning of the input speech. A possible third task of an NLP process is text-to-speech conversion: at the end, the programming language is converted into a textual or audible format understandable by humans. That's the ultimate goal of NLP: to build software that analyzes, understands, and can generate human languages in a natural way, making computers communicate as if they were humans.

Given a piece of text, there are three things that need to be considered and understood when implementing NLP:

- **Semantic information**: The specific meaning of a single word. Consider, for example, the word *pole*, which could have different meanings (one end of a magnet, a long stick, and others). In a sentence like *extreme right and extreme left are the two poles of the political system,* in order to understand the correct meaning, it is important to know the relevant definition of pole. A reader would easily infer which one it is, but a machine can't without ML or DL.
- **Syntax information**: The phrase structure. Consider the sentence *William joined the football team already with long international experience.* Depending on how it is read, it has different meanings (it could be William or the football team that has long international experience).

- **Context information**: The context where a word or a phrase appears. Consider, for example, the adjective *low*. It is often positive when part of a context of convenience (for example, *This mobile phone has a low price*), but it is almost always negative when talking about supplies (for example, *Supplies of drinkable water are running low*).

The following subsections will explain the main concepts of NLP supervised learning.

Tokenizers

Tokenization means defining what a word is in NLP ML algorithms. Given a text, tokenization is the task of cutting it down into pieces, called **tokens**, while at the same time also removing particular characters (such as punctuation or delimiters). For example, given this input sentence in the English language:

```
To be, or not to be, that is the question
```
The result of tokenization would produce the following 11 tokens:

```
To be or or not to be that is the question
```

One big challenge with tokenization is about what the correct tokens to use are. In the previous example, it was easy to decide: we cut down on white spaces and removed all the punctuation characters. But what if the input text isn't in English? For some other languages, such as Chinese for example, where there are no white spaces, the preceding rules don't work. So, any ML/DL model training for NLP should consider the specific rules for a language.

But even when limited to a single language, let's say English, there could be tricky cases. Consider the following example sentence:

```
David Anthony O'Leary is an Irish football manager and former player
```
How do you manage the apostrophe? There are five possible tokenizations in this case for `O'Leary`. These are as follows:

1. `leary`
2. `oleary`
3. `o'leary`
4. `o' leary`
5. `o leary`

But which one is the desired one? A simple strategy that comes quickly to mind could be to just split out all the non-alphanumeric characters in sentences. So, getting the `o` and `leary` tokens would be acceptable, because doing a Boolean query search with those tokens would match three cases out of five. But what about this following sentence?

```
Michael O'Leary has slammed striking cabin crew at Aer Lingus saying
"they aren't being treated like Siberian salt miners".
```

For *aren't*, there are four possible tokenizations, which are as follows:

1. `aren't`
2. `arent`
3. `are n't`
4. `aren t`

Again, while the `o` and `leary` split looks fine, what about the `aren` and `t` split? This last one doesn't look good; a Boolean query search with those tokens would match two cases only out of four.

Challenges and issues with tokenization are language-specific. A deep knowledge of the language of the input documents is required in this context.

Sentence segmentation

Sentence segmentation is the process of splitting up a text into sentences. From its definition, it seems a straightforward process, but several difficulties can occur with it, for example, the presence of punctuation marks that can be used to indicate different things:

```
Streamsets Inc. has released the new Data Collector 3.5.0. One of the
new features is the MongoDB lookup processor.
```

Looking at the preceding text, you can see that the same punctuation mark (`.`) is used for three different things, not just as a sentence separator. Some languages, such as Chinese for example, come with unambiguous sentence-ending markers, while others don't. So a strategy needs to be set. The quickest and dirtiest approach to locate the end of a sentence in a case like that in the previous example is the following:

- If it is a full stop, then it ends a sentence
- If the token preceding a full stop is present in a hand-precompiled list of abbreviations, then the full stop doesn't end the sentence
- If the next token after a full stop is capitalized, then the full stop ends the sentence

This gets more than 90% of sentences correct, but something smarter can be done, such as rule-based boundary disambiguation techniques (automatically learn a set of rules from input documents where the sentence breaks have been pre-marked), or better still, use a neural network (this can achieve more than 98% accuracy).

POS tagging

POS tagging in NLP is the process of marking a word, depending on its definition and context as well, inside a text as corresponding to a particular POS. Speech has nine main parts—nouns, verbs, adjectives, articles, pronouns, adverbs, conjunctions, prepositions, and interjections. Each of them is divided into sub-classes. This process is more complex than tokenization and sentence segmentation. POS tagging can't be generic because, depending on the context, the same word could have a different POS tag in sentences belonging to the same text, for example:

```
Please lock the door and don't forget the key in the lock.
```

Here, the word `lock` is used twice with two different meanings (as a verb and as a noun) in the same sentence. Differences across languages should be considered as well. So this is a process that can't be handled manually, but it should be machine-based. The algorithms used can be rule-based or stochastic. Rule-based algorithms, in order to assign tags to unknown (or at least ambiguous) words, make use of contextual information. Disambiguation is achieved by analyzing different linguistic features of a word, such as the preceding and following words. A rule-based model is trained from a starting set of rules and data, and attempts to infer execution instructions for POS tagging. Stochastic taggers relate to different approaches; basically, any model that includes probability or frequency can be labeled this way. A simple stochastic tagger can disambiguate words based only on the probability a word occurs with a particular tag. More complex stochastic taggers are more efficient, of course. One of the most popular is the hidden Markov model (https://en.wikipedia.org/wiki/Hidden_Markov_model), a statistical model in which the system being modeled is assumed to be a Markov process (https://en.wikipedia.org/wiki/Markov_chain) with hidden states.

Named entity extraction (NER)

NER is the sub-task of NLP, the goal of which is to locate and classify named entities in a text into predefined categories. Let's give an example. We have the following sentence:

```
Guglielmo is writing a book for Packt Publishing in 2018.
```

An NER process on it will produce the following annotated text:

```
[Guglielmo]Person is writing a book for [Packt Publishing]Organization in
[2018]Time .
```

Three entities have been detected, a person, `Guglielmo`, a two-token organization, `Packt Publishing`, and a temporal expression, `2018`.

Traditionally, NER has been applied to structured text, but lately the number of use cases for unstructured text has grown.

Challenges with automating this process implementation have been case sensitivity (earlier algorithms often failed to recognize, for example, that Guglielmo Iozzia and GUGLIELMO IOZZIA are the same entity), different uses of punctuation marks, and missing separation characters. Implementations of NER systems use linguistic grammar-based techniques or statistical models and ML. Grammar-based systems can give better precision, but have a huge cost in terms of months of work by experienced linguists, plus they have low recall. ML-based systems have a high recall, but require a large amount of manually annotated data for their training. Unsupervised approaches are coming through order to drastically reduce the effort of data annotation.

Another challenge for this process is the context domain—several studies have demonstrated that NER systems developed for one domain (reaching high performance on it) typically don't perform well the same way in other domains. An NER system that has been trained in a Twitter content, for example, can't be applied, expecting the same performance and accuracy, to medical records. This applies for both rule-based and statistical/ML systems; a considerable effort is needed when tuning NER systems in a new domain in order for them to reach the same level of performance they had in the original domain where they were successfully trained.

Chunking

Chunking in NLP is the process of extracting phrases from text. It is used because simple tokens may not represent the real meaning of the text under examination. As an example, consider the phrase *Great Britain*; while the two separate words make sense, it is more advisable to use *Great Britain* as a single word. Chunking works on top of POS tagging; typically POS tags are input, while chunks are the output from it. This process is very similar to the way the human brain chunks information together to make it easier to process and understand. Think about the way you memorize, for example, sequences of numbers (such as debit card pins, telephone numbers, and others); you don't tend to memorize them as individual numbers, but try to group them together in a way that makes them easier to remember.

Chunking can be up or down. Chunking up tends more to abstraction; chunking down tends to look for more specific details. As an example, consider the following scenario in a call with a ticket sales and distribution company. The operator asks the question *"which kind of tickets would you like to purchase?"* The customer's answer, *"Concert tickets"*, is chunking up, because it moves towards a higher level of abstraction. Then, the operator asks more questions, such as *"which genre,"* *"which artist or group,"* *"for which dates and locations,",* *"for how many people,",* *"which sector,",* and so on, in order to get more details and fulfill the customer's needs (this is chunking down). At the end, you can think about chunking as a hierarchy of sets. For a given context, there is always a higher-level set, which has subsets, and each subset can have other subsets. For example, consider a programming language as a higher-level subset; you can then have the following:

```
Programming Language

Scala (Subset of Programming Language)

Scala 2.11 (Subset of Scala)

Trait (a specific concept of Scala)

Iterator (a core Scala trait)
```

Parsing

Parsing in NLP is the process of determining the syntactic structure of a text. It works by analyzing the text constituent words and it bases itself on the underlying grammar of the specific language in which the text has been written. The outcome of parsing is a parse tree of each sentence part of the input text. A parse tree is an ordered, rooted tree that represents the syntactic structure of a sentence according to some context-free grammar (a set of rules that describe all the possible strings in a given formal language). Let's make an example. Consider the English language and the following example grammar:

```
sentence -> noun-phrase, verb-phrase

noun-phrase -> proper-noun

noun-phrase -> determiner, noun

verb-phrase -> verb, noun-phrase
```

Consider the phrase `Guglielmo wrote a book` and apply the parsing process to it. The output would be a parse tree like this:

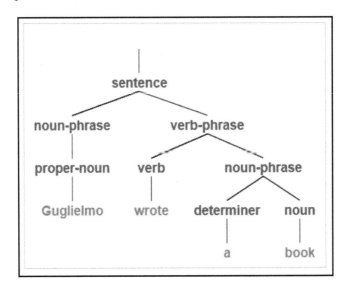

Currently, the approaches to automated machine-based parsing are statistical, probabilistic, or ML.

Hands-on NLP with Spark

In this section, some examples of the implementation of NLP (and its core concepts as described in the previous sections) with Apache Spark are going to be detailed. These examples don't include DL4J or other DL frameworks, as NLP with multilayer neural networks will be the main topic of the next chapter.

While one of the core components of Spark, MLLib, is an ML library, it doesn't provide any facility for NLP. So, you need to use some other NLP library or framework on top of Spark.

Hands-on NLP with Spark and Stanford core NLP

The first example covered in this chapter involves a Scala Spark wrapper of the Stanford core NLP (`https://github.com/stanfordnlp/CoreNLP`) library, which is open source and released with the GNU general public licence v3 (`https://www.gnu.org/licenses/gpl-3.0.en.html`). It is a Java library that provides a set of natural language analysis tools. Its basic distribution provides model files for the analysis of English, but the engine is compatible with models for other languages as well. It is stable and ready for production, and widely used across different areas of academic and industry. Spark CoreNLP (`https://github.com/databricks/spark-corenlp`) is a wrapper of the Stanford Core NLP Java library for Apache Spark. It has been implemented in Scala. The Stanford Core NLP annotators have been wrapped as Spark DataFrames.

The spark-corenlp library's current release contains a single Scala class function, which provides all of the high-level wrapper methods, as follows:

- `cleanXml`: Takes as input an XML document and removes all the XML tags.
- `tokenize`: Tokenizes the input sentence into words.
- `ssplit`: Splits its input document into sentences.
- `pos`: Generates the POS tags of its input sentence.
- `lemma`: Generates the word lemmas of its input sentence.
- `ner`: Generates the named entity tags of its input sentence.
- `depparse`: Generates the semantic dependencies of its input sentence.
- `coref`: Generates the `coref` chains of its input document.
- `natlog`: Generates the natural logic notion of polarity for each token in its input sentence. The possible returned values are up, down, or flat.

- openie: Generates a list of open IE triples as flat quadruples.
- sentiment: Measures the sentiment of its input sentence. The scale goes from zero (strongly negative) to four (strongly positive).

The first thing to do is to set up the dependencies for this example. It has dependencies on Spark SQL and the Stanford core NLP 3.8.0 (the importing of the models needs to be explicitly specified through the Models classifier), as follows:

```
groupId: edu.stanford.nlp
artifactId: stanford-corenlp
version: 3.8.0

groupId: edu.stanford.nlp
artifactId: stanford-corenlp
version: 3.8.0
classifier: models
```

When you need to work with a single language, let's say Spanish, you can also choose to import the models for that language only, through its specific classifier, as follows:

```
groupId: edu.stanford.nlp
 artifactId: stanford-corenlp
 version: 3.8.0
 classifier: models-spanish
```

No library is available for spark-corenlp on Maven central. So, you have to build its JAR file starting from the GitHub source code, and then add it to the classpath of your NLP application or, if your applications rely on an artifact repository, such as JFrog Artifactory (https://jfrog.com/artifactory/), Apache Archiva (https://archiva.apache.org/index.cgi), or Sonatype Nexus OSS (https://www.sonatype.com/nexus-repository-oss), store the JAR file there and then add the dependency to it in your project build file the same way as for any other dependency available in Maven central.

I previously mentioned that spark-corenlp wraps Stanford core NLP annotators as DataFrames. So, the first thing to do in the source code is to create a SparkSession, as follows:

```
val sparkSession = SparkSession
   .builder()
   .appName("spark-corenlp example")
   .master(master)
   .getOrCreate()
```

Create now a `Sequence` (`https://www.scala-lang.org/api/current/scala/collection/Seq.html`) for the input text content (in XML format) and then transform it into a DataFrame, as follows:

```
import sparkSession.implicits._
 val input = Seq(
   (1, "<xml>Packt is a publishing company based in Birmingham and Mumbai.
It is a great publisher.</xml>")
 ).toDF("id", "text")
```

Given this input, we could do different NLP operations using the `functions` available methods, such as cleaning from the tags the input XML included in the `text` field of the `input` DataFrame, splitting each sentence into single words, generating the named entity tags for each sentence, and measuring the sentiment of each sentence, for example:

```
val output = input
     .select(cleanxml('text).as('doc))
     .select(explode(ssplit('doc)).as('sen))
     .select('sen, tokenize('sen).as('words), ner('sen).as('nerTags),
sentiment('sen).as('sentiment))
```

At the end, we print the output of those operations (`output` itself is a DataFrame), as follows:

```
output.show(truncate = false)
```

Finally, we need to stop and destroy the `SparkSession`, as follows:

```
sparkSession.stop()
```

Executing this example, the output is as follows:

```
10/15/96 14:29:48 INFO DAGScheduler: Job 0 finished: show at SparkCoreNlpExample.scala:27, took 9.569711 s
+---------------------------------------------------+------------------------------------------------------+---------------------------------------------+---------+
|sen                                                |words                                                 |nerTags                                      |sentiment|
+---------------------------------------------------+------------------------------------------------------+---------------------------------------------+---------+
|Packt is a publishing company based in Birmingham and Mumbai .|[Packt, is, a, publishing, company, based, in, Birmingham, and, Mumbai, .]|[0, 0, 0, 0, 0, 0, 0, LOCATION, 0, LOCATION, 0]|3        |
|It is a great publisher .                          |[It, is, a, great, publisher, .]                      |[0, 0, 0, 0, 0, 0]                           |3        |
+---------------------------------------------------+------------------------------------------------------+---------------------------------------------+---------+
```

The XML content has been cleared from the tags, the sentences have been split into their single words as expected, and for some words (`Birmingham`, `Mumbai`) a named entity tag (`LOCATION`) has been generated. And, the sentiment is positive (3) for both input sentences!

This approach is a good way to start with NLP in Scala and Spark; the API provided by this library is simple and high level, and gives time to people to assimilate the core NLP concepts quickly, while leveraging the Spark DataFrames capabilities. But there are downsides with it. Where there is a need to implement more complex and custom NLP solutions, the available API is too simple to tackle them. Also a licensing problem could occur if your final system isn't for internal purposes only, but your company plan is to sell and distribute your solution to customers; the Stanford core NLP library and `spark-corenlp` models depend on, and are released under, the full GNU GPL v3 license, which forbids redistributing it as part of proprietary software. The next section presents a more viable alternative for Scala and Spark.

Hands-on NLP with Spark NLP

Another alternative library to integrate with Apache Spark in order to do NLP is `spark-nlp` (`https://nlp.johnsnowlabs.com/`) by the John Snow labs (`https://www.johnsnowlabs.com/`). It is open source and released under Apache License 2.0, so is different from `spark-corenlp` because its licensing model makes it possible to redistribute it as part of a commercial solution. It has been implemented in Scala on top of the Apache Spark ML module and it is available in Maven central. It provides NLP annotations for machine learning pipelines that at the same time are easy to understand and use, have great performance, and can scale easily in a distributed environment.

The release I am referring to in this section is 1.6.3 (the latest at the time this book was written).

The core concept of `spark-nlp` is the Spark ML pipeline (`https://spark.apache.org/docs/2.2.1/api/java/org/apache/spark/ml/Pipeline.html`). A pipeline consists of a sequence of stages. Each stage could be a transformer (`https://spark.apache.org/docs/2.2.1/api/java/org/apache/spark/ml/Transformer.html`) or an estimator (`https://spark.apache.org/docs/2.2.1/api/java/org/apache/spark/ml/Estimator.html`). Transformers transform an input dataset into another, while estimators fit a model to data. When the fit method of a pipeline is invoked, its stages are then executed in order. Three types of pre-trained pipelines are available: the basic, advanced, and sentiment. The library provides also several pre-trained models for NLP and several annotators. But, let's start with a simple first example in order to clarify the details of the main concepts of `spark-nlp`. Let's try to implement a basic pipeline for ML-based named entity tag extraction.

The following example depends on the Spark SQL and MLLib components and the `spark-nlp` library:

```
groupId: com.johnsnowlabs.nlp
  artifactId: spark-nlp_2.11
  version: 1.6.3
```

We need to start a `SparkSession` before anything else, as follows:

```
val sparkSession: SparkSession = SparkSession
            .builder()
            .appName("Ner DL Pipeline")
            .master("local[*]")
            .getOrCreate()
```

Before creating the pipeline, we need to implement its single stages. The first one is `com.johnsnowlabs.nlp.DocumentAssembler`, to specify the column of the application input to parse and the output column name (which will be the input column for the next stage), as follows:

```
val document = new DocumentAssembler()
        .setInputCol("text")
        .setOutputCol("document")
```

The next stage is a `Tokenizer` (`com.johnsnowlabs.nlp.annotators.Tokenizer`), as follows:

```
val token = new Tokenizer()
        .setInputCols("document")
        .setOutputCol("token")
```

After this stage, any input sentences should have been split into single words. We need to clean up those tokens, so the next stage is a `normalizer` (`com.johnsnowlabs.nlp.annotators.Normalizer`), as follows:

```
val normalizer = new Normalizer()
        .setInputCols("token")
        .setOutputCol("normal")
```

We can now use one of the pre-trained models of the `spark-nlp` library to generate the named entity tags, as follows:

```
val ner = NerDLModel.pretrained()
        .setInputCols("normal", "document")
        .setOutputCol("ner")
```

Here we are using the `NerDLModel` class
(`com.johnsnowlabs.nlp.annotators.ner.dl.NerDLModel`), which behind the scenes
uses a TensorFlow pre-trained model. The named entity tags generated by that model are
in IOB format (`https://en.wikipedia.org/wiki/`
`Inside%E2%80%93outside%E2%80%93beginning_(tagging)`), so we need to make them in a
more human readable format. We can achieve this using the `NerConverter` class
(`com.johnsnowlabs.nlp.annotators.ner.NerConverter`), as follows:

```
val nerConverter = new NerConverter()
    .setInputCols("document", "normal", "ner")
    .setOutputCol("ner_converter")
```

The last stage is to finalize the output of the pipeline, as follows:

```
val finisher = new Finisher()
    .setInputCols("ner", "ner_converter")
    .setIncludeMetadata(true)
    .setOutputAsArray(false)
    .setCleanAnnotations(false)
    .setAnnotationSplitSymbol("@")
    .setValueSplitSymbol("#")
```

For this, we use the `Finisher` transformer (`com.johnsnowlabs.nlp.Finisher`).

We can now create the pipeline using the stages created so far, as follows:

```
val pipeline = new Pipeline().setStages(Array(document, token, normalizer,
ner, nerConverter, finisher))
```

You have already probably noticed that each stage's output column is the input for the next
stage's input column. That's because the stages for a pipeline are executed in the exact order
they are listed in the input `Array` for the `setStages` method.

Let's now feed the application with some sentences, as follows:

```
val testing = Seq(
    (1, "Packt is a famous publishing company"),
    (2, "Guglielmo is an author")
  ).toDS.toDF( "_id", "text")
```

The same as for the `spark-corenlp` example in the previous section, we have created a
`Sequence` for the input text content and then transformed it into a Spark DataFrame.

By invoking the `fit` method of the `pipeline`, we can execute all of its stages, as follows:

```
val result =
pipeline.fit(Seq.empty[String].toDS.toDF("text")).transform(testing)
```

And, we get the resulting DataFrame output, as follows:

```
result.select("ner", "ner_converter").show(truncate=false)
```

This will give the following output:

When we take a closer look it is seen as follows:

```
-+-------------------------------------------+
|ner_converter                               |
-+-------------------------------------------+
]|[[chunk,0,4,Packt,Map(entity -> ORG)]]     |
 |[[chunk,0,8,Guglielmo,Map(entity -> PER)]]||
-+-------------------------------------------+
```

An `ORGANIZATION` named entity tag has been generated for the word `Packt` and a `PERSON` named entity tag has been generated for the word `Guglielmo`.

`spark-nlp` also provides a class, `com.johnsnowlabs.util.Benchmark`, to perform the benchmarking of pipeline execution, for example:

```
Benchmark.time("Time to convert and show") {result.select("ner",
"ner_converter").show(truncate=false)}
```

Finally, we stop the `SparkSession` at the end of the pipeline execution, as follows:

```
sparkSession.stop
```

Let's now do something more complex. The pipeline in this second example does tokenization with n-grams (https://en.wikipedia.org/wiki/N-gram), sequences of *n* tokens (typically words) from a given text or speech. The dependencies for this example are the same as for the previous one presented in this section—Spark SQL, Spark MLLib, and `spark-nlp`.

Create a `SparkSession` and configure some Spark properties, as follows:

```
val sparkSession: SparkSession = SparkSession
    .builder()
```

```
        .appName("Tokenize with n-gram example")
        .master("local[*]")
        .config("spark.driver.memory", "1G")
        .config("spark.kryoserializer.buffer.max","200M")
    .config("spark.serializer","org.apache.spark.serializer.KryoSerializer")
        .getOrCreate()
```

The first three stages for the pipeline are the same as for the previous example, as follows:

```
val document = new DocumentAssembler()
  .setInputCol("text")
  .setOutputCol("document")

val token = new Tokenizer()
  .setInputCols("document")
  .setOutputCol("token")

val normalizer = new Normalizer()
  .setInputCols("token")
  .setOutputCol("normal")
```

Put a `finisher` stage before using the n-gram stage, as follows:

```
val finisher = new Finisher()
    .setInputCols("normal")
```

The n-gram stage uses the NGram class (https://spark.apache.org/docs/2.2.1/api/scala/index.html#org.apache.spark.ml.feature.NGram) of Spark MLLib, as follows:

```
val ngram = new NGram()
  .setN(3)
  .setInputCol("finished_normal")
  .setOutputCol("3-gram")
```

NGram is a feature transformer that converts an input array of strings into an array of n-grams. The chosen value for *n* in this example is 3. We need now a further DocumentAssembler stage for the n-gram results, as follows:

```
val gramAssembler = new DocumentAssembler()
  .setInputCol("3-gram")
  .setOutputCol("3-grams")
```

Let's implement the pipeline, as follows:

```
val pipeline = new Pipeline().setStages(Array(document, token, normalizer,
finisher, ngram, gramAssembler))
```

Now feed the application with the same input sentences as for the previous example:

```
import sparkSession.implicits._
val testing = Seq(
  (1, "Packt is a famous publishing company"),
  (2, "Guglielmo is an author")
).toDS.toDF( "_id", "text")
```

And execute the stages of the pipeline, as follows:

```
val result =
pipeline.fit(Seq.empty[String].toDS.toDF("text")).transform(testing)
```

Print the results to the screen:

```
result.show(truncate=false)
```

This produces the following output:

```
#spark}
AILABLE.@Spark}

|3-gram                                                                           |3-grams
y][Packt is a, is a famous, a famous publishing, famous publishing company]|[[document.0.9,Packt is a,Map()], [document.0,10,is a famous,Map()], [document.0,18,a famous publishing,Map()], [document.0,24,famous publis
 |[Guglielmo is an, is an author]                                               |[[document.0,14,Guglielmo is an,Map()], [document,0,11,is an author,Map()]]
```

Finally, we stop the `SparkSession`, as follows:

```
sparkSession.stop
```

The final example is an ML sentiment analysis using the Vivek Narayanan (https:// github.com/vivekn) model. Sentiment analysis, which is a practical application of NLP, is the process of identifying and categorizing, through a computer, the opinion expressed in a text, in order to determine whether its writer's/speaker's attitude towards a product or topic is positive, negative, or neutral. In particular, for this example, we are going to train and validate the model on movie reviews. The dependencies for this example are the usual ones—Spark SQL, Spark MLLib, and `spark-nlp`.

As usual, create a `SparkSession` (while also configuring some Spark properties), as follows:

```
val spark: SparkSession = SparkSession
    .builder
    .appName("Train Vivek N Sentiment Analysis")
    .master("local[*]")
    .config("spark.driver.memory", "2G")
    .config("spark.kryoserializer.buffer.max","200M")
  .config("spark.serializer","org.apache.spark.serializer.KryoSerializer")
    .getOrCreate
```

We then need two datasets, one for training and one for testing. For simplicity, we define the training dataset as a `Sequence` and then transform it into a DataFrame, where the columns are the review text and the associated sentiment, as follows:

```
import spark.implicits._
val training = Seq(
  ("I really liked it!", "positive"),
  ("The cast is horrible", "negative"),
  ("Never going to watch this again or recommend it", "negative"),
  ("It's a waste of time", "negative"),
  ("I loved the main character", "positive"),
  ("The soundtrack was really good", "positive")
).toDS.toDF("train_text", "train_sentiment")

While the testing data set could be a simple Array:

val testing = Array(
  "I don't recommend this movie, it's horrible",
  "Dont waste your time!!!"
)
```

We can now define the stages for the pipeline. The first three stages are exactly the same as for the previous example pipelines (`DocumentAssembler`, `Tokenizer`, and `Normalizer`), as follows:

```
val document = new DocumentAssembler()
  .setInputCol("train_text")
  .setOutputCol("document")

val token = new Tokenizer()
  .setInputCols("document")
  .setOutputCol("token")

val normalizer = new Normalizer()
  .setInputCols("token")
  .setOutputCol("normal")
```

We can now use the `com.johnsnowlabs.nlp.annotators.sda.vivekn.VieknSentimentApproach` annotator, as follows:

```
val vivekn = new ViveknSentimentApproach()
  .setInputCols("document", "normal")
  .setOutputCol("result_sentiment")
  .setSentimentCol("train_sentiment")
```

And finally we use a Finisher transformer as last stage:

```
val finisher = new Finisher()
  .setInputCols("result_sentiment")
  .setOutputCols("final_sentiment")
```

Create the pipeline using the stages previously defined:

```
val pipeline = new Pipeline().setStages(Array(document, token, normalizer,
vivekn, finisher))
```

And then start the training, as follows:

```
val sparkPipeline = pipeline.fit(training)
```

Once the training has completed, we can use the following testing dataset to test it:

```
val testingDS = testing.toSeq.toDS.toDF("testing_text")
 println("Updating DocumentAssembler input column")
 document.setInputCol("testing_text")
 sparkPipeline.transform(testingDS).show()
```

The output will be as follows:

```
Updating DocumentAssembler input column
+--------------------+---------------+
|        testing_text|final_sentiment|
+--------------------+---------------+
|I don't recommend...|     [negative]|
|Dont waste your t...|     [negative]|
+--------------------+---------------+
```

Two sentences that are part of the testing dataset have been properly marked as negative.

It is of course possible to do a benchmark for sentiment analysis, too, through the spark-nlp Benchmark class, as follows:

```
Benchmark.time("Spark pipeline benchmark") {
   val testingDS = testing.toSeq.toDS.toDF("testing_text")
   println("Updating DocumentAssembler input column")
   document.setInputCol("testing_text")
   sparkPipeline.transform(testingDS).show()
 }
```

At the end of this section, we can state that `spark-nlp` provides more features than `spark-corenlp`, is well integrated with Spark MLLib, and, thanks to its licensing model, doesn't present the same issues concerning the distribution of the application/system in which it is used and integrated. It is a stable library and ready for production in Spark environments. Unfortunately, most of its documentation is missing and the existing documentation is minimal and not well maintained, despite project development being active.

In order to understand how a single feature works and how to combine them together, you have to go through the source code in GitHub. The library also uses existing ML models implemented through Python frameworks and provides a Scala class to represent them, hiding the underlying model implementation details from developers. This will work in several use case scenarios, but in order to build more robust and efficient models, you would probably have to move to implementing your own neural network model. Only DL4J will give you that level of freedom in development and training with Scala.

Summary

In this chapter, we became familiar with the main concepts of NLP and started to get hands-on with Spark, exploring two potentially useful libraries, `spark-corenlp` and `spark-nlp`.

In the next chapter, we will see how it is possible to achieve the same or better results by implementing complex NLP scenarios in Spark though DL (mostly RNN-based). We will explore different implementations by using DL4J, TensorFlow, Keras, the TensorFlow backend, and DL4J + Keras model imports.

Textual Analysis and Deep Learning

12

In the previous chapter, we became familiar with the core concepts of **Natural Language Processing** (**NLP**) and then we saw some implementation examples in Scala with Apache Spark, and two open source libraries for this framework. We also understood the pros and cons of those solutions. This chapter walks through hands-on examples of NLP use case implementations using DL (Scala and Spark). The following four cases will be covered:

- DL4J
- TensorFlow
- Keras and TensorFlow backend
- DL4J and Keras model import

The chapter covers some considerations regarding the pros and cons for each of those DL approaches in order, so that readers should then be ready to understand in which cases one framework is preferred over the others.

Hands-on NLP with DL4J

The first example we are going to examine is a sentiment analysis case for movie reviews, the same as for the last example shown in the previous chapter (the *Hands-on NLP with Spark-NLP* section). The difference is that here, we are going to combine Word2Vec (https://en.wikipedia.org/wiki/Word2vec) and an RNN model.

Word2Vec can be seen as a neural network with two layers only, which expects as input some text content and then returns vectors. It isn't a deep neural network, but it is used to turn text into a numerical format that deep neural networks can understand. Word2Vec is useful because it can group the vectors of similar words together in a vector space. It does this mathematically. It creates, without human intervention, distributed numerical representations of word features. The vectors that represent words are called **neural word embeddings**. Word2vec trains words against others that neighbor them in the input text. The way it does it is using context to predict a target word (**Continuous Bag Of Words (CBOW)**) or using a word to predict a target context (skip-gram). It has been demonstrated that the second approach produces more accurate results when dealing with large datasets. If the feature vector assigned to a word can't be used to accurately predict its context, an adjustment happens to the vector components. Each word's context in the input text becomes the teacher by sending errors back. This way the word vectors that have been estimated similar by the context where they are, are moved closer together.

The dataset used for training and testing is the *Large Movie Review Dataset,* which is available for download at `http://ai.stanford.edu/~amaas/data/sentiment/` and is free to use. It contains 25,000 highly popular movie reviews for training and another 25,000 for testing.

The dependencies for this example are DL4J NN, DL4J NLP, and ND4J.

Set up the RNN configuration using, as usual, the DL4J `NeuralNetConfiguration.Builder` class, as follows:

```
val conf: MultiLayerConfiguration = new NeuralNetConfiguration.Builder
   .updater(Updater.ADAM)
   .l2(1e-5)
   .weightInit(WeightInit.XAVIER)
 .gradientNormalization(GradientNormalization.ClipElementWiseAbsoluteValue)
   .gradientNormalizationThreshold(1.0)
   .list
   .layer(0, new GravesLSTM.Builder().nIn(vectorSize).nOut(256)
     .activation(Activation.TANH)
     .build)
   .layer(1, new RnnOutputLayer.Builder().activation(Activation.SOFTMAX)
 .lossFunction(LossFunctions.LossFunction.MCXENT).nIn(256).nOut(2).build)
   .pretrain(false).backprop(true).build
```

This network is made by a Graves LSTM RNN (please go back to `Chapter 6`, *Recurrent Neural Networks,* for more details on it) plus the DL4J—specific RNN output layer `RnnOutputLayer`. The activation function for this output layer is SoftMax.

We can now create the network using the preceding configuration set, as follows:

```
val net = new MultiLayerNetwork(conf)
 net.init()
 net.setListeners(new ScoreIterationListener(1))
```

Before starting the training, we need to prepare the training set to make it ready to be used. For this purpose, we are going to use the dataset iterator by Alex Black that can be found among the GitHub examples for DL4J (`https://github.com/deeplearning4j/dl4j-examples/blob/master/dl4j-examples/src/main/java/org/deeplearning4j/examples/recurrent/word2vecsentiment/SentimentExampleIterator.java`). It is in Java, so it has been adapted to Scala and added to the source code examples of this book. It implements the `DataSetIterator` interface (`https://static.javadoc.io/org.nd4j/nd4j-api/1.0.0-alpha/org/nd4j/linalg/dataset/api/iterator/DataSetIterator.html`) and it is specialized for the IMDB review datasets. It expects as input a raw IMDB dataset (it could be a training or testing dataset), plus a `wordVectors` object, and then generates the dataset ready to be used for training/test purposes. This particular implementation uses the Google News 300 pre-trained vectors as `wordVectors` objects; it can be freely downloaded in GZIP format from the `https://github.com/mmihaltz/word2vec-GoogleNews-vectors/` GitHub repo. It needs to be unzipped before it can be used. Once extracted, the model can be loaded though the `loadStaticModel` of the `WordVectorSerializer` class (`https://static.javadoc.io/org.deeplearning4j/deeplearning4j-nlp/1.0.0-alpha/org/deeplearning4j/models/embeddings/loader/WordVectorSerializer.html`) as follows:

```
val WORD_VECTORS_PATH: String =
getClass().getClassLoader.getResource("GoogleNews-vectors-
negative300.bin").getPath
 val wordVectors = WordVectorSerializer.loadStaticModel(new
File(WORD_VECTORS_PATH))
```

Training and test data can be now prepared through the custom dataset iterator `SentimentExampleIterator`:

```
val DATA_PATH: String =
getClass.getClassLoader.getResource("aclImdb").getPath
 val train = new SentimentExampleIterator(DATA_PATH, wordVectors,
batchSize, truncateReviewsToLength, true)
 val test = new SentimentExampleIterator(DATA_PATH, wordVectors, batchSize,
truncateReviewsToLength, false)
```

Then, we can test and evaluate the model in DL4J and Spark as explained in Chapter 6, *Recurrent Neural Networks*, Chapter 7, *Training Neural Networks with Spark*, and Chapter 8, *Monitoring and Debugging Neural Network Training*. Please be aware that the Google model used here is pretty big (about 3.5 GB), so take this into account when training the model in this example, in terms of resources needed (memory in particular).

In this first code example, we have used the common API of the DL4J main modules that are typically used for different MNNs in different use case scenarios. We have also explicitly used Word2Vec there. Anyway, the DL4J API also provides some basic facilities specific for NLP built on top of ClearTK (https://cleartk.github.io/cleartk/), an open source framework for ML, and NLP for Apache UIMA (http://uima.apache.org/). In the second example that is going to be presented in this section, we are going to use those facilities.

The dependencies for this second example are DataVec, DL4J NLP, and ND4J. While they are properly loaded as transitive dependencies by Maven or Gradle, the following two libraries. Need to be explicitly declared among the project dependencies to skip NoClassDefFoundError at runtime:

```
groupId: com.google.guava
  artifactId: guava
  version: 19.0
groupId: org.apache.commons
  artifactId: commons-math3
  version: 3.4
```

A file containing about 100,000 generic sentences has been used as input for this example. We need to load it in our application, as follows:

```
val filePath: String = new
ClassPathResource("rawSentences.txt").getFile.getAbsolutePath
```

The DL4J NLP library provides the SentenceIterator interface (https://static. javadoc.io/org.deeplearning4j/deeplearning4j-nlp/1.0.0-alpha/org/ deeplearning4j/text/sentenceiterator/SentenceIterator.html) and several implementations for it. In this specific example, we are going to use the BasicLineIterator implementation (https://static.javadoc.io/org. deeplearning4j/deeplearning4j-nlp/1.0.0-alpha/org/deeplearning4j/text/ sentenceiterator/BasicLineIterator.html) in order to remove white spaces at the beginning and the end of each sentence in the input text, as follows:

```
val iter: SentenceIterator = new BasicLineIterator(filePath)
```

We need to do the tokenization now in order to segment the input text into single words. For this, we use the `DefaultTokenizerFactory` implementation (https://static. javadoc.io/org.deeplearning4j/deeplearning4j-nlp/1.0.0-alpha/org/ deeplearning4j/text/tokenization/tokenizerfactory/DefaultTokenizerFactory.html) and set as tokenizer a `CommomPreprocessor` (https://static.javadoc.io/org. deeplearning4j/deeplearning4j-nlp/1.0.0-alpha/org/deeplearning4j/text/ tokenization/tokenizer/preprocessor/CommonPreprocessor.html) to remove punctuation marks, numbers, and special characters, and then force lowercase for all the generated tokens, as follows:

```
val tokenizerFactory: TokenizerFactory = new DefaultTokenizerFactory
  tokenizerFactory.setTokenPreProcessor(new CommonPreprocessor)
```

The model can now be built, as follows:

```
val vec = new Word2Vec.Builder()
   .minWordFrequency(5)
   .iterations(1)
   .layerSize(100)
   .seed(42)
   .windowSize(5)
   .iterate(iter)
   .tokenizerFactory(tokenizerFactory)
   .build
```

As mentioned earlier, we are using Word2Vec, so the model is built through the `Word2Vec.Builder` class (https://static.javadoc.io/org.deeplearning4j/ deeplearning4j-nlp/1.0.0-alpha/org/deeplearning4j/models/word2vec/Word2Vec. Builder.html), setting as tokenizer factory for the one created previously.

Let's start the model fitting:

```
vec.fit()
```

And save the word vectors in a file when finished, as follows:

```
WordVectorSerializer.writeWordVectors(vec, "wordVectors.txt")
```

The `WordVectorSerializer` utility class (https://static.javadoc.io/org. deeplearning4j/deeplearning4j-nlp/1.0.0-alpha/org/deeplearning4j/models/ embeddings/loader/WordVectorSerializer.html) handles word vector serialization and persistence.

The model can be tested this way:

```
val lst = vec.wordsNearest("house", 10)
 println("10 Words closest to 'house': " + lst)
```

The produced output is as follows:

```
Fitting the Word2Vec model....
Saving word vectors to text file....
10 Words closest to 'house': [office, company, family, country, life, program, court, center, market, second]
```

GloVe (https://en.wikipedia.org/wiki/GloVe_(machine_learning)), like Wor2Vec, is a model for distributed word representation, but it uses a different approach. While Word2Vec extracts the embeddings from a neural network that is designed to predict neighboring words, in GloVe the embeddings are optimized directly. This way the product of two-word vectors is equal to the logarithm of the number of times the two words occur near each other. For example, if the words *cat* and *mouse* occur near each other 20 times in a text, then *(vec(cat) * vec(mouse)) = log(20)*. The DL4J NLP library also provides a GloVe model implementation, GloVe.Builder (https://static.javadoc.io/org.deeplearning4j/deeplearning4j-nlp/1.0.0-alpha/org/deeplearning4j/models/glove/Glove.Builder.html). So, this example could be adapted for the GloVe model. The same file containing about 100,000 generic sentences used for the Word2Vec example is the input for this new one. The SentenceIterator and tokenization don't change (the same as for the Word2Vec example). What's different is the model to build, as follows:

```
val glove = new Glove.Builder()
    .iterate(iter)
    .tokenizerFactory(tokenizerFactory)
    .alpha(0.75)
    .learningRate(0.1)
    .epochs(25)
    .xMax(100)
    .batchSize(1000)
    .shuffle(true)
    .symmetric(true)
    .build
```

We can fit the model by invoking its fit method, as follows:

```
glove.fit()
```

After the fitting process completes, we can use model to do several things, such as find the similarity between two words, as follows:

```
val simD = glove.similarity("old", "new")
 println("old/new similarity: " + simD)
```

Or, find the *n* nearest words to a given one:

```
val words: util.Collection[String] = glove.wordsNearest("time", 10)
 println("Nearest words to 'time': " + words)
```

The output produced will look like this:

```
Load & Vectorize Sentences....
old/new similarity: 0.4553183913230896
Nearest words to 'time': [want, use, nt, who, work, have, do, much, our, you]
```

After seeing these last two examples, you are probably wondering which model, Word2Vec or GloVe, is better. There is no winner; it all depends on the data. It is possible to pick up one model and train it in a way that the encoded vectors at the end become specific for the domain of the use case scenario in which the model is working.

Hands-on NLP with TensorFlow

In this section, we are going to use TensorFlow (Python) to do DL sentiment analysis using the same *Large Movie Review Dataset* as for the first example in the previous section. Prerequisites for this example are Python 2.7.x, the PIP package manager, and Tensorflow. The *Importing Python Models in the JVM with DL4J* section in `Chapter 10`, *Deploying on a Distributed System*, covers the details of setting up the required tools. We are also going to use the TensorFlow hub library (`https://www.tensorflow.org/hub/`), which has been created for reusable ML modules. It needs to be installed through `pip`, as follows:

```
pip install tensorflow-hub
```

The example also requires the `pandas` (`https://pandas.pydata.org/`) data analysis library, as follows:

```
pip install pandas
```

Import the necessary modules:

```
import tensorflow as tf
 import tensorflow_hub as hub
 import os
 import pandas as pd
 import re
```

Next, we define a function to load all of the files from an input directory into a pandas DataFrame, as follows:

```
def load_directory_data(directory):
    data = {}
    data["sentence"] = []
    data["sentiment"] = []
    for file_path in os.listdir(directory):
      with tf.gfile.GFile(os.path.join(directory, file_path), "r") as f:
        data["sentence"].append(f.read())
        data["sentiment"].append(re.match("\d+_(\d+)\.txt",
file_path).group(1))
    return pd.DataFrame.from_dict(data)
```

Then, we define another function to merge the positive and negative reviews, add a column called `polarity`, and do some shuffling, as follows:

```
def load_dataset(directory):
    pos_df = load_directory_data(os.path.join(directory, "pos"))
    neg_df = load_directory_data(os.path.join(directory, "neg"))
    pos_df["polarity"] = 1
    neg_df["polarity"] = 0
    return pd.concat([pos_df, neg_df]).sample(frac=1).reset_index(drop=True)
```

Implement a third function to download the movie review dataset and use the `load_dataset` function to create the following training and test DataFrames:

```
def download_and_load_datasets(force_download=False):
    dataset = tf.keras.utils.get_file(
        fname="aclImdb.tar.gz",
origin="http://ai.stanford.edu/~amaas/data/sentiment/aclImdb_v1.tar.gz",
        extract=True)
    train_df = load_dataset(os.path.join(os.path.dirname(dataset),
                                      "aclImdb", "train"))
    test_df = load_dataset(os.path.join(os.path.dirname(dataset),
                                      "aclImdb", "test"))
    return train_df, test_df
```

This function downloads the datasets the first time the code is executed. Then, unless you delete them, the following executions get them from the local disk.

The two DataFrames are then created this way:

```
train_df, test_df = download_and_load_datasets()
```

We can also pretty-print the training DataFrame head to the console to check that everything went fine, as follows:

```
print(train_df.head())
```

The example output is as follows:

```
guglielmo@ubuntu:~/PythonCode/TensorFlow$ python ./tf-txtclassifier.py
                                              sentence sentiment   polarity
0   Oh what a condescending movie! Set in Los Ange...         2          0
1   Generally I like horror movies, but unfortunat...         1          0
2   It seems to me that Stephen King's "Bachman" p...         4          0
3   The film is very complete in what it is, keepi...         8          1
4   I'm in Iraq right now doing a job that gives p...         2          0
guglielmo@ubuntu:~/PythonCode/TensorFlow$
```

Now that we have the data, we can define the model. We are going to use the **Estimator** API (https://www.tensorflow.org/guide/estimators), a high-level TensorFlow API that has been introduced in the framework to simplify ML programming. *Estimator* provides some input functions that form the wrapper of the pandas DataFrames. So, we define the following function: `train_input_fn` to train on the whole training set with no limit on training epochs:

```
train_input_fn = tf.estimator.inputs.pandas_input_fn(
    train_df, train_df["polarity"], num_epochs=None, shuffle=True)
predict_train_input_fn
```

To do prediction on the whole training set execute the following:

```
predict_train_input_fn = tf.estimator.inputs.pandas_input_fn(
    train_df, train_df["polarity"], shuffle=False)
```

And we use `predict_test_input_fn` to do predictions on the test set:

```
predict_test_input_fn = tf.estimator.inputs.pandas_input_fn(
    test_df, test_df["polarity"], shuffle=False)
```

The TensorFlow hub library provides a feature column that applies a module on a given input text feature whose values are strings, and then passes the outputs of the module downstream. In this example, we are going to use the `nnlm-en-dim128` module (https://tfhub.dev/google/nnlm-en-dim128/1), which has been trained on the English Google News 200B corpus. The way we embed and use this module in our code is as follows:

```
embedded_text_feature_column = hub.text_embedding_column(
    key="sentence",
    module_spec="https://tfhub.dev/google/nnlm-en-dim128/1")
```

For classification purposes, we use a `DNNClassifier` (https://www.tensorflow.org/api_docs/python/tf/estimator/DNNClassifier) provided by the TensorFlow hub library. It extends `Estimator` (https://www.tensorflow.org/api_docs/python/tf/estimator/Estimator) and is a classifier for TensorFlow DNN models. So the `Estimator` in our example is created this way:

```
estimator = tf.estimator.DNNClassifier(
    hidden_units=[500, 100],
    feature_columns=[embedded_text_feature_column],
    n_classes=2,
    optimizer=tf.train.AdagradOptimizer(learning_rate=0.003))
```

Note that we are specifying `embedded_text_feature_column` as a feature column. The two hidden layers have `500` and `100` nodes respectively. `AdagradOptimizer` is the default optimizer for `DNNClassifier`.

The training of the model can be implemented with a single line of code, by invoking the `train` method of our `Estimator`, as follows:

```
estimator.train(input_fn=train_input_fn, steps=1000);
```

Given the size of the training dataset used for this example (25 KB), 1,000 steps is equivalent to five epochs (using the default batch size).

After the training has completed, we can then do predictions for the training dataset, as follows:

```
train_eval_result = estimator.evaluate(input_fn=predict_train_input_fn)
  print("Training set accuracy: {accuracy}".format(**train_eval_result))
```

And the test dataset as well, as follows:

```
test_eval_result = estimator.evaluate(input_fn=predict_test_input_fn)
  print("Test set accuracy: {accuracy}".format(**test_eval_result))
```

Here's the output of the application, showing the accuracy for both predictions:

```
Training set accuracy: 0.800639986992
Test set accuracy: 0.792360007763
Execution completed!
guglielmo@ubuntu:~/PythonCode/TensorFlow$
```

We can also do evaluation of the model and, as explained in Chapter 9, *Interpreting Neural Network Output*, in the *Evaluation for Classification* section, calculate the confusion matrix in order to understand the distribution of wrong classifications. Let's define a function to get the predictions first, as follows:

```
def get_predictions(estimator, input_fn):
    return [x["class_ids"][0] for x in estimator.predict(input_fn=input_fn)]
```

Now, create the confusion matrix starting on the training dataset, as follows:

```
with tf.Graph().as_default():
    cm = tf.confusion_matrix(train_df["polarity"],
                             get_predictions(estimator,
predict_train_input_fn))
    with tf.Session() as session:
        cm_out = session.run(cm)
```

And, normalize it to have each row sum equals to 1, as follows:

```
cm_out = cm_out.astype(float) / cm_out.sum(axis=1)[:, np.newaxis]
```

The output of the confusion matrix on screen will look like this:

```
[[0.78944 0.21056]
 [0.18728 0.81272]]
Execution completed!
guglielmo@ubuntu:~/PythonCode/TensorFlow$
```

However, you can also render it in a more elegant way using some chart library available in Python of your choice.

You have noticed that, while this code is compact and doesn't require advanced Python knowledge, it isn't an easy entry point for a starter in ML and DL, as TensorFlow implicitly requires a good knowledge of ML concepts in order to understand its API. Making a comparison with the DL4J API, you can tangibly feel this difference.

Hand-on NLP with Keras and a TensorFlow backend

As mentioned in `Chapter 10`, *Deploying on a Distributed System*, in the *Importing Python Models in the JVM with DL4J* section, when doing DL in Python, an alternative to TensorFlow is Keras. It can be used as a high-level API on top of a TensorFlow backed. In this section, we are going to learn how to do sentiment analysis in Keras, and finally we will make a comparison between this implementation and the previous one in TensorFlow.

We are going to use the exact same IMDB dataset (25,000 samples for training and 25,000 for test) as for the previous implementations through DL4J and TensorFlow. The prerequisites for this example are the same as for the TensorFlow example (Python 2.7.x, the PIP package manager, and Tensorflow), plus of course Keras. The Keras code module has that dataset built in:

```
from keras.datasets import imdb
```

So, we just need to set the vocabulary size and load the data from there, and not from any other external location, as follows:

```
vocabulary_size = 5000

(X_train, y_train), (X_test, y_test) = imdb.load_data(num_words = vocabulary_size)
```

At the end of the download, you can print a sample of the downloaded reviews for inspection purposes, as follows:

```
print('---review---')
print(X_train[6])
print('---label---')
print(y_train[6])
```

The output is shown as follows:

```
Loaded dataset with 25000 training samples, 25000 test samples
---review---
[1, 2, 365, 1234, 5, 1156, 354, 11, 14, 2, 2, 7, 1016, 2, 2, 356, 44, 4, 1349, 500, 746, 5, 200, 4, 4132, 11, 2, 2, 1117, 1831, 2, 5, 4831, 26, 6, 2, 4183, 17, 369,
37, 215, 1345, 143, 2, 5, 1838, 8, 1974, 15, 36, 119, 257, 85, 52, 486, 9, 6, 2, 2, 63, 271, 6, 196, 96, 949, 4121, 4, 2, 7, 4, 2212, 2436, 819, 63, 47, 77, 2, 180,
6, 227, 11, 94, 2494, 2, 13, 423, 4, 168, 7, 4, 22, 5, 89, 665, 71, 270, 56, 5, 13, 197, 12, 161, 2, 99, 76, 23, 2, 7, 419, 665, 40, 91, 85, 108, 7, 4, 2084, 5, 4773
, 81, 55, 52, 1901]
---label---
1
```

You can see that at this stage the reviews are stored as a sequence of integers, IDs that have been preassigned to single words. Also the label is an integer (0 means negative, 1 means positive). It is possible anyway to map the downloaded reviews back to their original words by using the dictionary returned by the `imdb.get_word_index()` method, as follows:

```
word2id = imdb.get_word_index()
  id2word = {i: word for word, i in word2id.items()}
  print('---review with words---')
  print([id2word.get(i, ' ') for i in X_train[6]])
  print('---label---')
  print(y_train[6])
```

```
---review with words---
[u'the', u'and', u'full', u'involving', u'to', u'impressive', u'boring', u'this', u'as', u'and', u'and', u'br', u'villain', u'and', u'and', u'need', u'has', u'of', u
'costumes', u'b', u'message', u'to', u'may', u'of', u'props', u'this', u'and', u'and', u'concept', u'issue', u'and', u'to', u'god's', u'he', u'is', u'and', u'unfolds
', u'movie', u'women', u'like', u'isn't', u'surely', u'i'm', u'and', u'to', u'toward', u'in', u'here's', u'for', u'from', u'did', u'having', u'because', u'very', u'q
uality', u'it', u'is', u'and', u'and', u'really', u'book', u'is', u'both', u'too', u'worked', u'carl', u'of', u'and', u'br', u'of', u'reviewer', u'closer', u'figure'
, u'really', u'there', u'will', u'and', u'things', u'is', u'far', u'this', u'make', u'mistakes', u'and', u'was', u'couldn't', u'of', u'few', u'br', u'of', u'you', u'
to', u'don't', u'female', u'than', u'place', u'she', u'to', u'was', u'between', u'that', u'nothing', u'and', u'movies', u'get', u'are', u'and', u'br', u'yes', u'fema
le', u'just', u'its', u'because', u'many', u'br', u'of', u'overly', u'to', u'descent', u'people', u'time', u'very', u'bland']
---label---
1
```

In the preceding screenshot, you can see the returned dictionary of the words used in the input reviews. We are going to use an RNN model for this example. In order to feed data to it, all the inputs should have the same length. Looking at the maximum and minimum lengths of the downloaded reviews (following is the code to get this info and its output):

```
print('Maximum review length: {}'.format(
  len(max((X_train + X_test), key=len))))
  print('Minimum review length: {}'.format(
  len(min((X_test + X_test), key=len))))
```

The output is shown as follows:

```
Maximum review length: 2697
Minimum review length: 14
```

We can see that they don't have all the same length. So, we need to limit the maximum review length to, let's say, 500 words by truncating the longer reviews and padding the shorter ones with zeros. This can be done through the `sequence.pad_sequences` Keras function, as follows:

```
from keras.preprocessing import sequence

max_words = 500
X_train = sequence.pad_sequences(X_train, maxlen=max_words)
X_test = sequence.pad_sequences(X_test, maxlen=max_words)
```

Let's design the RNN model, as follows:

```
from keras import Sequential
 from keras.layers import Embedding, LSTM, Dense, Dropout

 embedding_size=32
 model=Sequential()
 model.add(Embedding(vocabulary_size, embedding_size,
input_length=max_words))
 model.add(LSTM(100))
 model.add(Dense(1, activation='sigmoid'))
```

It is a simple RNN model, with three layers, embedding, LSTM, and dense, as follows:

Layer (type)	Output Shape	Param #
embedding_1 (Embedding)	(None, 500, 32)	160000
lstm_1 (LSTM)	(None, 100)	53200
dense_1 (Dense)	(None, 1)	101

Total params: 213,301
Trainable params: 213,301
Non-trainable params: 0

The input for this model is a sequence of integer word IDs with a maximum length of 500, and its output is a binary label (0 or 1).

The configuration of the learning process for this model can be done through its `compile` method, as follows:

```
model.compile(loss='binary_crossentropy',
              optimizer='adam',
              metrics=['accuracy'])
```

After setting up the batch size and number of training epochs, as follows:

```
batch_size = 64
 num_epochs = 3
```

We can start the training, as follows:

```
X_valid, y_valid = X_train[:batch_size], y_train[:batch_size]
 X_train2, y_train2 = X_train[batch_size:], y_train[batch_size:]

 model.fit(X_train2, y_train2, validation_data=(X_valid, y_valid),
batch_size=batch_size, epochs=num_epochs)
```

```
Train on 24936 samples, validate on 64 samples
Epoch 1/3
2018-10-15 02:31:00.401234: I tensorflow/core/platform/cpu_feature_guard.cc:141] Your CPU supports instructions that this Tenso
FMA
24936/24936 [==============================] - 162s 7ms/step - loss: 0.4380 - acc: 0.7911 - val_loss: 0.1959 - val_acc: 0.9219
Epoch 2/3
24936/24936 [==============================] - 162s 7ms/step - loss: 0.2821 - acc: 0.8880 - val_loss: 0.1710 - val_acc: 0.9219
Epoch 3/3
24936/24936 [==============================] - 166s 7ms/step - loss: 0.2373 - acc: 0.9083 - val_loss: 0.2135 - val_acc: 0.9375
```

When the training completes, we can evaluate the model to assess its level of accuracy using the test dataset, as follows:

```
scores = model.evaluate(X_test, y_test, verbose=0)
 print('Test accuracy:', scores[1])
```

```
Epoch 3/3
24936/24936 [==================
('Test accuracy:', 0.87308)
```

Looking at the code of this example, you should have noticed that it is more high-level if than the previous example with TensorFlow, and that the focus at development time is mostly on the specific problem model implementation details rather than the ML/DL mechanisms behind it.

Hands-on NLP with Keras model import into DL4J

In `Chapter 10`, *Deploying on a Distributed System, Importing Python Models in the JVM with DL4J* section, we learned how to import existing Keras models into DL4J and use them to make predictions or re-train them in a JVM-based environment.

This applies to the model we implemented and trained in the *Hand-on NLP with Keras and TensorFlow backend* section in Python, using Keras with a TensorFlow backed. We need to modify the code for that example to serialize the model in HDF5 format by doing the following:

```
model.save('sa_rnn.h5')
```

The `sa_rnn.h5` file produced needs to be copied into the resource folder for the Scala project to be implemented. The dependencies for the project are the DataVec API, the DL4J core, ND4J, and the DL4J model import library.

We need to import and transform the Large Movie Review database as explained in section 12.1, in case we want to retrain the model through DL4J. Then, we need to import the Keras model programmatically, as follows:

```
val saRnn = new ClassPathResource("sa_rnn.h5").getFile.getPath
val model = KerasModelImport.importKerasSequentialModelAndWeights(saRnn)
```

Finally, we can start to do predictions by invoking the `predict` method of `model` (which is an instance of `MultiLayerNetwork`, as usual in DL4J), passing the input data as an ND4J DataSet (`https://static.javadoc.io/org.nd4j/nd4j-api/1.0.0-alpha/org/nd4j/linalg/dataset/api/DataSet.html`).

Summary

This chapter closes the explanation of the NLP implementation process with Scala. In this chapter and the previous one, we evaluated different frameworks for this programming language, and the pros and cons of each have been detailed. In this chapter, the focus has been mostly on a DL approach to NLP. For that, some Python alternatives have been presented, and the potential integration of those Python models in a JVM context with the DL4J framework has been highlighted. At this stage, a reader should be able to accurately evaluate what will be the best fit for his/her particular NLP use case.

Starting from the next chapter, we will learn more about convolution and how CNNs apply to image recognition problems. Image recognition will be explained by presenting different implementations using different frameworks, including DL4J, Keras, and TensorFlow.

13
Convolution

The previous two chapters have covered real use case implementation of NLP done through RNNs/LSTMs in Apache Spark. In this and the following chapter, we are going to do something similar for CNNs: we are going to explore how they can be used in image recognition and classification. This chapter in particular covers the following topics:

- A quick recap on what convolution is, from both the mathematical and DL perspectives
- The challenges and strategies for object recognition in real-world problems
- How convolution applies to image recognition and a walk-through of hands-on practical implementations of an image recognition use case through DL (CNNs) by adopting the same approach, but using the following two different open source frameworks and programming languages:
    - Keras (with a TensorFlow backend) in Python
    - DL4J (and ND4J) in Scala

Convolution

Chapter 5, *Convolutional Neural Networks*, covered the theory behind CNNs, and convolution of course has been part of that presentation. Let's do a recap of this concept from a mathematical and practical perspective before moving on to object recognition. In mathematics, convolution is an operation on two functions that produces a third function, which is the result of the integral of the product between the first two, one of which is flipped:

$$[f * g](t) = \int_0^t f(\tau)g(t - \tau)d\tau$$

Convolution is heavily used in 2D image processing and signal filtering.

To better understand what happens behind the scenes, here's a simple Python code example of 1D convolution with NumPy (http://www.numpy.org/):

```python
import numpy as np

x = np.array([1, 2, 3, 4, 5])
y = np.array([1, -2, 2])
result = np.convolve(x, y)
print result
```

This produces the following result:

```
>>> import numpy as np
>>> x = np.array([1, 2, 3, 4, 5])
>>> y = np.array([1, -2, 2])
>>> result = np.convolve(x, y)
>>> print result
[ 1  0  1  2  3 -2 10]
```

Let's see how the convolution between the x and y arrays produces that result. The first thing the convolve function does is to horizontally flip the y array:

[1, -2, 2] becomes [2, -2, 1]

Then, the flipped y array slides over the x array:

```
Step 1)
    1 2 3 4 5                        1 x 1 = 1

2-2 1

Step 2)
    1 2 3 4 5                        (1 x -2) + (2 x 1) = 0

  2-2 1

Step 3)
    1 2 3 4 5                        (1 x 2) + (2 x -2) + (3 x 1) = 1

    2-2 1

Step 4)
    1 2 3 4 5                        (2 x 2) + (3 x -2) + (4 x 1) = 2

      2-2 1

Step 5)
    1 2 3 4 5                        (3 x 2) + (4 x -2) + (5 x 1) = 3

        2-2 1

Step 6)
    1 2 3 4 5                        (4 x 2) + (5 x -2) = -2

          2-2 1

Step 7)
    1 2 3 4 5                        5 x 2 = 10

            2 -2 1
```

That's how the `result` array [1   0   1   2   3 -2 10] is generated.

2D convolution happens with a similar mechanism. Here's a simple Python code example with NumPy:

```
import numpy as np
from scipy import signal

a = np.matrix('1 3 1; 0 -1 1; 2 2 -1')
print(a)
w = np.matrix('1 2; 0 -1')
print(w)

f = signal.convolve2d(a, w)
print(f)
```

This time, the SciPy (https://www.scipy.org/) signal.convolve2d function is used to do the convolution. The result of the preceding code is as follows:

```
>>> f = signal.convolve2d(a, w)
>>> print(f)
[[ 1  5  7  2]
 [ 0 -2 -4  1]
 [ 2  6  4 -3]
 [ 0 -2 -2  1]]
>>>
```

When the flipped matrix is totally inside the input matrix, the results are called valid convolutions. It is possible to calculate the 2D convolution, getting only the valid results this way, as follows:

```
f = signal.convolve2d(a, w, 'valid')
```

This will give output as follows:

```
>>> f = signal.convolve2d(a, w, 'valid')
>>> print(f)
[[-2 -4]
 [ 6  4]]
```

Here's how those results are calculated. First, the w array is flipped:

$$\begin{bmatrix} 1 & 2 \\ 0 & -1 \end{bmatrix}_{\text{becomes}} \begin{bmatrix} -1 & 0 \\ 2 & 1 \end{bmatrix}$$

Then, the same as for the 1D convolution, each window of the a matrix is multiplied, element by element, with the flipped w matrix, and the results are finally summed as follows:

$$\begin{bmatrix} 1 & 3 \\ 0 & -1 \end{bmatrix} \quad (1 \text{ x } -1) + (0 \text{ x } 3) + (0 \text{ x } 2) + (-1 \text{ x } 1) = -2$$

$$\begin{bmatrix} 3 & 1 \\ -1 & 1 \end{bmatrix} \quad (3 \text{ x } -1) + (1 \text{ x } 0) + (-1 \text{ x } 2) + (1 \text{ x } 1) = -4$$

And so on.

Object recognition strategies

This section presents different computational techniques used in implementing the automated recognition of objects in digital images. Let's start by giving a definition of object recognition. In a nutshell, it is the task of finding and labeling parts of a 2D image of a scene that correspond to objects inside that scene. The following screenshot shows an example of object recognition performed manually by a human using a pencil:

Figure 13.1: An example of manual object detection

The image has been marked and labeled to show fruits recognizable as a banana and a pumpkin. This is exactly the same as what happens for calculated object recognition; it can be simply thought of as the process of drawing lines and outlining areas of an image, and finally attaching to each structure a label corresponding to the model that best represents it.

A combination of factors, such as the semantics of a scene context or information present in the image, must be used in object recognition. Context is particularly important when interpreting images. Let's first have a look at the following screenshot:

Figure 13.2: Object in isolation (no context)

It is nearly impossible to identify in isolation the object in the center of that image. Let's have a look now at the following screenshot, where the same object appears in the position as it had in the original image:

Figure 13.3: The object from figure 13.2 in its original context

Providing no further information, it is still difficult to identify that object, but not as difficult as for *Figure 13.2*. Given context information that the image in the preceding screenshot is a circuit board, the initial object is more easily recognized as a polarized capacitor. Cultural context plays a key role in enabling the proper interpretation of a scene.

Let's now consider a second example (shown in the following screenshot), a consistent 3D image of a stairwell:

Figure 13.4: A consistent 3D image showing a stairwell

By changing the light in that image, the final result could make it harder for the eye (and also a computer) to see a consistent 3D image (as shown in the following screenshot):

Figure 13.5: The result of applying a different light to the image in figure 13.4

Compared with the original image (*Figure 13.3*) its brightness and contrast have been modified (as shown in the following screenshot):

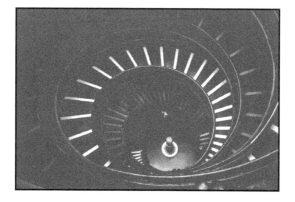

Figure 13.6: The image in figure 13.3 with changed brightness and contrast

The eye can still recognize three-dimensional steps. However, using different brightness and contrast values to the original image looks as shown in following screenshot:

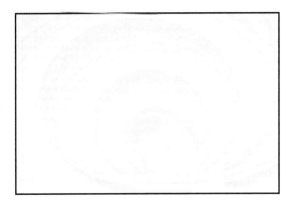

Figure 13.7: The image in figure 13.3 with different brightness and contrast

It is almost impossible to recognize the same image. What we have learned is that although the retouched image in the previous screenshot retains a significant part of the important visual information in the original one (*Figure 13.3*), the images in *Figure 13.4* and the preceding screenshot became less interpretable because of the 3D details that have been removed by retouching them. The examples presented provide evidence that computers (like human eyes) need appropriate context models in order to successfully complete object recognition and scene interpretation.

Computational strategies for object recognition can be classified based on their suitability for complex image data or for complex models. Data complexity in a digital image corresponds to its signal-to-noise ratio. An image with semantic ambiguity corresponds to complex (or noisy) data. Data consisting of perfect outlines of model instances throughout an image is called simple. Image data with poor resolution, noise, or other kinds of anomalies, or with easily confused false model instances, is referred to as complex. Model complexity is indicated by the level of detail in the data structures in an image, and in the techniques required to determine the form of the data. If a model is defined by a simple criterion (such as a single shape template or the optimization of a single function implicitly containing a shape model), then no other context may be needed to attach model labels to a given scene. But, in cases where many atomic model components must be assembled or some way hierarchically related to establish the existence of the desired model instance, complex data structures and non-trivial techniques are required.

Based on the previous definitions, object recognition strategies can then be classified into four main categories, as follows:

- **Feature vector classification**: This relies on a trivial model of an object's image characteristics. Typically, it is applied only to simple data.
- **Fitting model to photometry**: This is applied when simple models are sufficient but the photometric data of an image is noisy and ambiguous.
- **Fitting model to symbolic structures**: Applied when complex models are required, but reliable symbolic structures can be accurately inferred from simple data. These approaches look for instances of objects by matching data structures that represent relationships between globally object parts.
- **Combined strategies**: Applied when both data and desired model instances are complex.

The implementation of the available API to build and train CNNs for object recognition provided by the major open source frameworks detailed in this book have been done keeping these considerations and strategies in mind. While those APIs are very high-level, the same mindset should be taken when choosing the proper combination of hidden layers for a model.

Convolution applied to image recognition

In this section, we are now going hands-on by implementing an image recognition model, taking into account the considerations discussed in the first part of this chapter. We are going to implement the same use case using two different frameworks and programming languages.

Keras implementation

The first implementation of object recognition we are going to do is in Python and involves the Keras framework. To train and evaluate the model, we are going to use a public dataset called CIFAR-10 (`http://www.cs.toronto.edu/~kriz/cifar.html`). It consists of 60,000 (50,000 for training and 10,000 for testing) small (32 x 32 pixels) color images divided into 10 classes (airplane, automobile, bird, cat, deer, dog, frog, horse, ship, and truck). These 10 classes are mutually exclusive. The CIFAR-10 dataset (163 MB) is freely downloadable from `http://www.cs.toronto.edu/~kriz/cifar-10-python.tar.gz`.

The prerequisites for this implementation are Python 2.7.x, Keras, TensorFlow (it is used as the Keras backend), NumPy, and `scikit-learn` (http://scikit-learn.org/stable/index.html), an open source tool for ML. Chapter 10, *Deploying on a Distributed System*, covers the details to set up the Python environment for Keras and TensorFlow. `scikit-learn` can be installed as follows:

```
sudo pip install scikit-learn
```

First of all, we need to import all of the necessary NumPy, Keras, and `scikit-learn` namespaces and classes, as follows:

```
import numpy as np
from keras.models import Sequential
from keras.layers import Dense
from keras.layers import Dropout
from keras.layers import Flatten
from keras.constraints import maxnorm
from keras.optimizers import SGD
from keras.layers.convolutional import Conv2D
from keras.layers.convolutional import MaxPooling2D
from keras.utils import np_utils
from keras.datasets import cifar10
from keras import backend as K
from sklearn.model_selection import train_test_split
```

Now, we need to load the CIFAR-10 dataset. No need to download it separately; Keras provides a facility to download it programmatically, as follows:

```
K.set_image_dim_ordering('th')
  (X_train, y_train), (X_test, y_test) = cifar10.load_data()
```

The `load_data` function downloads it the first time it is executed. Successive runs will use the dataset already downloaded locally.

We initialize the `seed` with a constant value, in order to ensure that the results are then reproducible, as follows:

```
seed = 7
  np.random.seed(seed)
```

The pixel values for the input datasets are in the range 0 to 255 (for each of the RGB channels). We can normalize this data to a range from 0 to 1 by dividing the values by 255.0, then doing the following:

```
X_train = X_train.astype('float32')
 X_test = X_test.astype('float32')

 X_train = X_train / 255.0
 X_test = X_test / 255.0
```

We can hot encode the output variables to transform them into a binary matrix (it could be a one-hot encoding, because they are defined as vectors of integers in the range between 0 and 1 for each of the 10 classes), as follows:

```
y_train = np_utils.to_categorical(y_train)
 y_test = np_utils.to_categorical(y_test)
 num_classes = y_test.shape[1]
```

Let's start the model implementation. Let's start by implementing a simple CNN first, verify its accuracy level and, if the case, we will go to make the model more complex. The following is a possible first implementation:

```
model = Sequential()
model.add(Conv2D(32,(3,3), input_shape = (3,32,32), padding = 'same',
activation = 'relu'))
model.add(Dropout(0.2))
model.add(Conv2D(32,(3,3), padding = 'same', activation = 'relu'))
model.add(MaxPooling2D(pool_size=(2,2)))
model.add(Conv2D(64,(3,3), padding = 'same', activation = 'relu'))
model.add(MaxPooling2D(pool_size=(2,2)))
model.add(Flatten())
model.add(Dropout(0.2))
model.add(Dense(512,activation='relu',kernel_constraint=maxnorm(3)))
model.add(Dropout(0.2))
model.add(Dense(num_classes, activation='softmax'))
```

You can see the model layer details at runtime in the console output before the training starts (see the following screenshot):

Layer (type)	Output Shape	Param #
conv2d_1 (Conv2D)	(None, 32, 32, 32)	896
dropout_1 (Dropout)	(None, 32, 32, 32)	0
conv2d_2 (Conv2D)	(None, 32, 32, 32)	9248
max_pooling2d_1 (MaxPooling2	(None, 32, 16, 16)	0
conv2d_3 (Conv2D)	(None, 64, 16, 16)	18496
max_pooling2d_2 (MaxPooling2	(None, 64, 8, 8)	0
flatten_1 (Flatten)	(None, 4096)	0
dropout_2 (Dropout)	(None, 4096)	0
dense_1 (Dense)	(None, 512)	2097664
dropout_3 (Dropout)	(None, 512)	0
dense_2 (Dense)	(None, 10)	5130

Total params: 2,131,434
Trainable params: 2,131,434
Non-trainable params: 0

The model is a `Sequential` model. As we can see from the preceding output, the input layer is convolutional, with 32 feature maps of size 3 x 3 and a **Rectified Linear Unit (ReLU)** activation function. After applying a 20% dropout to the input to reduce overfitting, the following layer is a second convolutional layer with the same characteristics as the input layer. Then, we set a max pooling layer of size 2 x 2. After it, there is a third convolutional layer with 64 feature maps of size 3 x 3 and a ReLU activation function, and a second max pooling layer of size 2 x 2 is set. After this second max pooling, we put a flattened layer and apply a 20% dropout, before sending the output to the next layer, which is a fully connected layer with 512 units and a ReLU activation function. We apply another 20% dropout before the output layer, which is another fully-connected layer with 10 units and a softmax activation function.

We can now define the following training properties (number of epochs, learning rate, weight decay, and optimizer, which for this specific case has been set as a **Stochastic Gradient Descent (SGD)**:

```
epochs = 25
  lrate = 0.01
  decay = lrate/epochs
  sgd = SGD(lr=lrate, momentum=0.9, decay=decay, nesterov=False)
```

Configure the training process for the model, as follows:

```
model.compile(loss='categorical_crossentropy', optimizer=sgd,
metrics=['accuracy'])
```

The training can be now started, using the CIFAR-10 training data, as follows:

```
model.fit(X_train, y_train, validation_data=(X_test, y_test),
epochs=epochs, batch_size=32)
```

When it completes, the evaluation can be done using the CIFAR-10 test data, as follows:

```
scores = model.evaluate(X_test,y_test,verbose=0)
  print("Accuracy: %.2f%%" % (scores[1]*100))
```

The accuracy of this model is around 75%, as can be seen in the following screenshot:

```
Epoch 21/25
50000/50000 [==============================] - 426s 9ms/step - loss: 0.1879 - acc: 0.9318 - val_loss: 0.8800 - val_acc: 0.7484
Epoch 22/25
50000/50000 [==============================] - 427s 9ms/step - loss: 0.1728 - acc: 0.9397 - val_loss: 0.9243 - val_acc: 0.7470
Epoch 23/25
50000/50000 [==============================] - 427s 9ms/step - loss: 0.1676 - acc: 0.9419 - val_loss: 0.9170 - val_acc: 0.7498
Epoch 24/25
50000/50000 [==============================] - 429s 9ms/step - loss: 0.1580 - acc: 0.9451 - val_loss: 0.9065 - val_acc: 0.7500
Epoch 25/25
50000/50000 [==============================] - 425s 8ms/step - loss: 0.1497 - acc: 0.9485 - val_loss: 0.9329 - val_acc: 0.7500
Accuracy: 75.00%
```

Not a great result then. We have executed the training on 25 epochs, which is a small number. So, the accuracy will improve when training for a greater number of epochs. But, let's see first whether things can be improved by making changes to the CNN model, making it deeper. Add two extra imports, as follows:

```
from keras.layers import Activation
  from keras.layers import BatchNormalization
```

The only change to the code implemented previously is for the network model. Here's the new one:

```
model = Sequential()
model.add(Conv2D(32, (3,3), padding='same', input_shape=x_train.shape[1:]))
model.add(Activation('elu'))
model.add(BatchNormalization())
model.add(Conv2D(32, (3,3), padding='same'))
model.add(Activation('elu'))
model.add(BatchNormalization())
model.add(MaxPooling2D(pool_size=(2,2)))
model.add(Dropout(0.2))

model.add(Conv2D(64, (3,3), padding='same'))
model.add(Activation('elu'))
model.add(BatchNormalization())
model.add(Conv2D(64, (3,3), padding='same'))
model.add(Activation('elu'))
model.add(BatchNormalization())
model.add(MaxPooling2D(pool_size=(2,2)))
model.add(Dropout(0.3))

model.add(Conv2D(128, (3,3), padding='same'))
model.add(Activation('elu'))
model.add(BatchNormalization())
model.add(Conv2D(128, (3,3), padding='same'))
model.add(Activation('elu'))
model.add(BatchNormalization())
model.add(MaxPooling2D(pool_size=(2,2)))
model.add(Dropout(0.4))

model.add(Flatten())
model.add(Dense(num_classes, activation='softmax'))
```

Basically, what we have done is to repeat the same pattern, each one with a different number of feature maps (32, 64, and 128). The advantage of adding layers is that each of them will learn features at different levels of abstraction. In our case, training a CNN to recognize objects, we can check that the first layer trains itself to recognize basic things (for example, the edges of objects), the next one trains itself to recognize shapes (which can be considered as collections of edges), the following layer trains itself to recognize collections of shapes (with reference to the CIFAR-10 dataset, they could be legs, wings, tails, and so on), and the following layer learns higher-order features (objects). Multiple layers are better because they can learn all the intermediate features between the input (raw data) and the high-level classification:

Layer (type)	Output Shape	Param #
conv2d_1 (Conv2D)	(None, 32, 32, 32)	896
activation_1 (Activation)	(None, 32, 32, 32)	0
batch_normalization_1 (Batch	(None, 32, 32, 32)	128
conv2d_2 (Conv2D)	(None, 32, 32, 32)	9248
activation_2 (Activation)	(None, 32, 32, 32)	0
batch_normalization_2 (Batch	(None, 32, 32, 32)	128
max_pooling2d_1 (MaxPooling2	(None, 32, 16, 16)	0
dropout_1 (Dropout)	(None, 32, 16, 16)	0
conv2d_3 (Conv2D)	(None, 64, 16, 16)	18496
activation_3 (Activation)	(None, 64, 16, 16)	0
batch_normalization_3 (Batch	(None, 64, 16, 16)	64
conv2d_4 (Conv2D)	(None, 64, 16, 16)	36928
activation_4 (Activation)	(None, 64, 16, 16)	0
batch_normalization_4 (Batch	(None, 64, 16, 16)	64
max_pooling2d_2 (MaxPooling2	(None, 64, 8, 8)	0
dropout_2 (Dropout)	(None, 64, 8, 8)	0
conv2d_5 (Conv2D)	(None, 128, 8, 8)	73856
activation_5 (Activation)	(None, 128, 8, 8)	0
batch_normalization_5 (Batch	(None, 128, 8, 8)	32
conv2d_6 (Conv2D)	(None, 128, 8, 8)	147584
activation_6 (Activation)	(None, 128, 8, 8)	0
batch_normalization_6 (Batch	(None, 128, 8, 8)	32
max_pooling2d_3 (MaxPooling2	(None, 128, 4, 4)	0
dropout_3 (Dropout)	(None, 128, 4, 4)	0
flatten_1 (Flatten)	(None, 2048)	0
dense_1 (Dense)	(None, 10)	20490

```
Total params: 307,946
Trainable params: 307,722
Non-trainable params: 224
```

Running the training again and doing the evaluation for this new model, the result, is `80.57%`:

```
Accuracy: 80.57%
Application end.
```

This is a sensible improvement compared to the previous model, and considering that we are still running 25 epochs only. But, let's see now if we can improve more by doing image data augmentation. Looking at the training dataset, we can see that the objects in the images change their position. Typically, in a dataset, images have a variety of conditions (different brightness, orientation, and so on). We need to address these situations by training a neural network with additional modified data. Consider the following simple example, a training dataset of car images with two classes only, Volkswagen Beetle and Porsche Targa. Assume that all of the Volkswagen Beetle cars are aligned to the left, such as in the following screenshot:

Figure 13.8: Volkswagen Beetle training image

However, all of the Porsche Targa cars are aligned to the right, such as in the following screenshot:

Figure 13.9: Porsche Targa training image

After completing the training and reaching a high accuracy (90 or 95%), feeding the model with an image such as the following screenshot:

Figure 13.10: Volkswagen Beetle input image

There is a concrete risk that this car is classified as a Porsche Targa. In order to prevent situations such as this, we need to reduce the number of irrelevant features in the training dataset. With reference to this car example, one thing we can do is to horizontally flip the training dataset images, so that they face the other way. After training the neural network again on this new dataset, the performance of the model is more likely to be what is expected. Data augmentation could happen offline (which is suitable for small datasets) or online (which is suitable for large datasets, because transformations apply on the mini-batches that feed the model). Let's try the programmatic online data augmentation of the training dataset for the latest implementation of a model for this section's example, using the `ImageDataGenerator` class from Keras, as follows:

```
from keras.preprocessing.image import ImageDataGenerator

datagen = ImageDataGenerator(
    rotation_range=15,
    width_shift_range=0.1,
    height_shift_range=0.1,
    horizontal_flip=True,
    )
datagen.fit(X_train)
```

And the using it when fitting the model, as follows:

```
batch_size = 64

model.fit_generator(datagen.flow(X_train, y_train, batch_size=batch_size),\
                steps_per_epoch=X_train.shape[0] //
batch_size,epochs=125,\
verbose=1,validation_data=(X_test,y_test),callbacks=[LearningRateScheduler(
lr_schedule)])
```

One more thing to do before starting the training is to apply a kernel regularizer (https://keras.io/regularizers/) to the convolutional layers of our model, as follows:

```
weight_decay = 1e-4
model = Sequential()
model.add(Conv2D(32, (3,3), padding='same',
kernel_regularizer=regularizers.l2(weight_decay),
input_shape=X_train.shape[1:]))
model.add(Activation('elu'))
model.add(BatchNormalization())
model.add(Conv2D(32, (3,3), padding='same',
kernel_regularizer=regularizers.l2(weight_decay)))
model.add(Activation('elu'))
model.add(BatchNormalization())
model.add(MaxPooling2D(pool_size=(2,2)))
model.add(Dropout(0.2))

model.add(Conv2D(64, (3,3), padding='same',
kernel_regularizer=regularizers.l2(weight_decay)))
model.add(Activation('elu'))
model.add(BatchNormalization())
model.add(Conv2D(64, (3,3), padding='same',
kernel_regularizer=regularizers.l2(weight_decay)))
model.add(Activation('elu'))
model.add(BatchNormalization())
model.add(MaxPooling2D(pool_size=(2,2)))
model.add(Dropout(0.3))

model.add(Conv2D(128, (3,3), padding='same',
kernel_regularizer=regularizers.l2(weight_decay)))
model.add(Activation('elu'))
model.add(BatchNormalization())
model.add(Conv2D(128, (3,3), padding='same',
kernel_regularizer=regularizers.l2(weight_decay)))
model.add(Activation('elu'))
model.add(BatchNormalization())
model.add(MaxPooling2D(pool_size=(2,2)))
model.add(Dropout(0.4))

model.add(Flatten())
model.add(Dense(num_classes, activation='softmax'))
```

Regularizers allow us to apply penalties (which are incorporated into the loss function) on layer parameters during network optimization.

After these code changes, train the model with a still relatively small number of epochs (64) and basic image data augmentation. The following screenshot shows that the accuracy improves to almost 84%:

```
703/703 [===============================] - 786
Accuracy: 83.57%
Application end.
```

By training for a greater number of epochs, the accuracy of the model could increase up to around 90 or 91%.

DL4J implementation

The second implementation of object recognition we are going to do is in Scala and involves the DL4J framework. To train and evaluate the model, we are still going to use the CIFAR-10 dataset. The dependencies for this project are a DataVec data image, DL4J, NN, and ND4J, plus Guava 19.0 and Apache commons math 3.4.

If you look at the CIFAR-10 dataset download page (see the following screenshot), you can see that there are specific archives available for the Python, MatLab, and C programming languages, but not for Scala or Java:

Download

Version	Size	md5sum
CIFAR-100 python version	161 MB	eb9058c3a382ffc7106e4002c42a8d85
CIFAR-100 Matlab version	175 MB	6a4bfa1dcd5c9453dda6bb54194911f4
CIFAR-100 binary version (suitable for C programs)	161 MB	03b5dce01913d631647c71ecec9e9cb8

Figure 13.11: The CIFAR-10 dataset download page

There's no need to separately download and then convert the dataset for our Scala application; the DL4J dataset library provides the `org.deeplearning4j.datasets.iterator.impl.CifarDataSetIterator` iterator to get the training and test datasets programmatically, as follows:

```
val trainDataSetIterator =
              new CifarDataSetIterator(2, 5000, true)
val testDataSetIterator =
              new CifarDataSetIterator(2, 200, false)
```

The `CifarDataSetIterator` constructor expects three arguments: the number of batches, the number of samples, and a Boolean to specify whether the dataset is for training (`true`) or test (`false`).

We can now define the neural network. We implement a function to configure the model, as follows:

```
def defineModelConfiguration(): MultiLayerConfiguration =
    new NeuralNetConfiguration.Builder()
        .seed(seed)
        .cacheMode(CacheMode.DEVICE)
        .updater(new Adam(1e-2))
        .biasUpdater(new Adam(1e-2*2))
        .gradientNormalization(GradientNormalization.RenormalizeL2PerLayer)
.optimizationAlgo(OptimizationAlgorithm.STOCHASTIC_GRADIENT_DESCENT)
        .l1(1e-4)
        .l2(5 * 1e-4)
        .list
        .layer(0, new ConvolutionLayer.Builder(Array(4, 4), Array(1, 1),
Array(0, 0)).name("cnn1").convolutionMode(ConvolutionMode.Same)
.nIn(3).nOut(64).weightInit(WeightInit.XAVIER_UNIFORM).activation(Activatio
n.RELU)
            .biasInit(1e-2).build)
        .layer(1, new ConvolutionLayer.Builder(Array(4, 4), Array(1, 1),
Array(0, 0)).name("cnn2").convolutionMode(ConvolutionMode.Same)
.nOut(64).weightInit(WeightInit.XAVIER_UNIFORM).activation(Activation.RELU)
            .biasInit(1e-2).build)
        .layer(2, new SubsamplingLayer.Builder(PoolingType.MAX,
Array(2,2)).name("maxpool2").build())

        .layer(3, new ConvolutionLayer.Builder(Array(4, 4), Array(1, 1),
Array(0, 0)).name("cnn3").convolutionMode(ConvolutionMode.Same)
.nOut(96).weightInit(WeightInit.XAVIER_UNIFORM).activation(Activation.RELU)
            .biasInit(1e-2).build)
        .layer(4, new ConvolutionLayer.Builder(Array(4, 4), Array(1, 1),
Array(0, 0)).name("cnn4").convolutionMode(ConvolutionMode.Same)
.nOut(96).weightInit(WeightInit.XAVIER_UNIFORM).activation(Activation.RELU)
            .biasInit(1e-2).build)

        .layer(5, new ConvolutionLayer.Builder(Array(3,3), Array(1, 1),
Array(0, 0)).name("cnn5").convolutionMode(ConvolutionMode.Same)
.nOut(128).weightInit(WeightInit.XAVIER_UNIFORM).activation(Activation.RELU
)
            .biasInit(1e-2).build)
        .layer(6, new ConvolutionLayer.Builder(Array(3,3), Array(1, 1),
Array(0, 0)).name("cnn6").convolutionMode(ConvolutionMode.Same)
.nOut(128).weightInit(WeightInit.XAVIER_UNIFORM).activation(Activation.RELU
```

```
)
            .biasInit(1e-2).build)

        .layer(7, new ConvolutionLayer.Builder(Array(2,2), Array(1, 1),
Array(0, 0)).name("cnn7").convolutionMode(ConvolutionMode.Same)
.nOut(256).weightInit(WeightInit.XAVIER_UNIFORM).activation(Activation.RELU
)
            .biasInit(1e-2).build)
        .layer(8, new ConvolutionLayer.Builder(Array(2,2), Array(1, 1),
Array(0, 0)).name("cnn8").convolutionMode(ConvolutionMode.Same)
.nOut(256).weightInit(WeightInit.XAVIER_UNIFORM).activation(Activation.RELU
)
            .biasInit(1e-2).build)
        .layer(9, new SubsamplingLayer.Builder(PoolingType.MAX,
Array(2,2)).name("maxpool8").build())

        .layer(10, new
DenseLayer.Builder().name("ffn1").nOut(1024).updater(new
Adam(1e-3)).biasInit(1e-3).biasUpdater(new Adam(1e-3*2)).build)
        .layer(11,new
DropoutLayer.Builder().name("dropout1").dropOut(0.2).build)
        .layer(12, new
DenseLayer.Builder().name("ffn2").nOut(1024).biasInit(1e-2).build)
        .layer(13,new
DropoutLayer.Builder().name("dropout2").dropOut(0.2).build)
        .layer(14, new
OutputLayer.Builder(LossFunctions.LossFunction.NEGATIVELOGLIKELIHOOD)
            .name("output")
            .nOut(numLabels)
            .activation(Activation.SOFTMAX)
            .build)
        .backprop(true)
        .pretrain(false)
        .setInputType(InputType.convolutional(height, width, channels))
        .build
```

All the exact same considerations as for the model implemented in the *Keras implementation* section apply here. So, we are skipping all the intermediate steps and directly implementing a complex model, as shown in following screenshot:

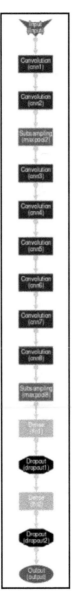

Figure 13.12: The graphical representation of the model for this section's example

These are the details of the model:

Layer type	Input size	Layer size	Parameter count	Weight init	Updater	Activation function
Input Layer						
Convolution	3	64	3,136	XAVIER_UNIFORM	Adam	ReLU
Convolution	64	64	65,600	XAVIER_UNIFORM	Adam	ReLU
Subsampling (max pooling)						
Convolution	64	96	98,400	XAVIER_UNIFORM	Adam	ReLU
Convolution	96	96	147,552	XAVIER_UNIFORM	Adam	ReLU
Convolution	96	128	110,720	XAVIER_UNIFORM	Adam	ReLU
Convolution	128	128	147,584	XAVIER_UNIFORM	Adam	ReLU
Convolution	128	256	131,328	XAVIER_UNIFORM	Adam	ReLU
Convolution	256	256	262,400	XAVIER_UNIFORM	Adam	ReLU
Subsampling (max pooling)						
Dense	16,384	1,024	16,778,240	XAVIER	Adam	Sigmoid
Dropout	0	0	0			Sigmoid
Dense	1,024	1,024	1,049,600	XAVIER	Adam	Sigmoid
Dropout	0	0	0			Sigmoid
Output	1,024	10	10,250	XAVIER	Adam	Softmax

Let's then initialize the model, as follows:

```
val conf = defineModelConfiguration
 val model = new MultiLayerNetwork(conf)
 model.init
```

Then, start the training, as follows:

```
val epochs = 10
 for(idx <- 0 to epochs) {
     model.fit(trainDataSetIterator)
 }
```

Finally, evaluate it, as follows:

```
val eval = new Evaluation(testDataSetIterator.getLabels)
  while(testDataSetIterator.hasNext) {
      val testDS = testDataSetIterator.next(batchSize)
      val output = model.output(testDS.getFeatures)
      eval.eval(testDS.getLabels, output)
  }
  println(eval.stats)
```

The neural network we have implemented here has quite a large number of hidden layers, but, following the suggestions from the previous section (adding more layers, doing data augmentation, and training for a bigger number of epochs) would drastically improve the accuracy of the model.

The training of course can be done with Spark. The changes needed to the preceding code are, as detailed in Chapter 7, *Training Neural Networks with Spark*, related to Spark context initialization, training data parallelization, TrainingMaster creation, and training execution using a SparkDl4jMultiLayer instance, as follows:

```
// Init the Spark context
val sparkConf = new SparkConf
sparkConf.setMaster(master)
  .setAppName("Object Recognition Example")
val sc = new JavaSparkContext(sparkConf)
// Parallelize data
val trainDataList = mutable.ArrayBuffer.empty[DataSet]
while (trainDataSetIterator.hasNext) {
    trainDataList += trainDataSetIterator.next
}
val paralleltrainData = sc.parallelize(trainDataList)
// Create the TrainingMaster
var batchSizePerWorker: Int = 16
val tm = new
  ParameterAveragingTrainingMaster.Builder(batchSizePerWorker)
  .averagingFrequency(5)
  .workerPrefetchNumBatches(2)
  .batchSizePerWorker(batchSizePerWorker)
  .build
// Training
val sparkNet = new SparkDl4jMultiLayer(sc, conf, tm)
for (i <- 0 until epochs) {
    sparkNet.fit(paralleltrainData)
    println("Completed Epoch {}", i)
}
```

Summary

After a recap of the concept of convolution and the classification of object recognition strategies, in this chapter, we have been implementing and training CNNs for object recognition using different languages (Python and Scala) and different open source frameworks (Keras and TensorFlow in the first case, DL4J, ND4J, and Apache Spark in the second) in a hands-on manner.

In the next chapter, we are going to implement a full image classification web application which, behind the scenes, uses a combination of Keras, TensorFlow, DL4J, ND4J, and Spark.

14
Image Classification

In the previous chapter, after a quick recap on the concept of convolution, we learned more about the strategies for object recognition and more implementation details through examples in Python (Keras) and Scala (DL4J). This chapter covers the implementation of a full image classification web application or web service. The goal here is to show you how to apply the concepts from the previous chapter to an end-to-end classification system.

The steps to complete this goal are as follows:

- Pick up a proper Keras (with TensorFlow backend) pre-trained CNN model
- Load it and test it in DL4J (and Spark)
- Understand how to retrain the Python model on Apache Spark
- Implement an image classification web application that uses it
- Implement an alternative image classification web service that uses it

All of the open source technologies that we have come across in the previous chapters of this book while learning to use DL scenarios are involved in the implementation process that's explained here.

Implementing an end-to-end image classification web application

Using all of the things that we learned about in the previous chapters of this book, we should now be able to implement a real-world web application that allows users to upload an image and then properly classify it.

Picking up a proper Keras model

We are going to use an existing, pre-trained Python Keras CNN model. Keras applications (`https://keras.io/applications/`) are a set of DL models that are available as part of the framework with pre-trained weights. Among those models is **VGG16**, a 16-layer CNN that was implemented by the Visual Geometry Group at the University of Oxford in 2014. This model is compatible with a TensorFlow backend. It has been trained on the ImageNet database (`http://www.image-net.org/`). The ImageNet dataset is an excellent training set for general image classification, but it isn't suitable for facial recognition model training. Here is the way you can load and use the **VGG16** model in Keras. We are using a TensorFlow backend. Let's import the model:

```
from keras.applications.vgg16 import VGG16
```

Then, we need to import the other necessary dependencies (including NumPy and Pillow):

```
from keras.preprocessing import image
from keras.applications.vgg16 import preprocess_input
import numpy as np
from PIL import Image
```

Now, we can create an instance of the model:

```
model = VGG16(weights='imagenet', include_top=True)
```

The pre-trained weights are automatically downloaded the first time we run this application. Successive runs will pick up the weights from the local `~/.keras/models/` directory.

Here's the model architecture:

```
FMA

Layer (type)                    Output Shape               Param #
input_1 (InputLayer)            (None, None, None, 3)      0
block1_conv1 (Conv2D)           (None, None, None, 64)     1792
block1_conv2 (Conv2D)           (None, None, None, 64)     36928
block1_pool (MaxPooling2D)      (None, None, None, 64)     0
block2_conv1 (Conv2D)           (None, None, None, 128)    73856
block2_conv2 (Conv2D)           (None, None, None, 128)    147584
block2_pool (MaxPooling2D)      (None, None, None, 128)    0
block3_conv1 (Conv2D)           (None, None, None, 256)    295168
block3_conv2 (Conv2D)           (None, None, None, 256)    590080
block3_conv3 (Conv2D)           (None, None, None, 256)    590080
block3_pool (MaxPooling2D)      (None, None, None, 256)    0
block4_conv1 (Conv2D)           (None, None, None, 512)    1180160
block4_conv2 (Conv2D)           (None, None, None, 512)    2359808
block4_conv3 (Conv2D)           (None, None, None, 512)    2359808
block4_pool (MaxPooling2D)      (None, None, None, 512)    0
block5_conv1 (Conv2D)           (None, None, None, 512)    2359808
block5_conv2 (Conv2D)           (None, None, None, 512)    2359808
block5_conv3 (Conv2D)           (None, None, None, 512)    2359808
block5_pool (MaxPooling2D)      (None, None, None, 512)    0

Total params: 14,714,688
Trainable params: 14,714,688
Non-trainable params: 0
```

We can test the model by loading an image:

```
img_path = 'test_image.jpg'
img - image.load_img(img_path, target_size-(224, 224))
```

We can then prepare it to be passed as input to the model (by transforming the image pixels into a NumPy array and preprocessing it):

```
x = image.img_to_array(img)
x = np.expand_dims(x, axis=0)
x = preprocess_input(x)
```

Then, we can make predictions:

```
features = model.predict(x)
```

Finally, we save the model configuration (in JSON format):

```
model_json = model.to_json()
with open('vgg-16.json', 'w') as json_file:
    json_file.write(model_json)
```

We can also save the weights of the model that we want to import into DL4J:

```
model.save_weights("vgg-16.h5")
```

Then, we pass the following image into the model as input:

The image is correctly classified as a tabby cat, with a likelihood of almost 64%.

Importing and testing the model in DL4J

In Chapter 10, *Deploying on a Distributed System*, we learned how to import a pre-trained Keras model into DL4J. Let's apply the same process here.

The dependencies for the Scala project are DL4J DataVec, NN, model import, zoo, and ND4J plus Apache common math 3.

The first thing we need to do is copy the model configuration (from the `vgg-16.json` file) and weights (from the `vgg-16.h5` file) into the resource folder of the project. Then, we can load them through the `importKerasModelAndWeights` method of the `KerasModelImport` class:

```
val vgg16Json = new ClassPathResource("vgg-16.json").getFile.getPath
 val vgg16 = new ClassPathResource("vgg-16.h5").getFile.getPath
 val model = KerasModelImport.importKerasModelAndWeights(vgg16Json, vgg16,
 false)
```

The third argument to pass to the method is a Boolean; if `false`, this means that the pre-trained model has been imported to do inference only and won't be re-trained.

Let's test the model using the image in the preceding screenshot. We need to copy it into the resource directory for the application. Then, we can load it and resize it to be the required size (224 × 224 pixels):

```
val testImage = new ClassPathResource("test_image.jpg").getFile
 val height = 224
 val width = 224
 val channels = 3
 val loader = new NativeImageLoader(height, width, channels)
```

For this, we are using the `NativeImageLoader` class (`https://jar-download.com/javaDoc/org.datavec/datavec-data-image/1.0.0-alpha/org/datavec/image/loader/NativeImageLoader.html`) of the DataVec Image API.

Then, we need to transform the image into an NDArray and preprocess it:

```
val image = loader.asMatrix(testImage)
 val scaler = new VGG16ImagePreProcessor
 scaler.transform(image)
```

Afterwards, we need to do inference through the model:

```
val output = model.output(image)
```

To consume the result in a human readable format, we use the
`org.deeplearning4j.zoo.util.imagenet.ImageNetLabels` class, which is available
in the DL4J zoo library. The input for the `decodePredictions` method of this class is the
array of the NDArray that's returned from the `output` method of the model:

```
val imagNetLabels = new ImageNetLabels
  val predictions = imagNetLabels.decodePredictions(output(0))
  println(predictions)
```

The following screenshot shows the output of the preceding code. It presents the prediction
results (in descending order) for the uploaded image. According to the model, the highest
probability (around 53.3%) is that the main subject in the input picture is a tabby cat (which
is the correct one):

```
Predictions for batch   :
        53.297222%, tabby
        24.008511%, Egyptian_cat
        20.766859%, tiger_cat
        0.767307%, lynx
        0.208587%, bow_tie
--- Application end.---
```

You should have noticed that, once the model has been imported, the steps to load an
image and make an inference through the DL4J API are the same as for the example in
Keras that we presented in the previous section.

After the model has been tested, it is a good practice to save it through the
`ModelSerializer` class:

```
val modelSaveLocation = new File("Vgg-16.zip")
  ModelSerializer.writeModel(model, modelSaveLocation, true)
```

Then, we can load it through the same class because it is less expensive in terms of resource
usage than loading from Keras.

Re-training the model in Apache Spark

To improve the accuracy of the Keras VGG16 pre-trained model that we have considered for the use case of this chapter, we could also decide to retrain it and apply all of the best practices we have learned from the previous chapter (running more epochs, image augmentation, and so on). Once the model has been imported into DL4J, its training can be done exactly the same way it was explained in Chapter 7, *Training Neural Networks with Spark* (training with DL4J and Apache Spark). After loading, an instance of org.deeplearning4j.nn.graph.ComputationGraph is created, so the exact same principles for training multilayer networks apply here.

For completeness of information, you have to know that it is possible to train Keras models in parallel mode on Apache Spark, too. This can be done through the dist-keras Python framework (https://github.com/cerndb/dist-keras/), which was created for **Distributed Deep Learning** (**DDL**). The framework can be installed through pip:

```
sudo pip install dist-keras
```

It requires TensorFlow (this will be used as a backend) and the following variables to be set:

```
export SPARK_HOME=/usr/lib/spark
 export PYTHONPATH="$SPARK_HOME/python/:$SPARK_HOME/python/lib/py4j-0.9-
src.zip:$PYTHONPATH"
```

Let's have a quick look at the typical flow for distributed training with dist-keras. The following code isn't a complete working example; the goal here is to make you aware of how data parallelism training could be set.

First, we need to import all of the required classes for Keras, PySpark, Spark MLLib, and dist-keras. We will import Keras first:

```
from keras.optimizers import *
 from keras.models import Sequential
 from keras.layers.core import Dense, Dropout, Activation
```

Then, we can import PySpark:

```
from pyspark import SparkContext
 from pyspark import SparkConf
```

Then, we import Spark MLLib:

```
from pyspark.ml.feature import StandardScaler
 from pyspark.ml.fcaturc import VectorAssembler
 from pyspark.ml.feature import StringIndexer
 from pyspark.ml.evaluation import MulticlassClassificationEvaluator
 from pyspark.mllib.evaluation import BinaryClassificationMetrics
```

Finally, we import `dist-keras`:

```
from distkeras.trainers import *
 from distkeras.predictors import *
 from distkeras.transformers import *
 from distkeras.evaluators import *
 from distkeras.utils import *
```

We then need to create the Spark configuration, like so:

```
conf = SparkConf()
 conf.set("spark.app.name", application_name)
 conf.set("spark.master", master)
 conf.set("spark.executor.cores", num_cores)
 conf.set("spark.executor.instances", num_executors)
 conf.set("spark.locality.wait", "0")
 conf.set("spark.serializer",
"org.apache.spark.serializer.KryoSerializer");
```

We can then use this to create a `SparkSession`:

```
sc = SparkSession.builder.config(conf=conf) \
    .appName(application_name) \
    .getOrCreate()
```

The dataset is now as follows:

```
raw_dataset = sc.read.format('com.databricks.spark.csv') \
                    .options(header='true',
inferSchema='true').load("data/some_data.csv")
```

We can use this dataset to perform data preprocessing and normalization using the API provided by the Spark core and Spark MLLib (the strategy depends on the nature of the dataset, so it doesn't make sense to present some code here). Once this phase has been completed, we can define our model using the Keras API.

Here's an example with a simple `Sequential` model:

```
model = Sequential()
  model.add(Dense(500, input_shape=(nb_features,)))
  model.add(Activation('relu'))
  model.add(Dropout(0.4))
  model.add(Dense(500))
  model.add(Activation('relu'))
  model.add(Dense(nb_classes))
  model.add(Activation('softmax'))
```

Finally, you can start the training process by choosing one of the multiple optimization algorithms that's available with `dist-keras`:

- Sequential trainer
- ADAG
- Dynamic SDG
- AEASGD
- AEAMSGD
- DOWNPOUR
- Ensemble training
- Model averaging

While those later in this list are more performant, the first one, `SingleTrainer`, which is typically used as a benchmarking `trainer`, could be a good `trainer` choice in situations where a dataset is too big to fit in memory. Here's a code example of training with `SingleTrainer`:

```
trainer = SingleTrainer(keras_model=model, worker_optimizer=optimizer,
                        loss=loss, features_col="features_normalized",
                        label_col="label", num_epoch=1, batch_size=32)
  trained_model = trainer.train(training_set)
```

Implementing the web application

Let's go back to our main task and start implementing a web application that allows users to upload an image, and then use the serialized VGG16 model to make an inference on it. Several frameworks exist for the JVM to implement web applications. In this case, to minimize our efforts, we are going to use SparkJava (http://sparkjava.com/, not to be confused with Apache Spark), a micro framework for JVM programming languages, which has being implemented to keep rapid prototyping in mind. Compared to other web frameworks, it has a minimal boilerplate. SparkJava isn't for web applications only; it is possible to implement the REST API in very few lines of code (it will also be used in the next section to implement our image classification web service).

We have to add SparkJava to the dependencies list of the Java project for the web app:

```
groupId: com.sparkjava
  artifactId: spark-core
  version: 2.7.2
```

The reference version for this example is `2.7.2` (the latest at the time of writing this book).

In its simplest implementation, a SparkJava web application can be made of a single line of code in the `main` method:

```
get("/hello", (req, res) -> "Hello VGG16");
```

Running the application, the `hello` page is accessible from a web browser at the following URL:

```
http://localhost:4567/hello
```

`4567` is the default port for SparkJava web apps.

The main building block of a SparkJava application is a route. A route is made up of three pieces: a verb (`get`, `post`, `put`, `delete`, `head`, `trace`, `connect`, and `options` are the available verbs), a path (`/hello` in the preceding code example), and a callback (`request` or `response`). The SparkJava API also includes classes for sessions, cookies, filters, redirection, and custom errors handling.

Let's start implementing our web application. The other dependencies for the project are DL4J core, DataVec, NN, model import and zoo, and ND4J. We need to add the DL4J serialized model (the `Vgg-16.zip` file) to the resources of the project. The model can then be loaded programmatically through the `ModelSerializer` class:

```
ClassLoader classLoader = getClass().getClassLoader();
  File serializedModelFile = new
```

```
File(classLoader.getResource("Vgg-16.zip").getFile());
 ComputationGraph vgg16 =
ModelSerializer.restoreComputationGraph(serializedModelFile);
```

We need to create a directory where the images from the users will be uploaded:

```
File uploadDir = new File("upload");
 uploadDir.mkdir();
```

The next step is the creation of the form where users can upload an image. In SparkJava, it is possible to use custom styles for web pages. In this example, we are going to add the responsive Foundation 6 framework (`https://foundation.zurb.com/`), CSS. We add the minimal Foundation CSS library (`foundation-float.min.css`) in a subdirectory called `public` of the resource folder of the project. This way, the web application can access it within its classpath. The registration of the static file's location can be done programmatically:

```
staticFiles.location("/public");
```

The Foundation CSS and any other static CSS files can be registered in the header of the pages. Here's the method that has been implemented for this example:

```
private String buildFoundationHeader() {
    String header = "<head>\n"
           + "<link rel='stylesheet' href='foundation-float.min.css'>\n"
           + "</head>\n";
    return header;
 }
```

We now implement a method called `buildUploadForm` that returns the HTML content for it:

```
private String buildUploadForm() {
    String form =
           "<form method='post' action='getPredictions'
enctype='multipart/form-data'>\n" +
           " <input type='file' name='uploadedFile'>\n" +
           " <button class='success button'>Upload picture</button>\n" +
           "</form>\n";
    return form;
 }
```

We then use this when defining the route to the upload page:

```
String header = buildFoundationHeader();
 String form = buildUploadForm();
 get("Vgg16Predict", (req, res) -> header + form);
```

We can now define the `post` request:

```
post("/doPredictions", (req, res)
```

We do this to handle the image upload and classification. In the body of this `post` request, we have to take the following actions:

1. Upload the image file to the `upload` directory
2. Convert the image to NDArray
3. Delete the file (there's no need to keep it in the web server disk after the conversion)
4. Preprocess the image
5. Do an inference
6. Display the results

When translated into Java, this is as follows:

```
// Upload the image file
Path tempFile = Files.createTempFile(uploadDir.toPath(), "", "");

req.attribute("org.eclipse.jetty.multipartConfig", new
MultipartConfigElement("/temp"));

try (InputStream input =
req.raw().getPart("uploadedFile").getInputStream()) {
    Files.copy(input, tempFile, StandardCopyOption.REPLACE_EXISTING);
}

// Convert file to INDArray
File file = tempFile.toFile();

NativeImageLoader loader = new NativeImageLoader(224, 224, 3);
INDArray image = loader.asMatrix(file);

// Delete the physical file
file.delete();

// Pre-processing the image to prepare it for the VGG-16 model
DataNormalization scaler = new VGG16ImagePreProcessor();
scaler.transform(image);
```

```
// Do inference
INDArray[] output = vgg16.output(false,image);

// Get the predictions
ImageNetLabels imagNetLabels = new ImageNetLabels();
String predictions = imagNetLabels.decodePredictions(output[0]);

// Return the results
return buildFoundationHeader() + "<h4> '" + predictions + "' </h4>" +
  "Would you like to try another image?" +
  form;
```

You will notice that the image preparation and the inference part that's done through DL4J is the exact same as for the standalone application.

After starting the application, it will be accessible at the following URL:

```
http://localhost:4567/Vgg16Predict
```

It is possible to programmatically set up a different listening port:

```
port(8998);
```

The following screenshot shows the upload page layout:

The following screenshot shows us uploading the required image:

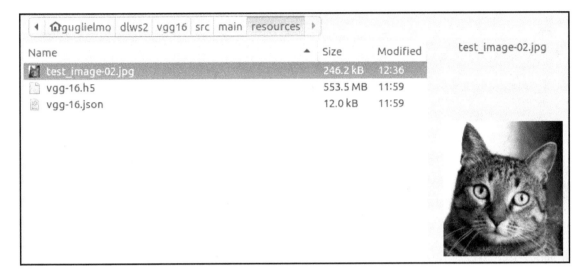

The results for this are as follows:

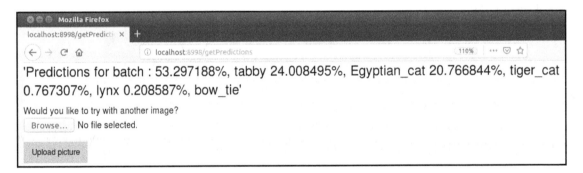

Implementing a web service

As we mentioned in the previous section, SparkJava can be used to quickly implement a REST API. The example web application we implemented in the previous section is monolithic, but looking back at its source code, we can notice how easily it would be to separate the frontend from the backend and move this to a REST API.

The frontend client presenting a form for image submission could be implemented with any web frontend framework. The client would then make a call to a REST service that's implemented through SparkJava, which performs the inference with the VGG16 model and finally returns the prediction results in JSON format. Let's see how easy it is to implement this service, starting from the existing code for the web application.

The web service is a Java class with the main method as an entry point. Let's define a custom listening port:

```
port(8998);
```

Now that we've done this, we need to define the upload endpoint:

```
post("/upload", (req, res) -> uploadFile(req));
```

We need to move the code that was part of the original post body into the uploadFile method (the only difference is the returned value, which is the prediction content only and not the full HTML content):

```
private String uploadFile(Request req) throws IOException, ServletException
{
    // Upload the image file
    Path tempFile = Files.createTempFile(uploadDir.toPath(), "", "");

    req.attribute("org.eclipse.jetty.multipartConfig", new
MultipartConfigElement("/temp"));

    try (InputStream input = req.raw().getPart("file").getInputStream()) {
      Files.copy(input, tempFile, StandardCopyOption.REPLACE_EXISTING);
    }

    // Convert file to INDArray
    File file = tempFile.toFile();

    NativeImageLoader loader = new NativeImageLoader(224, 224, 3);
    INDArray image = loader.asMatrix(file);

    // Delete the physical file
    file.delete();

    // Pre-processing the image to prepare it for the VGG-16 model
    DataNormalization scaler = new VGG16ImagePreProcessor();
    scaler.transform(image);

    // Do inference
    INDArray[] output = vgg16.output(false,image);
```

```
    // Get the predictions
    ImageNetLabels imagNetLabels = new ImageNetLabels();
    String predictions = imagNetLabels.decodePredictions(output[0]);

    // Return the results
    return predictions;
}
```

After running the application, you can test it with a simple `curl` (https://curl.haxx.se/) command:

```
curl -s -X POST http://localhost:8998/upload -F
'file=@/home/guglielmo/dlws2/vgg16/src/main/resources/test_image-02.jpg'
```

The output will be as follows:

```
guglielmo@ubuntu:~$ sudo curl -s -X POST http://localhost:8998/upload -F 'file=@
/home/guglielmo/dlws2/vgg16/src/main/resources/test_image-02.jpg'
Predictions for batch  :
        53.297222%, tabby
        24.008511%, Egyptian_cat
        20.766859%, tiger_cat
        0.767307%, lynx
        0.208587%, bow_tieguglielmo@ubuntu:~$
```

If we want to return the output in JSON format, this is the only change to the web service code that we have to perform:

```
Gson gson = new Gson();
  post("/upload", (req, res) -> uploadFile(req), gson::toJson);
```

We just need to create an instance of `com.google.gson.Gson` and pass it as the last argument to the `post` method. The output from our example will be as follows:

```
guglielmo@ubuntu:~$ sudo curl -s -X POST http://localhost:8998/upload -F 'file=@
/home/guglielmo/dlws2/vgg16/src/main/resources/test_image-02.jpg'
"Predictions for batch  :\n\t53.297188%, tabby\n\t24.008495%, Egyptian_cat\n\t20
.766844%, tiger_cat\n\t0.767307%, lynx\n\t0.208587%, bow_tie"guglielmo@ubuntu:~$
```

Summary

In this chapter, we have implemented our first end-to-end image classification web application by putting together several open source frameworks that we got familiar with throughout the previous chapters of this book. The readers should now have all of the knowledge of the building blocks to start working on their DL models or applications using Scala and/or Python and DL4J and/or Keras or TensorFlow.

This chapter ends the hands-on section of this book. The next and final chapter will discuss the future of DL and AI, with particular focus on DL4J and Apache Spark.

What's Next for Deep Learning?

15

This final chapter will try to give an overview of what's in store for the future of **deep learning** (**DL**) and, more generally, for AI.

We will be covering the following topics in this chapter:

- DL and AI
- Hot topics
- Spark and **Reinforcement Learning** (**RL**)
- Support for **Generative Adversarial Networks** (**GANs**) in DL4J

The rapid advancement of technology not only speeds up the implementation of existing AI ideas, it creates new opportunities in this space that would have been unthinkable one or two years ago. Day by day, AI is finding new practical applications in diverse areas and is radically transforming the way we do business in them. Therefore, it would be impossible to cover all of the new scenarios, so we are going to focus on some particular contexts/areas where we have been directly or indirectly involved.

What to expect next for deep learning and AI

As mentioned previously, there are daily advances in technology and there's a growing availability of greater, but at the same time cheaper, computational power, along with a greater availability of data, which is driving toward the implementation of deeper and more complex models. So, at the same time, the limit for both DL and AI seems to be the sky. Trying to understand what we have to expect for these fields is speculation that could help us clearly understand what would happen in a short period of time (2-3 years), but what can happen next could be less predictable, as it has been observed that any new idea in this space is bringing up other ideas and is contributing to radically transforming ways of doing business in several areas. So, what I am going to describe in this section is related to the immediate future rather than a long-term period.

DL has played a key role in shaping the future of AI. In some areas, such as, for example, image classification and recognition, object detection, and NLP, DL has outperformed ML, but this doesn't mean that ML algorithms became obsolete. For some particular problems, DL is probably overkill, so ML would still be enough. In some other more complex cases, a combination of algorithms (DL and non-DL) have led to significant results; a perfect example is the AlphaGo system (`https://deepmind.com/research/alphago/`) by the DeepMind team, which uses a combination of the **Monte Carlo tree search** (**MCTS**): `http://mcts.ai/about/`, with a DL network to quickly search for winning moves. This huge progress in DL has also led to other more complex and advanced techniques such as RL and GANs, which are discussed in the last two sections of this chapter.

However, while algorithms and models are making incredibly fast progress, there are still plenty of obstacles that require significant human intervention (and extra time) to remove them before data can be taken and turned into machine intelligence. As discussed in the paper *Hidden Technical Debt in Machine Learning Systems* (`https://papers.nips.cc/paper/5656-hidden-technical-debt-in-machine-learning-systems.pdf`) by a research group at Google, in DL and ML systems the cost of data dependencies is difficult to detect and it could easily become higher than the cost of code dependencies. The following diagram, which has been taken from the same Google research paper, shows the proportion of the dependencies in ML or DL code versus the rest of the dependencies in an ML or DL system:

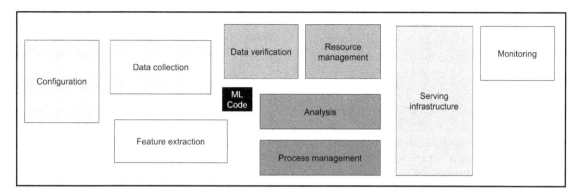

Figure 15.1: Only a small fraction (the black rectangle at the center of the image) of real-world ML/DL systems are composed of ML/DL code

As you can see from the preceding diagram, things such as data collection and the setup and maintenance of the serving infrastructure are more time and money consuming than the model's implementation and training. Therefore, I would expect significant improvements when automating these tasks.

Topics to watch for

In the past few months, a new debate started about the so-called explainable AI, an AI which isn't a sort of black box (where we understand only the underlying mathematical principles) and whose actions or decisions can be easily understood by humans. Criticism has been also been made (in general for AI, but in particular DL) about the generated results from models not being compliant with **GDPR** (short for **General Data Protection Regulation**): https://ec.europa.eu/commission/priorities/justice-and-fundamental-rights/data-protection/2018-reform-eu-data-protection-rules_en for data related to EU citizens, or other data regulations that will probably be defined next in other parts of the world, which require the right to an explanation to prevent discriminatory effects based on different factors.

While this is a real hot and not negligible topic, and since several interesting analyze and proposals (such as `https://www.academia.edu/18088836/Defeasible_Reasoning_and_Argument-Based_Systems_in_Medical_Fields_An_Informal_Overview` from Dr. Luca Longo (`https://ie.linkedin.com/in/drlucalongo`) from the Dublin Institute of Technology) have been done, I (and the readers of this book most probably too) have had the chance to listen to a few others' opinions and points of view in predicting a bad future for DL in particular, where DL applications will be restricted to non-business apps and games. In this section, I am not going to make comments on that point of view, which is often based more on opinions than facts, and is sometimes done by people who are not fully involved in production or research projects in the DL or ML spaces. Instead, I would prefer to present a list of practical DL applications that should still stay valid for a while.

Healthcare is one of the sectors that has a higher number of practical applications of AI and DL. Optum (`https://www.optum.com/`), a tech company that's part of the UnitedHealth Group, has achieved, as part of its overall strategy to transform healthcare operations, significant results when applying NLP to several of its business use cases. The ability of AI to understand both structured and unstructured data plays a critical role in medical record review (where most parts of the data are unstructured). Optum's so-called clinically intelligent NLP unlocks the unstructured content to get structured data elements, such as diagnoses, procedures, drugs, labs, and more that make up complete and accurate clinical documentation.

Data from unstructured sources is automatically retrieved through NLP technology that complements the structured data coming through more *traditional* clinical models and rules engines. This level of automation can accurately identify diagnoses, along with related conditions and procedures to implement the care that's provided, but it is also necessary to define the appropriate reimbursement, quality initiatives, and other critical healthcare operations. But understanding what has been documented in a record is only a part of what makes NLP so valuable in healthcare. Clinically intelligent NLP technology can also identify documentation gaps; it can understand not only what is in a record, but also what is missing. This way, clinicians can get valuable feedback so that they can improve documentation. Other remarkable applications of AI in Optum have been related to payment integrity, simplified population analysis, and call centers.

Another hot topic in AI is robotics. While, technically speaking, it is a separate branch, it has a lot of overlap with AI. Advances in DL and RL provide answers to several questions in robotics. Robots have being defined by first being able to sense, then compute the inputs of their sensors, and finally take action based on the results of those computations. AI comes into play to move them away from an industrial step-and-repeat model and make them smarter.

A perfect example of a successful user story in this direction is the German startup Kewazo (`https://www.kewazo.com/`). They have implemented a smart robotic scaffolding transportation system that addresses several problems such as understaffing, efficiency, high costs, time-consuming activities, and worker's safety. AI has made it possible for them to implement a robotic system that, through data about the overall scaffolding assembly process delivered in real time, allows constant control and significant optimization or tuning. AI has also helped Kewazo engineers to identify other use cases, such as roofing or solar panel installations, where their robots can work and help achieve the same results as a scaffolding assembly.

The **Internet of Things** (**IoT**) is another area where AI is becoming more pervasive every day. IoT is based on the concept that daily use physical devices are connected to the internet and can communicate with each other to exchange data. The data that's collected could be processed intelligently to make devices smarter. The number of AI and IoT use cases is constantly growing due to the rapidly increasing number of connected devices (and the data that's generated by them).

Among these use cases, I would like to mention the potential of AI for smart buildings. The rapid growth of the Irish economy in the past 5 years, which has been driven by industries such as IT, banking, finance, and pharma, has led to a radical transformation of the area where I work at the present time, the Dublin city center between the Docklands and the Grand Canal Dock. To address the constant increasing need for office space from new or expanding companies, hundreds of new buildings have been built (and many more are coming). All of these recent buildings use some AI, combined with IoT, to become smarter. Significant results have been achieved in the following areas:

- Making buildings more comfortable for humans
- Making building safer for humans
- Improving energy savings (and helping the environment)

Traditional controllers (for temperature, lights, doors, and so on) use a limited number of sensors to automatically adjust the devices to a constant end result. This paradigm used to leave out an important thing: buildings are occupied by humans, but they are controlled the same, regardless of whether occupants are present or not. This means that things like making the people comfortable or saving energy, just to mention a couple issues, weren't taken into account. IoT combined with AI can add this critical missing piece. Therefore, buildings can have priorities and not simply follow a rigid programming paradigm.

Another interesting real-world use case for IoT and AI is farming. The farming sector (dairy, in particular) is a significant part of the Irish GDP and not a negligible voice in Irish exports. Farming has new and old challenges (such as producing more food on the same acres, meeting strict emissions requirements, protecting plantations from pests, taking the climate into account and global climate change, controlling water flow, monitoring extensive orchards, fighting fires, monitoring soil quality, monitoring the health of animals, and so on). This means that farmers can't rely just on traditional practices. AI, IoT, and IoT-enabled sensors are now helping them in solving the challenges we mentioned previously, and many others. Lots of practical applications of smart farming are in place in Ireland (some of them were presented at the Predict 2018 conference: `https://www.tssg.org/projects/precision-dairy/`) and more are to be expected across 2019.

Speaking about AI and IoT, edge analytics is another hot topic. Edge analytics, which is an alternative to traditional big data analytics that is performed in centralized ways, is the analysis of data from some non-central point in a system, such as a connected device or sensor. Several real-world applications of edge analytics are currently in place, but are not restricted to it, in the industry 4.0 space (`https://en.wikipedia.org/wiki/Industry_4.0`). Analyzing data as it is generated can decrease latency in the decision-making process on connected devices.

Imagine, for example, a situation where sensor data from a manufacturing system points to the probable failure of a specific part; rules built into a ML or DL algorithm interpreting the data at the network edge can automatically shut down the machine and send an alert to maintenance managers so that that part can be promptly replaced. This can save lot of time compared to transmitting the data to a centralize data location for processing and analysis and reduce, if not avoid, the risk of unplanned machinery downtime.

Edge analytics also brings benefits in terms of scalability. In those cases where the number of connected devices in an organization increases (and the amount of generated and collected data too), by pushing algorithms to sensors and network devices, it is possible to alleviate the processing strain on enterprise data management and centralized analytics systems. There are some promising open source projects in this space to keep an eye on. One is DL4J itself; its mobile features allow multi-layer neural network model definition, training, and inference on Android devices (there's no support for other mobile platforms, since Android is the natural choice as it's a DL4J a framework for the JVM). TensorFlow Lite (`https://www.tensorflow.org/lite/`) enables on-device ML inference with low latency and a small binary size on several mobile operating systems (Android, iOS, and others) and embedded devices. The latest releases of the StreamSets data collector edge (`https://streamsets.com/products/sdc-edge`) allow you to trigger advanced analytics and ML (TensorFlow) in devices (Linux, Android, iOS, Windows, and MacOS are the supported operating systems for it). I would expect much more to come from the open source world on this front.

The rise of DL has led researchers to develop hardware chips that can directly implement neural network architectures. They are designed to mimic the human brain at the hardware level. In a traditional chip, the data needs to be transferred between CPUs and storage blocks, while in an neuromorphic chip, data is both processed and stored in the chip and can generate synapses when required. This second approach results in no time overhead and an energy saving. Therefore, the future of AI would most probably be more neuromorphic than based on CPUs or GPUs. With about 100 billion neurons densely packed into a small volume, the human brain can handle complex computations at lightning speed using very little energy. These past few years saw brain-inspired algorithms that can do things like identify faces, mimic voices, play games, and more. But software is only part of the bigger picture. Our state-of-the-art computers can't really run these powerful algorithms. That's where neuromorphic computing comes into the game.

The scenarios that have been presented in this section definitely confirm that, when considering GDPR or other data regulations, DL and AI definitely wouldn't be restricted to useless applications.

Is Spark ready for RL?

Throughout this book, we have understood how DL can address several problems in computer vision, natural language processing, and time series forecasting. This combination of DL with RL can lead to more astonishing applications to solve more complex problems. But what is RL? It is a specific area of ML, where agents have to take action to maximize the reward in a given environment. The term reinforcement comes from the similarity of this learning process to what happens when children are incentivized by sweets; the RL algorithms are rewarded when making the right decision and penalized when making a wrong one. RL differs from supervised learning, where the training data brings the answer key with it and a model is then trained with the correct answer itself. In RL, the agents decide what to do to perform the given task and, if no training dataset is available, they are tied to learn only from their experience.

One of the principal practical applications of RL is in computer gaming (one of the best and most popular results is from AlphaGo (`https://deepmind.com/research/alphago/`), from Alphabet's DeepMind team), but it can also be used in other areas such as robotics, industrial automation, chatbot systems, autonomous cars, data processing, and many others.

Let's look at the basics of RL before we understand what the availability of support for it in Apache Spark is and what it could become.

Here are the main concepts:

- **Agent**: It is the algorithm that takes actions.
- **Action**: It is one of the possible moves that an agent can make.
- **Discount factor**: It quantifies the difference, in terms of importance, between immediate and future rewards.
- **Environment**: It is the world through which agents move. The environment takes the agent's current state and action as input. It returns the agent reward and next state as output.
- **State**: It is a concrete situation in which an agent finds itself.
- **Reward**: It is the feedback by which the success or failure of an agent's action (which makes a transition from one state to another) can be measured.
- **Policy**: It is the strategy that an agent follows to determine its next action, based on the current state.
- **Value**: It is the expected long-term return of the current state under a given policy.
- **Q-value**: It is similar to value, but it also takes into account the current action.
- **Trajectory**: It is a sequence of states and actions that influence them.

We can summarize RL as follows:

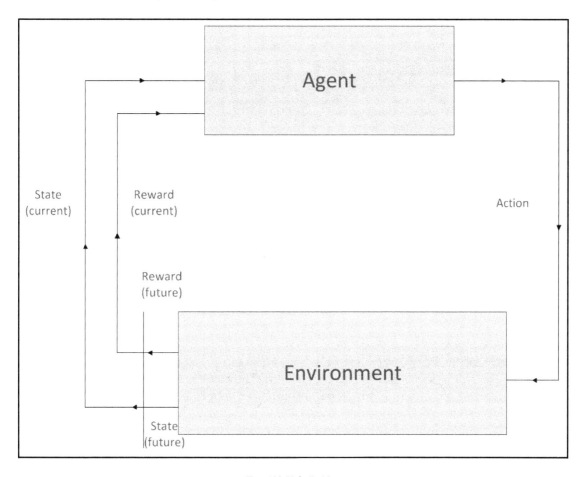

Figure 15.2: RL feedback loop

A good example to explain these concepts is the popular Pac-Man video game (`https://en.wikipedia.org/wiki/Pac-Man`); see the following screenshot:

Figure 15.3: The Pac-Man video game

Here, the agent is the Pac-Man character, whose goal is to eat all of the food items in a maze, while avoiding some ghosts that try to kill it. The maze is the environment for the agent. It receives a reward for eating food and punishment (game over) when it gets killed by a ghost. The states are the locations of the agent in the maze. The total cumulative reward is the agent winning the game and moving to the next level. After starting its exploration, Pac-Man (agent) might find one of the four power pellets (which make it invulnerable to the ghosts) near the four corners of the maze and decide to spend all its time exploiting that discovery by continually going around that small portion of the overall maze and never going further into the rest of the environment to pursue the bigger prize. To build an optimal policy, the agent faces the dilemma of exploring new states while maximizing its reward at the same time. This way, it would then miss out on the ultimate reward (moving to the next level). This is called an exploration versus exploitation trade-off.

The most popular algorithms for RL are the **Markov decision process** (**MDP**): `https://en.wikipedia.org/wiki/Markov_decision_process`, **Q-learning** (`https://en.wikipedia.org/wiki/Q-learning`), and **A3C** (`https://arxiv.org/pdf/1602.01783.pdf`).

Q-learning is widely use in gaming (or gaming-like) spaces. It can be summarized with the following equation (the source code is from the Wikipedia page for Q-learning):

$$Q^{new}(s_t, a_t) \leftarrow (1 - \alpha) \cdot Q(s_t, a_t) + \alpha \cdot (r_t + \gamma \cdot max_a Q(s_{t+1}, a))$$

Here, s_t is the state at time t, a_t is the action taken by the agent, r_t is the reward at time t, s_{t+1} is the new state (time $t+1$), α is the learning rate ($0 \leq \alpha \leq 1$), and γ is the discount factor. This last one determines the importance of future rewards. If it is zero, it will make the agent short-sighted because it means that it will only consider current rewards. If its value is close to one, the agent will work hard to achieve a long-term high reward. If the discount factor value is or exceeds one, then the action values could diverge.

The MLLib component of Apache Spark currently doesn't have any facility for RL and it seems that there is no plan, at the time of writing this book, to implement support for it in future Spark releases. However, there are some open source stable initiatives for RL that integrate with Spark.

The DL4J framework provides a specific module for RL, RL4J, which was originally a separate project. As for all of the other DL4J components, it is fully integrated with Apache Spark. It implements the DQN (Deep Q Learning with double DQN) and AC3 RL algorithms.

Interesting implementations have been done by Yuhao Yang (`https://www.linkedin.com/in/yuhao-yang-8a150232`) from Intel, which led to the analytics zoo initiative (`https://github.com/intel-analytics/analytics-zoo`). Here's the link to the presentation he did at the Spark-AI summit 2018 (`https://databricks.com/session/building-deep-reinforcement-learning-applications-on-apache-spark-using-bigdl`). Analytics zoo provides a unified analytics and AI platform that seamlessly puts the Spark, TensorFlow, Keras, and BigDL programs into an integrated pipeline that can scale out to a large Spark cluster for distributed training or inference.

While RL4J, as part of DL4J, provides APIs for the JVM languages (including Scala) and BigDL provides APIs for both Python and Scala, a Python-only, end-to-end, open source platform for large-scale RL is available from Facebook. The name of this platform is Horizon (`https://github.com/facebookresearch/Horizon`). It is used by Facebook itself in production to optimize systems in large-scale environments. It supports the discrete-action DQN, parametric-action DQN, double DQN, DDPG (`https://arxiv.org/abs/1509.02971`), and SAC (`https://arxiv.org/abs/1801.01290`) algorithms. The workflows and algorithms included in this platform have been built on open source frameworks (PyTorch 1.0, Caffe2, and Apache Spark). There's currently no support for their use with other popular Python ML frameworks such as TensorFlow and Keras.

The Ray framework (`https://ray-project.github.io/`) by RISELab (`https://rise.cs.berkeley.edu/`) deserves a special mention. While DL4J and the other frameworks that we mentioned previously work in a distributed mode on top of Apache Spark, in the mind of the Berkley researchers, Ray is a replacement for Spark itself, which is seen by them as more general purpose and not the perfect fit for some real-world AI applications. Ray has been implemented in Python; it is fully compatible with the most popular Python DL frameworks, including TensorFlow and PyTorch; and it allows us to use a combination of more than one of them in the same application.

In the specific case of RL, the Ray framework also provides a dedicated library, RLLib (`https://ray.readthedocs.io/en/latest/rllib.html`), which implements the AC3, DQN, evolution strategy (`https://en.wikipedia.org/wiki/Evolution_strategy`), and PPO (`https://blog.openai.com/openai-baselines-ppo/`) algorithms. At the time of writing this book, I am not aware of any real-world AI applications that are using this framework, but I believe it is worth following how it is going to evolve and its level of adoption by the industry.

DeepLearning4J future support for GANs

Generative Adversarial Networks (**GANs**) are deep neural network architectures that include two nets that are pitted against each other (that's the reason for the *adversarial* adjective in the name). GAN algorithms are used in unsupervised machine learning. The main focus for GANs is to generate data from scratch. Among the most popular use cases of GANs, there's image generation from text, image-to-image-translation, increasing image resolution to make more realistic pictures, and doing predictions on the next frames of videos.

As we mentioned previously, a GAN is made up of two deep networks, the **generator** and the **discriminator**; the first one generates candidates, while the second one evaluates them. Let's see how generative and discriminative algorithms work at a very high level. Discriminative algorithms try to classify the input data. Therefore, they predict a label or category to which that input data belongs. Their only concern is to map features to labels. Generative algorithms, instead of predicting a label when given certain features, attempt to predict features when given a certain label. Essentially, they do the opposite thing from what the discriminative algorithms do.

Here's how a GAN works. The generator generates new data instances, while the discriminator evaluates them to assess their authenticity. Using the same MNIST dataset (`http://yann.lecun.com/exdb/mnist/`) that has been considered to illustrate more than one code example throughout this book, let's think of a scenario to make it clear what happens in GANs. Suppose we have the generator generating an MNIST dataset like hand-written numerals and then we're passing them to the discriminator. The goal of the generator is to generate passable hand-written digits without being caught, while the goal of the discriminator is to identify those images coming from the generator as fake hand-written digits. With reference to the following diagram, these are the steps that this GAN takes:

1. The generator net takes some random numbers as input and then returns an image.
2. The generated image is used to feed the discriminator net alongside a stream of other images that have been taken from the training dataset.
3. While taking in both real and fake images, the discriminator returns probabilities, which are numbers between zero and one. Zero represents a prediction of fake, while one represents a prediction of authenticity:

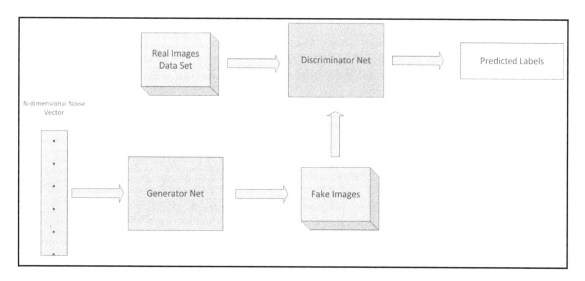

Figure 15.4: The typical flow of the MNIST example GAN

In terms of implementation, the **Discriminator Net** is a standard CNN that can categorize the images fed to it, while the **Generator Net** is an inverse CNN. Both nets try to optimize a different and opposing loss function in a zero-sum game. This model is essentially an actor-critic model (`https://cs.wmich.edu/~trenary/files/cs5300/RLBook/node66.html`), whereas the **Discriminator Net** changes its behavior, so does the generator net, and vice versa.

At the time of writing this book, DL4J doesn't provide any direct API for GANs, but it allows you to import existing Keras (like those you can find it at `https://github.com/eriklindernoren/Keras-GAN`, which is our GitHub repository) or TensorFlow (like this one: `https://github.com/aymericdamien/TensorFlow-Examples/blob/master/examples/3_NeuralNetworks/gan.py`) GAN models and then retrain them and/or make predictions using the DL4J API in a JVM environment (which can include Spark), as explained in `Chapter 10`, *Deploying on a Distributed System*, and `Chapter 14`, *Image Classification*. No direct capabilities for GANs are in the immediate plan for DL4J, but the Python model's import is a valid way to train and make inference with them.

Summary

This chapter wraps up this book. In this book, we got familiar with Apache Spark and its components, and then we moved on to discover the fundamentals of DL before getting practical. We started our Scala hands-on journey with the DL4J framework by understanding how to ingest training and testing data from diverse data sources (in both batch and streaming modes) and transform it into vectors through the DataVec library. The journey then moved on to exploring the details of CNNs and RNNs the implementation of those network models through DL4J, how to train them in a distributed and Spark-based environment, how to get useful insights by monitoring them using the visual facilities of DL4J, and how to evaluate their efficiency and do inference.

We also learned some tips and best practices that we should use when configuring a production environment for training, and how it is possible to import Python models that have been implemented in Keras and/or TensorFlow and make them run (or be retrained) in a JVM-based environment. In the last part of this book, we applied what we learned previously to implementing NLP use cases with DL first and then an end-to-end image classification application.

I hope that all of the readers who went through all of the chapters of this book have reached my initial goal: they have all of the building blocks to start tackling their own specific DL use case scenarios in Scala and/or Python, in a distributed system such as Apache Spark.

Appendix A: Functional Programming in Scala

Scala combines functional programming and object-oriented programming in a single high-level language. This appendix contains a reference to the principles of functional programming in Scala.

Functional programming (FP)

In FP, functions are first-class citizens—this means that they are treated like any other values and can be passed as arguments to other functions or be returned as a result of a function. In FP, it is also possible to work with functions in the so-called literal form, with no need to name them. Let's look at the following Scala example:

```scala
val integerSeq = Seq(7, 8, 9, 10)
integerSeq.filter(i => i % 2 == 0)
```

`i => i % 2 == 0` is a function literal without a name. It checks whether a number is even. It can be passed as another function argument or it can be used as a return value.

Purity

One of the pillars of functional programming is pure functions. A pure programming function is a function that is analogous of a mathematical function. It depends only on its input parameters and its internal algorithm and always returns an expected result for a given input, since it doesn't rely on anything from outside. (This is a big difference compared to the OOP methods.) You can easily understand that this makes a function easier to test and maintain. The fact that a pure function doesn't rely on anything else from the outside means that it doesn't have side effects.

Purely functional programs work on immutable data. Rather than altering existing values, altered copies are created while the originals are preserved. This means that they can be shared between the old and new copies because the unchanged parts of the structure cannot be modified. An outcome of this behavior is a significant saving in terms of memory.

Examples of pure functions in Scala (and Java) include the `size` method of `List` (https://docs.oracle.com/javase/8/docs/api/java/util/List.html) or the `lowercase` method of `String` (https://docs.oracle.com/javase/8/docs/api/java/lang/String.html). `String` and `List` are both immutable, and, as a consequence, all of their methods act like pure functions.

But not all abstractions can be directly implemented with pure functions (some such as reading and writing from a database or object storage or logging). FP provides two approaches that allow developers to deal with impure abstractions in a pure way, therefore making the final code much cleaner and maintainable. The first approach, which is used in some other FP languages but not in Scala, is to extend the language's purely functional core with side effects. Then, the responsibility to avoid using impure functions in situations where only pure functions are expected is up to the developers. The second approach, which happens in Scala, is by introducing side effects to the pure language simulating them with *monads* (https://www.haskell.org/tutorial/monads.html). This way, while the programming language remains pure and referentially transparent, the monads can provide implicit state by threading it inside them. The compiler doesn't have to know about the imperative features because the language itself stays pure, while, usually, the implementations know about them due to efficiency reasons.

Since pure computations are referentially transparent, they can be performed at any time while still yielding the same result, making it possible to defer the computation of values until they are really needed (lazy computation). This lazy evaluation avoids unnecessary computations and allows infinite data structures to be defined and used.

Allowing side effects only through monads as in Scala and keeping the language pure makes it possible to have a lazy evaluation that doesn't conflict with the effects of impure code. While lazy expressions can be evaluated in any order, the monad structure forces these effects to be executed in the correct order.

Recursion

Recursion is heavily used in FP, as it is the canonical, and often the only, way to iterate. Functional language implementations will often include optimizations based on the so-called **tail recursion** (https://alvinalexander.com/scala/fp-book/tail-recursive-algorithms) to ensure that heavy recursion doesn't have a significant or excessive impact on memory consumption. Tail recursion is a particular instance of recursion where the return value of a function is calculated only as a call to itself. Here is a Scala example of calculating a Fibonacci sequence recursively. This first piece of code represents an implementation of the recursive function:

```
def fib(prevPrev: Int, prev: Int) {
    val next = prevPrev + prev
    println(next)
    if (next > 1000000) System.exit(0)
    fib(prev, next)
}
```

This other piece of code represents an implementation of the same function in a tail-recursive way:

```
def fib(x: Int): BigInt = {
    @tailrec def fibHelper(x: Int, prev: BigInt = 0, next: BigInt = 1):
BigInt = x match {
        case 0 => prev
        case 1 => next
        case _ => fibHelper(x - 1, next, (next + prev))
    }
    fibHelper(x)
}
```

While the return line of the first function contains a call to itself, it also does something to its output, so the return value isn't really the recursive call's return value. The second implementation is a regular recursive (and in particular tail-recursive) function.

Appendix B: Image Data Preparation for Spark

CNNs are among the main topics of this book. They are used in lots of practical applications of image classification and analysis. This Appendix explains how to create a `RDD<DataSet>` to train a CNN model for image classification.

Image preprocessing

The approach described in this section, image preprocessing into batches of files, relies on the ND4J `FileBatch` class (`https://static.javadoc.io/org.nd4j/nd4j-common/1.0.0-beta3/org/nd4j/api/loader/FileBatch.html`), which is available starting from the 1.0.0-beta3 release of that library. This class can store the raw content of multiple files in byte arrays (one per file), including their original paths. A `FileBatch` object can be stored to disk in ZIP format. This can reduce the number of disk reads that are required (because of fewer files) and network transfers when reading from remote storage (because of the ZIP compression). Typically, the original image files that are used to train a CNN make use of an efficient (in terms of space and network) compression format (such as JPEG or PNG). But when it comes to a cluster, there is the need to minimize disk reads due to latency issues with remote storage. Switching to one file read/transfer will be faster compared to `minibatchSize` remote file reads.

Doing image preprocessing into batches comes with the following limitation in DL4J – the class labels need to be provided manually. Images should reside in directories whose names are their corresponding labels. Let's look at an example – assuming that we have three classes, that is, car, truck, and motorbike, the image directory structure should be as follows:

```
imageDir/car/image000.png
imageDir/car/image001.png
...
imageDir/truck/image000.png
imageDir/truck/image001.png
...
imageDir/motorbike/image000.png
imageDir/motorbike/image001.png
...
```

The names of the image files don't matter. All that matters is that the subdirectories of the root directory have the names of the classes.

Strategies

Two strategies are possible for preprocessing images before we starting training on a Spark cluster. The first strategy is about preprocessing the images locally by using the `SparkDataUtils` class of `dl4j-spark`. For example:

```
import org.datavec.image.loader.NativeImageLoader
import org.deeplearning4j.spark.util.SparkDataUtils
...
val sourcePath = "/home/guglielmo/trainingImages"
val sourceDir = new File(sourcePath)
val destinationPath = "/home/guglielmo/preprocessedImages"
val destDir = new File(destinationPath)
val batchSize = 32
SparkDataUtils.createFileBatchesLocal(sourceDir,
NativeImageLoader.ALLOWED_FORMATS, true, destDir, batchSize)
```

In this example, `sourceDir` is the root directory of the local images, `destDir` is the local directory where the preprocessed images will be saved, and `batchSize` is the number of images to put into a single `FileBatch` object. The `createFileBatchesLocal` method is responsible for the import. Once all of the images have been preprocessed, the content of the destination, `dir`, can be copied/moved to a cluster for training purposes.

The second strategy is about preprocessing the images using Spark. In those cases where the original images are stored in a distributed filesystem, such as HDFS, or a distributed object storage, such as S3, the `SparkDataUtils` class is still used, but a different method, `createFileBatchesLocal`, which expects a SparkContext among its arguments, has to be invoked. Here's an example:

```
val sourceDirectory = "hdfs:///guglielmo/trainingImages";
val destinationDirectory = "hdfs:///guglielmo/preprocessedImages";
val batchSize = 32

val conf = new SparkConf
...
val sparkContext = new JavaSparkContext(conf)

val filePaths = SparkUtils.listPaths(sparkContext, sourceDirectory, true,
NativeImageLoader.ALLOWED_FORMATS)
SparkDataUtils.createFileBatchesSpark(filePaths, destinationDirectory,
batchSize, sparkContext)
```

In this case, the original images are stored in HDFS (the location is specified through `sourceDirectory`) and the preprocessed images are saved in HDFS as well (in a location specified through `destinationDirectory`). Before starting the preprocessing, the `SparkUtils` class of dl4j-spark has to be used to create a `JavaRDD<String>` (`filePaths`) of the source images paths. The `SparkDataUtils.createFileBatchesSpark` method takes `filePaths`, the destination HDFS path (`destinationDirectory`), the number of images (`batchSize`) to put into a single `FileBatch` object, and the SparkContext (`sparkContext`) as input. The training can start once all of the images have been preprocessed by Spark.

Training

Whatever preprocessing strategy (local or Spark) has been chosen, here is how training using Spark happens.

First, you create the SparkContext, set up the `TrainingMaster`, and build the neural network model using the following instances:

```
val conf = new SparkConf
...
val sparkContext = new JavaSparkContext(conf)
val trainingMaster = ...
val net:ComputationGraph = ...
val sparkNet = new SparkComputationGraph(sparkContext, net, trainingMaster)
sparkNet.setListeners(new PerformanceListener(10, true))
```

After this, a data loader needs to be created, as in the following example:

```
val imageHeightWidth = 64
val imageChannels = 3
val labelMaker = new ParentPathLabelGenerator
val rr = new ImageRecordReader(imageHeightWidth, imageHeightWidth,
imageChannels, labelMaker)
rr.setLabels(new TinyImageNetDataSetIterator(1).getLabels())
val numClasses = TinyImageNetFetcher.NUM_LABELS
val loader = new RecordReaderFileBatchLoader(rr, minibatch, 1, numClasses)
loader.setPreProcessor(new ImagePreProcessingScaler)
```

The input images have a resolution 64 x 64 pixels (`imageHeightWidth`) and three channels (RGB, `imageChannels`). 0-255 valued pixels are scaled by the loader through a range of 0-1 through the `ImagePreProcessingScaler` class (`https://deeplearning4j.org/api/latest/org/nd4j/linalg/dataset/api/preprocessor/ImagePreProcessingScaler.html`).

The training can then start, as in the following example:

```
val trainPath = "hdfs:///guglielmo/preprocessedImages"
val pathsTrain = SparkUtils.listPaths(sc, trainPath)
val numEpochs = 10
for (i <- 0 until numEpochs) {
    println("--- Starting Training: Epoch {} of {} ---", (i + 1),
numEpochs)
    sparkNet.fitPaths(pathsTrain, loader)
}
```

Other Books You May Enjoy

If you enjoyed this book, you may be interested in these other books by Packt:

Apache Spark Deep Learning Cookbook
Ahmed Sherif, Amrith Ravindra

ISBN: 978-1-78847-422-1

- Set up a fully functional Spark environment
- Understand practical machine learning and deep learning concepts
- Apply built-in machine learning libraries within Spark
- Explore libraries that are compatible with TensorFlow and Keras
- Explore NLP models such as Word2vec and TF-IDF on Spark

Machine Learning with Apache Spark Quick Start Guide
Jillur Quddus

ISBN: 978-1-78934-656-5

- Understand how Spark fits in the context of the big data ecosystem
- Understand how to deploy and configure a local development environment using Apache Spark
- Understand how to design supervised and unsupervised learning models
- Build models to perform NLP, deep learning, and cognitive services using Spark ML libraries
- Design real-time machine learning pipelines in Apache Spark

Leave a review - let other readers know what you think

Please share your thoughts on this book with others by leaving a review on the site that you bought it from. If you purchased the book from Amazon, please leave us an honest review on this book's Amazon page. This is vital so that other potential readers can see and use your unbiased opinion to make purchasing decisions, we can understand what our customers think about our products, and our authors can see your feedback on the title that they have worked with Packt to create. It will only take a few minutes of your time, but is valuable to other potential customers, our authors, and Packt. Thank you!

Index

R

raw data transformation
  with Spark 79, 80, 81, 82, 83
Ray framework
  reference 288
RDD
  programming 15, 17, 18, 19, 20, 22, 23
Receiver Operating Characteristic (ROC)
  about 172
  exact 173
  reference 172
  ROC 172
  ROCBinary 172
  ROCMultiClass 172
  thresholded 173
receptive field 101
RecordReaderDataSetIterator
  reference 108
Rectified Linear Unit (ReLU) 105, 244
Recurrent Neural Network (RNN)
  about 58, 60, 61
  architectures 62, 63
  issues 117, 118
  multiple CSVs, loading from RNN data pipelines
    125, 126
  use cases 119
  with DL4J 120, 121, 122
  with DL4J and Spark 122, 124, 125
  with Spark 119
Red-Blue-Green (RGB) 100
RegexLineRecordReader
  reference 80
RegressionEvaluation class
  reference 172
Reinforcement Learning (RL)
  action 284
  agent 284
  discount factor 284
  environment 284
  policy 284
  Q-value 284
  reward 284
  state 284
  trajectory 284

value 284
  with Spark 283, 286
relational database
  data ingestion, training 71, 72, 73
reliability diagram
  reference 174
residual plot
  reference 174
ResourceManager 44
RL4J 66
RLLib
  reference 288
RNN distributed training
  with Spark and DL4J 134, 135

S

S3
  data ingestion 76, 77, 79
  reference 76
Scala
  BigDL, using 193, 194
  DeepLearning.scala, using 194, 195
  reference 7
Scalaz library
  reference 195
scikit-learn
  reference 242
SciPy
  reference 236
Secure Shell (SSH) 40
sentence segmentation 200
serializable interface
  reference 137
Shade plugin
  reference 181
Sonatype Nexus OSS
  reference 206
Spark applications
  submitting, on YARN 45
Spark CoreNLP
  reference 205
Spark DStreams, transformation
  cogroup(otherStream, [numTasks]) 34
  count() 34
  countByValue() 34

reference 123
transformation
  about 16
  through Spark 67, 69, 70
transformer
  reference 208
TreeAggregate
  reference 185

V

Vanishing Gradients 117
visualization
  neural networks, tuning 158, 159, 161

W

weights 101, 103, 104

Word2Vec
  about 218
  reference 217
Write Ahead Logs (WAL) 85

Y

YARN, deployment modes
  client mode 45
  cluster mode 45
YARN
  cluster mode 43, 44
  reference 43
  Spark applications, submitting 45

Z

ZooKeeper
  reference 92

www.ingramcontent.com/pod-product-compliance
Lightning Source LLC
LaVergne TN
LVHW081516050326
832903LV00025B/1511